HARVARD ECONOMIC STUDIES, Volume 144

The studies in this series are published under the
direction of the Department of Economics of
Harvard University. The Department does not
assume responsibility for the views expressed.

# Advertising and Market Power

William S. Comanor and Thomas A. Wilson

Harvard University Press, Cambridge, Massachusetts, 1974

Library of Congress Catalog Card Number 73–90849
ISBN 0–674–00580–5
Printed in the United States of America

FOR OUR PARENTS

LeRoy and Sylvia Comanor
Gordon and Edith Dunlop

# Contents

## FIGURES

## TABLES

# Foreword

Does advertising misinform us and make us buy things we do not "really" want? Does it impress on us the mercantile values of a materialistic society? Should we ban or limit the advertising of dubious commodities (cigarettes) or muffle the ears of immature consumers (children's television)? Or should we only require that the advertisers tell the truth about the tar and nicotine?

While the public debate over the economic and cultural significance of advertising has proceeded, a more technical debate among professional economists has swirled about two issues: Does advertising simply allow the seller to announce his wares and inform the market, or do heavy advertising outlays primarily permit established sellers in certain industries to put new entrants at a hopeless disadvantage and thus create market power for themselves? Does the volume of advertising messages offered to the public amount to an efficient supply of information, or is this market for information subject to structural failures? In this study Comanor and Wilson contribute important analytical and empirical evidence leading toward the conclusion that advertising outlays in certain sectors of the American economy do generate market power and comprise an inefficient supply of information to the public.

Any teacher knows that a debate is more interesting than a monologue, and teachers and students of industrial organization have enjoyed decades of stimulation from these issues. The debate over advertising and market power in particular has traveled over a long and twisting set of tracks. That a monopolist will restrict his supply below what a group of competitive sellers would offer is a theoretical proposition so firmly established that students of introductory economics remember it a year later! Yet some economists have resisted its policy implications, holding that the excess profits gleaned by the monopolist must lure new sellers into the market (unless the government fends them off) and ultimately restore the bliss of pure competition. A major challenge to this sanguine view was hurled down by Joe S. Bain, who showed in his *Barriers to New Competition* (1956) that new entrants to certain industries are at a structural disadvantage in relation to going firms. The going sellers can exploit their advantage by restricting output and thus gaining some excess profits without attracting new competitors.

Bain's contribution, important though it was, left some issues of analysis and policy unsettled. First, he failed to silence all believers in the ultimate triumph of pure competition. Putting aside the problem created by scale economies in production, they argued that Bain's other sources of advantage for going firms disappear when costs are correctly measured in a long-run context. If new firms must invest in advertising to build up intangible goodwill assets or seek out scarce resources that their going rivals already possess, they are still at no disadvantage because the going firms' current costs (properly measured) would include an equal user cost or rent for these assets. That scale economies of nationwide sales promotion might create an advantage for going firms they sought to reject by arguing that any such economies are social ones—not the result of large firms' bargaining power—and thus do not reflect any failure of the market. Second, Bain's findings left even economists who did not share these doubts at loose ends for drawing policy conclusions. If the barriers to entry are structural and the work of a malevolent god, what can man (especially man in the Antitrust Division) do to tear them down? The suspicion arose that some entry barriers, however, might well reflect not the state of nature but the past behavior of going firms, whether by luck or design serving to put market newcomers at a disadvantage.

The present volume goes far toward resolving both of these issues left open by Bain's seminal work and reaffirms the reality of product differentiation as a principal source of disadvantage to *de novo* entrants and to small firms in certain industries. The authors carefully review the evidence on the market for advertising messages and show that it does contain imperfections favoring the big advertisers. They also show that the association between advertising and excess profits—the signal that market power is in use—survives various supplemental tests to ward off the effects of two-way causation (profits to advertising, as well as vice versa) and the peculiar problems that arise because advertising is a form of investment that gets treated as a current cost by the firm's accountants. They conclude that the cost inflicted on consumers by certain industries that are heavy advertisers can be as high as 16 percent of the industry's value added. A clear case emerges for public action to limit advertising outlays by dominant firms in these industries.

This study also contributes to the debate over advertising as information. The authors show that the necessary bias in seller-supplied advertising messages and the joint consumption of advertising along with other information or entertainment (magazines, television programs) provide the basis for misallocation in the market for information. They also supply statistical evidence that advertising does affect the allocation of consumers' expenditures among types of products. Although they carefully qualify the significance of this finding for economic welfare, their conclusions surely amplify the nervousness long felt by economists about "consumer sovereignty" as the immutable hook from which dangles our justification for the allocation of resources produced by capitalistic markets.

Happily for the full employment of scholars, debates are seldom settled— only exhausted or transmuted. Already we can spot issues left open by Comanor and Wilson. What determines in which industries high advertising outlays can serve to erect massive entry barriers? Would a great elevation of selling outlays similarly affect the market for upholstered funiture or wooden spring clothespins? Advertising outlays are profitable because they strike responsive nerves in the consumer, and we have not established rigorously what makes some nerves susceptible, others not. Closely related to this problem is the fact that our studies of market power have so far neglected the role of the retailing sector through which goods are transmitted to the consumer. Forthcoming research by Michael E. Porter has shown that for certain products the manufacturer's advertising suffices to differentiate his product, but for others the retailer's collaboration is essential, and the structure of the retailing sector (in turn reflecting traits of consumers' preferences) has a critical influence on the manufacturer's market power. Finally, important theoretical and empirical work is underway on information, uncertainty, and their effects on resource allocation and market power. These contributions seem unlikely to upset the main policy implications of Comanor and Wilson's work, but they do promise an important sharpening and refinement.

Harvard University                                        Richard E. Caves

# Preface

This book is the culmination of research on advertising and market power which we have carried out for the past several years. Those familiar with the literature will recognize that the analysis of Chapters 4 and 6 owes much to our first article on the subject, "Advertising Market Structure and Performance," published in the *Review of Economics and Statistics* in 1967. Chapter 10 draws on a paper we delivered at the Meetings of the American Economic Association in December 1968. Entitled "Advertising and the Advantages of Size," it was subsequently published in the *American Economic Association Papers and Proceedings*, May 1969. Additional materials in these chapters and all of the remaining chapters are published in this volume for the first time.

Our joint research began while we were both on the faculty at Harvard University and our collaboration continued following our appointments at the University of Toronto and Stanford University in 1967 and 1968. A complete first draft of the manuscript was originally submitted for publication in the Harvard Economic Studies Series in December 1971. The final revised version was delivered to Harvard University Press in April 1973.

Naturally, in a collaboration of this magnitude, extending over several years, we owe many debts. For financial support, we are indebted to the Ford Foundation and Harvard University which supported our initial research in 1965–1966 under the Foundation's Small Grants Program; to the Sloan Foundation which supplied general support for Comanor's research cativities that enabled him to work on advertising among other topics in

1966–1967; to the Brookings Institution for grants that supported work on the study in 1967–1968; and to the Graduate School of Business, Stanford University, and the Institute for Policy Analysis, University of Toronto, for various forms of research support, including released time from teaching duties, computer time, and programming assistance.

Our debts to individuals are almost too numerous to enumerate. We have been unusually fortunate in having had excellent research assistants over the years. These included Barbara Clapp, Edward Wolff, James Sweeney, Richard Inman, and Robert Smiley. George Ugray helped with the regression estimates and the nonlinear estimation work. Our thanks also go to John Peterman for providing some unpublished data on television advertising rates.

For computer programming help, we had access to two of the best in the business, Les Cseh of the Institute for Policy Analysis, Toronto, and Aram Grayson. For secretarial assistance we are indebted to Dorothy Peet and Jane Klink at Stanford University and to Annette Ankow and Myrja Mogensen at the University of Toronto who typed and retyped the many drafts of the manuscript.

We are also much indebted to many colleagues, and ex-colleagues, for advice and criticism which has helped us sharpen our argument. Marc Roberts, William Massey, and William G. Shepherd provided extensive comments on early drafts of the study. Hendrik Houthakker and Lester Taylor provided detailed comments on Chapter 5. Richard Caves went far beyond his call of duty as editor of the Harvard Economic Studies Series in providing a detailed evaluation of the whole volume.

Finally, we want to express our considerable appreciation to our wives, Lorraine Comanor and Julia Wilson for bearing with us during this collaboration, which surely must have seemed to them, as it often did to us, unending.

In a collaboration extending over so many years, it is virtually impossible to separate the contributions of the two authors. While three or four chapters might have owed their original conception to one or the other of us, the process of mutual criticism, writing and rewriting, and editing has undermined the accuracy of even so limited an attribution. We therefore assume joint responsibility for each chapter in the monograph.

W.S.C.
T.A.W.

# Advertising and Market Power

CHAPTER 1 **Introduction**

This book deals with the impact of advertising on the structure and performance of the American economy. Various theoretical issues are examined, but emphasis is given to empirical analyses of the determinants and effects of advertising expenditures. Quantitative estimates of these effects constitute the major findings of this study.

OBJECTIVES

Our primary objective is to assess the economic consequences of the current volumes of advertising expenditures, and particularly to examine the effect of advertising on competition. We do not deal with the important issues of fraud or of patently misleading or deceptive advertisements. While the extent of "truthful" information in advertising may influence the economic effects of a given volume of advertising, our purpose is to appraise the effects of the existing volume of these expenditures on market behavior and performance.

Although the issue of advertising content is avoided, our analysis is necessarily concerned with the impact of advertising on consumer decisions, and therefore the general content of these messages assumes some importance. The fact that a message which describes a product is called advertising suggests that it has a self-serving character. It is provided by the seller of the product to prospective buyers to influence the demand for the seller's product. Even if the Federal Trade Commission were fully successful in alleviating problems of deceptive and misleading advertising, the major economic effects of a high volume of advertising might remain.

Consider the following statement by a columnist for *Advertising Age:* "Most advertising down the years has done little more than say sweet nothings about a product . . . It has contained the least information, the fewest facts of almost anything written. We have relied mainly on adjectives, on charm, on manner of presentation, coupled with unspecific, unsupported claims of superiority."[1] Whether or not this statement is a correct description of most advertising, we can note that a typical ad, especially for a final consumer product, gives the name and use of a product offered for sale, but infrequently mentions the price at which it is offered, and rarely provides much more information. At the same time, however, the message does indicate that the product is available and, what may be even more important, that the product is advertised. To the extent that advertised and unadvertised products compete in the same market, the fact that some products are highly advertised may have important implications for market behavior and performance.

An examination of the market effects of advertising must distinguish between two sets of markets. The first is the various markets in which advertising messages are purchased and sold. In these markets, the information media play a vital role and advertisers operate on the demand side of the market. Equally important are the markets for advertised products, where advertisers are sellers. In both cases, final consumers are elements of the demand side of the market. The distinction between these market concepts is important, and the failure to recognize this distinction has been the source of much confusion in studies of the effects of advertising. In the analysis that follows, we examine markets for both advertising messages and advertised products, as well as the interaction that exists between them.

Although an analysis of the market for advertising messages yields some important insights, the economic impact of advertising is felt in the product markets where advertised goods are sold. Three broad effects of advertising may be distinguished. The first is the possible impact of advertising on the total volume of spending in the economy, or more particularly on the distribution of consumer disposable income between spending and saving. This issue is of some interest, and has recently been studied by others,[2] but it is not part of the present study. The second effect of advertising is upon the total demand for products in an industry or, alternatively, upon the distribution of consumer spending among industries. What is at issue here is the extent to which advertising affects the total demand for industry output. In the analysis below,

1. William D. Tyler, "Is Competitive Comparison Really Bad in Advertising? Reform with Care," *Advertising Age*, 37 (March 14, 1966), 61; as quoted in David A. Aaker and George S. Day, *Consumerism: Search for the Consumer Interest* (Glencoe, Ill., Free Press, 1971), p. 97.
2. Lester D. Taylor and Daniel Weiserbs, "Advertising and the Aggregate Consumption Function," *American Economic Review*, 62 (September 1972), 642–655.

demand functions are estimated for a large number of industries in the consumer-goods sector of the economy.

The third effect of advertising is upon the distribution of sales among firms in the same industry. Since the distribution of sales among firms must influence the structure of an industry and thereby the state of competition, it is here where the effects of advertising on competition are likely to be greatest.

The effect of advertising on the intraindustry distribution of demand has a number of facets. Advertising serves as a major vehicle of rivalry in many industries. Advertising may affect the sales of the major firms in such an industry, and hence the relative positions of leading firms.[3] Advertising may also affect the relative demands for the outputs of large and of small firms. To the extent that it conveys advantages to large firms relative to their smaller rivals, advertising affects the relative growths of small and of large firms in industries where these outlays have a substantial effect on consumer demand. Finally, advertising may also influence the relative demands for the products of established firms and for the products of new entrants into the industry. To the extent that it conveys advantages to established firms relative to new entrants, advertising may also constitute a barrier to the entry of new firms. Analyses of intraindustry effects of advertising, examined from the latter two perspectives, constitute an important part of this study.

Throughout the analysis, we ignore the effects of other forms of promotion and focus exclusively on advertising expenditures. Since consistent data are available only for advertising, this limitation is unavoidable. Although the effects of other promotional activities may be similar to those of advertising, this cannot be inferred from our empirical results.

As indicated above, advertising refers to the messages provided by sellers to prospective buyers. This definition, however, covers a large number of situations where market effects may be widely different. Some advertising is carried on by most firms, but the importance of advertising relative to other forms of promotion may vary widely among industries. In particular, advertising by the sellers and distributors of producer goods may be relatively small as compared with their direct selling activities. In these industries, the number of prospective buyers may be sufficiently small that direct selling becomes a feasible strategy. As a result, our empirical analysis is concerned exclusively with firms and industries that produce consumer goods rather than producer goods. Not only are buyers likely to be more informed in the producer-goods sector of the economy, but also advertising expenditures appear

---

3. An amusing discussion of the use of advertising to influence the relative sales of leading firms in an industry is given in Thomas Whiteside, "The Suds Conflict," *The New Yorker*, December 19, 1964, pp. 42–65.

to be a much less important vehicle for selling efforts, so that the effects of advertising should vary greatly between the two sectors. The empirical analysis is applied to the consumer-goods sector, and no inferences should be drawn regarding the effects of advertising in other sectors of the economy.

Not only do we confine our attention to consumer goods, but also we deal only with advertising by firms in the manufacturing sector of the economy. Advertising is of course carried on by firms at both the wholesale and the retail levels of distribution, and much of this advertising concerns manufactured products. Although these outlays may influence consumer choices among alternative products, it has been suggested that advertising at the distribution stage is likely to have economic consequences that differ from those due to advertising by manufacturers.[4] Our attention is therefore confined to the effects of advertising by manufacturing firms in the consumer-goods sector of the economy.

A striking feature of the pattern of advertising expenditures across consumer-goods industries is the extent to which these expenditures are concentrated in a small number of industries. The interindustry distribution of advertising: sales ratios is highly skewed, with relatively low ratios found in most industries and high ratios found in a small number of industries. This suggests that the impact of advertising is unlikely to be distributed evenly across the consumer-goods sector of the economy, but is probably concentrated in a small number of industries. Although advertising may have major economic consequences in these industries, its effects will therefore be much less important in others.

This study includes an examination of this phenomenon. What is it about these industries that gives rise to heavy advertising expenditures, and how can these industries be distinguished from others in the economy? Two sets of factors are relevant. Of primary importance are those factors that reflect the nature of consumer demand for products of the industry. Because consumers may depend more heavily on advertising messages in some industries than in others, the effectiveness of advertising may differ significantly among industries. What is important here is the nature of consumer behavior and the ways in which consumers react to alternative products in the presence of extensive advertising. In addition, the volume of advertising expenditures should be influenced by the relations that exist among firms in the market and by the structure of the product market. We examine the importance of both sets of factors as determinants of the volume of advertising in an industry.

4. Nicholas Kaldor, "The Economic Aspects of Advertising," *Review of Economic Studies*, 18 (1949–50), reprinted in his *Essays on Value and Distribution* (Glencoe, Ill., Free Press, 1960), pp. 123–140.

## CHARACTERISTICS OF THE DATA

Most of the findings presented in later chapters are derived from analyses of statistics on advertising expenditures gathered from tax returns by the Internal Revenue Service. Since advertising is a legitimate deduction from gross revenues, the volume of these expenditures is reported on tax returns, and compilations of those expenditures are published in the IRS statistics. What is reported as advertising expenditures is therefore what the individual firms consider to be such expenditures. The definition may vary from firm to firm, but it seems likely that most use roughly comparable definitions which include primarily payments made to the information media for messages distributed via those media. In this manner, advertising outlays are distinguished from general promotional expenditures, which generally concern efforts made directly by the firm rather than via the various information media.

Although this distinction seems relatively apparent, there may be problems of interpretation, so that firms may differ regarding what is reported as advertising. To the extent that firms distribute and produce their own communication media, which include their advertising messages, it is unlikely that these outlays are reported as advertising expenditures even though they play the same role and function. When carried on within the firm, the expenditures are likely to be reported as salaries and other direct deductions from income, so that advertising is understated. To this extent, the true volume of advertising may be larger than that reported in the IRS statistics.

Since the IRS statistics are limited to corporate tax returns, they do not include advertising outlays by unincorporated enterprises. However, given the overwhelming importance of corporations in the manufacturing sector of the economy, this omission is relatively unimportant.

Industrial diversification poses a potentially greater problem. A corporate tax return is allocated to a specific industry even though the firm operates in several industries. Because of the reasonably broad industry definitions used, however (the IRS minor industries correspond reasonably closely to the three-digit SIC definitions), the possible distortions from this source are reduced. Although many firms have activity in more than one three-digit industry, the bulk of their activity is typically concentrated within a single industry.[5]

5. For data on the industrial diversification of multiunit companies see U.S. Bureau of the Census, *Enterprise Statistics: 1958, Part 1, General Report* (Washington, D.C., U.S. Government Printing Office, 1963). For cross-classification of Census and Internal Revenue Service data see U.S. Bureau of the Census, *Enterprise Statistics: 1958, Part 3, Link of Census Establishment and IRS Corporation Data* (Washington, D.C., U.S. Government Printing Office, 1964).

Many of the analyses that follow are cross-section analyses based on average values for the years 1954 through 1957, a period that has the advantage of representing a full business cycle. Although the results represent relations that existed some time ago, there is some evidence that they have not changed much in recent years. One of our basic relations was reestimated for the period 1963–1964, and similiar results were obtained.[6] Thus, it is unlikely that the results reported are sensitive to the time period selected for the analysis.

The statistical analyses of Chapter 5 are time-series analyses of the effects upon sales of advertising and other variables. Many of the series used are also based upon IRS statistics and run from the early postwar years to 1964. Some of the results obtained from the time-series analysis are used in later cross-section equations. In addition, it should be noted that the period for the cross-section analysis, 1954–1957, lies in the middle of the period of the time-series analysis.

## ORGANIZATION OF THE STUDY

Chapter 2 deals with the market for advertising messages, which, as indicated above, should be distinguished from the markets for advertised and unadvertised products. In this analysis, three important elements in the market are distinguished: sellers of advertising space, generally the information media; buyers of advertising space, generally the sellers of advertised products; and consumers, who also represent a demand for advertising messages. The interrelations among these three elements are examined, and some consideration is given to the question whether the volume of advertising is or is not excessive.

Since the way in which advertising affects consumer behavior has a critical effect on the relative demands for the output of established and new firms, Chapter 3 deals with the relation between advertising and consumer behavior. A model of consumer choice is presented in which the role of advertising is emphasized. This model takes explicitly into account consumer ignorance regarding the merits of competing but differentiated products, and specifies the effects of advertising on the process by which consumers cope with this ignorance.

In Chapter 4, this model is used to explain some of the circumstances in which advertising may constitute a barrier to the entry of new firms. The nature of such barriers is explored, and emphasis is placed on the circumstances in which such barriers are likely to exist. We also consider the extent to which

6. Compare the empirical results presented in Chapter 6 below with those presented in Leonard W. Weiss, "Advertising, Profits and Corporate Taxes," *The Review of Economics and Statistics*, 51 (November 1969), 429.

quantity discounts are present in the sale of advertising messages on the single most important advertising medium: network television.

In Chapter 5, attention is directed to the impact of advertising on industry demand. Dynamic demand functions are estimated for each industry in which the effects on sales of advertising as well as of price and income are estimated.

Chapter 6 presents an empirical analysis of the relation between profit rates, advertising, and other market factors. To the extent that a significant positive relation is observed between advertising and profit rates, this is viewed as providing evidence of the presence of barriers to the entry of new firms. In the absence of such barriers, high profits would encourage entry, which would lead to lower profits. Without additional barriers, high profits can be maintained in the long run only to the extent that advertising serves to restrict entry.

In Chapter 7, the question of the determinants of advertising expenditures is examined. Not only is theoretical analysis provided, but also an empirical analysis is carried out of the factors likely to affect advertising. Following this analysis, a two-equation model is presented in which the determinants of advertising and of profit rates are examined jointly. Since both profit rates and advertising are essentially endogenous variables, this approach is required to obtain clear evidence of the interrelations that exist between these variables. This analysis provides further evidence regarding the relation between advertising and entry barriers.

In Chapters 6 and 7, advertising is considered a current expense despite the possibility that it may have a lasting impact on sales. The theoretical implications of this issue are examined in Chapter 8, and estimates of the goodwill capital created by advertising are derived from the demand equations estimated in Chapter 5. These estimates are used to make adjustments in the profit-rate data used in previous chapters, and cross-section analyses of the adjusted profit rates are presented.

In Chapters 9 and 10, we consider the distribution of advertising expenditures among firms in different size classes within the same industry. The pattern of expenditures among firms is examined in Chapter 9, and Chapter 10 appraises the extent to which advertising expenditures convey significant advantages of size.

In the final chapter, some general questions regarding public policy toward advertising are raised, and the impact of advertising and of market power in consumer-goods industries is assessed. The conclusions and calculations presented in that chapter are based on findings presented in earlier parts of the study.

CHAPTER 2 **The Market for Advertising Messages**

Because the volume of advertising affects the price consumers will pay for a product, it is sometimes argued that sellers supply advertising messages jointly with the product, and that the price charged includes the price of the message as well as the price of the product.[1] As a result, the price differential between advertised and unadvertised products reflects the price set for these messages as a component of the former. Although this is a tempting approach to the analysis of the market for advertising, it involves a number of conceptual difficulties.

As explicitly recognized in later chapters, advertising can in a meaningful way be regarded as a characteristic or attribute of a product, which helps to explain why consumers react differently to advertised and unadvertised products. However, the fact that advertising influences consumer decisions does not by itself imply that consumers purchase advertising when they purchase the advertised product. Indeed, it is apparent that consumer demand for information from advertising or other sources generally precedes the effective demand for the individual product, since the decision to purchase a product must be based on information available prior to the actual purchase, rather than on information acquired by virtue of the purchase itself.[2] As a result of this separation of information gathering from purchase decisions, consumers not only may demand a particular product without demanding its advertising

1. Lester G. Telser, "Demand and Supply for Advertising Messages," *American Economic Review*, 56 (May 1966), 457–458.

2. Of course, past purchases can have significant effect on consumer demand. See the theoretical discussion of the role of advertising and experience in the next chapter, and the empirical analysis of demand functions in Chapter 5 below.

but also may demand the informational content of the advertising without demanding the product. Note that if advertising or information were viewed solely as an attribute or component of the product described, there should be little demand for information regarding products that are not purchased. Since this is patently false, and information is often required about alternative products in order to make a better choice of one of them, consumer decision-making is better viewed as a sequential process in which the demand for information precedes the demand for the product.

The provision of advertising messages and advertised products does not constitute joint supply in the standard economic sense of this term since the two do not arise from the same production process. There are no technical reasons why advertising must be supplied with the product. Furthermore, it should be obvious that some consumers who purchase the product may receive few advertising messages, whereas many or even most advertising messages may be received by those who do not purchase the product. Hence, although the costs of providing the advertising messages as well as the costs of producing and distributing the product are paid by the same firm, the product and the advertising messages are not in joint supply, and the sale of the product cannot be regarded as tied to the sale of the advertising messages.

Not only is the supply of advertising messages distinct from the supply of the advertised product, but the respective demands are also quite separate. Although the demand for advertising messages with respect to a particular branded product is tied generally to the decision to purchase some product within the commodity class, consumers generally demand information on a number of products in the same class and may be willing to allocate some portion of their budget for such messages. Also, consumers may require information rather infrequently, whereas the product may be bought continuously without much information processing between "decision points." Hence, although the demands for advertising and for commodities are related, they are not identical and must be distinguished.

It appears, therefore, that two allocation problems exist which are usefully separated. The first concerns the allocation of resources to the production and distribution of advertising messages; the second concerns the supply and demand of highly advertised and unadvertised products. Although these problems are related, advertising messages and advertised products are in fact provided separately, and an analysis of their respective markets must recognize this separation. In the remainder of this chapter we consider the factors that determine the volume of advertising messages and discuss the efficiency of existing institutional arrangements in the production and distribution of advertising.

## MODELS OF THE DEMAND FOR INFORMATION

Existing studies in this area trace their origin generally to the work of Stigler,[3] and it is therefore instructive to examine his analysis in some detail. Limiting himself to the case of fully homogeneous products, he examines the determinants of consumers' search for information on market prices. The gains from new information are obtained from lower prices, which depend on the minimum asking price of those sellers that are canvassed. Increased search yields diminishing returns, so the relevant demand curve for information is downward sloping. Moreover, consumers continue to search for information on asking prices so long as the expected saving in cost exceeds the marginal cost of searching. Where the two variables are equal, an optimal amount of information is determined. In this analysis, the costs of search may be indicated either by the opportunity cost, in income or leisure, of canvassing sellers or by the price charged for information services.[4]

Although this model is essentially static, Stigler emphasizes that the optimal quantity of search depends on the correlation of individual asking prices in successive time periods. When this correlation is perfect, the initial search is the only one undertaken, whereas if asking prices are uncorrelated, the gains from search are limited to the immediate time period. At intermediate values, this information will aid the consumer at various times, although "customer search will be larger in the initial period than in subsequent periods."[5]

Since this model refers strictly to the case of fully homogeneous products, some extensions are required before it can be applied more generally to the demand for information. Farley proposes a simple extension by noting that, where brands in the same commodity class are viewed as good substitutes for one another, buyers search for the lowest price among alternative brands rather than simply for the lowest price for a given brand.[6] In these circumstances, the gains from additional information are still defined by the expected price reduction times the quantity to be purchased. Although different brands of the same commodity are used for the same purpose, significant perceived quality differences among brands may be present. As a result, the search for

3. George J. Stigler, "The Economics of Information," *Journal of Political Economy*, 69 (June 1961), 213–225.

4. An extension of Stigler's analysis which emphasizes the effect of wage rates and information prices on the amount of search is presented in Jacob Mincer, "Market Prices, Opportunity Costs, and Income Effects," in Carl F. Christ and others, *Measurement in Economics* (Stanford, Calif., Stanford University Press, 1963), pp. 79–81. See also Richard H. Holton, "Consumer Behavior, Market Imperfections, and Public Policy," in Jesse W. Markham and Gustav F. Papanek, eds., *Industrial Organization and Economic Development — In Honor of E. S. Mason* (Boston, Houghton Mifflin, 1970), pp. 105–108.

5. Stigler, "The Economics of Information," p. 218.

6. John U. Farley, "Brand Loyalty and the Economics of Information," *Journal of Business*, 37 (October 1964), 370–371.

consumer information in this case is probably motivated more strongly by the goal of improved product quality than by that of lower prices.

One approach to this problem would be to view the gains from information as derived from the expected price reduction per unit of search for given product qualities, but this ignores the prospect that trade-offs may exist between lower prices and improved product qualities. An alternative approach, which incorporates these trade-offs, is to measure the gains from additional search by the increase in perceived performance that is due to searching further for a better product as well as for lower prices. In this framework, the gains from increased search depend not only on the dispersion of asking prices in the market but also on the perceived variance in product performance among brands in the commodity class, so that the higher the variance, the greater the gains from increased information.

An important feature of the extended model is that information costs should be far greater than in the case of fully homogeneous products. These costs refer now to the process of obtaining information on relative product qualities as well as on relative prices. Though prices can easily be canvassed, quality is a multidimensional characteristic about which it may be difficult to obtain factual information. This is especially important where the consumer is unable to evaluate the relative quality of an individual brand through personal inspection. Information costs may be so high in such circumstances that, even after spending considerable time and effort, the consumer may have gathered remarkably little factual information and still feel very much in the dark.

Furthermore, where new products are frequently introduced and standards of product performance frequently altered, the correlation of product quality in successive time periods may be sufficiently low that the high costs of gathering factual information are not easily spread across purchases separated in time. One result of rapid rates of new product introduction is to increase substantially the cost of information.[7] When the marginal costs of search are quite high, consumers may find it optimal to do very little searching. The consumer's primary problem may be one of coping with significant ignorance rather than of obtaining factual information with which to make decisions. These two problems, however, are two sides of the same coin, for we can reinterpret the problem of ignorance as one of making do with relatively little objective but costly information while making maximum use of whatever low-cost information is available.

7. The classic example of this phenomenon is the U.S. pharmaceutical industry where rapid rates of new product introduction during the postwar period increased information costs so much that substantial ignorance remained regarding product performance among prescribing physicians. See Herman M. Somers and Anne R. Somers, *Doctors, Patients, and Health Insurance* (Washington, D.C., Brookings Institution, 1962), pp. 95–101.

## THE ROLE OF ADVERTISING

Consumer information is derived from various sources, and each has distinct costs and characteristics. A major source is personal inspection by the prospective consumer. For homogeneous products, obtaining the required information may involve little more than learning the asking price. Where style or appearance is an important product characteristic, this source of information will also provide much of the information required to make a purchase decision. Where appearance is irrelevant but products are heterogeneous, however, as in the case of proprietary drug products, personal inspection, though inexpensive, yields little relevant information about product quality.

Direct consumer experience with a product is another major source of information, but one with an unusual price structure. When the consumer has previously purchased the product, the informational value of prior use is provided freely, so that the price is effectively zero, whereas if the product has not yet been purchased, prior experience *cannot* be gained at this time, so that the price is effectively infinite. Alternatively, it might be argued that the price of gaining experience is the price of the product itself. However, in the typical instance, where knowledge based on experience is acquired from consumption of a product over time, it may be impossible for the consumer to obtain this experience at a given time.

Consumer information is also gained indirectly from the experience of others through word-of-mouth communication. A further source of consumer information is that provided by journals such as *Consumer Reports* or obtained from knowledgeable and informed individuals. Although the cost may be high in these cases, the factual content of the information provided may also be substantial.

A final major source of consumer information consists of advertising messages. This category covers a vast variety of kinds of messages, which have in common the characteristic that they are provided by the sellers of the product. The spectrum of advertising runs from classified advertisements in newspapers to commercials on network television, and substantial differences exist among these various types. Our concern, however, is with advertising messages supplied by manufacturers of consumer goods directly to actual or potential customers.[8]

Advertising messages of this type are concerned primarily with providing a

---

8. That important differences exist between retailer and manufacturer advertising, which have implications for public policy, has been noted by other economists. Thus, Hicks suggests that "advertising by retailers is more harmonious with customers' interests than is advertising by manufacturer." John R. Hicks, "Economic Theory and the Evaluation of Consumers' Wants," *Journal of Business*, 35 (July 1962), 258.

summary of the product to prospective customers. Its presence on the market is made known, and on repetition the messages may instill a degree of familiarity with the product. In addition, some messages provide information on various product attributes and on prospective prices, although data on the latter are not contained in most advertising in this class. Most important, however, the messages provide information that the product is advertised.[9]

The demand for advertising as an information source is strongly influenced by the fact that it does not generally provide *objective* information. By this we mean simply that its content is determined by those with a direct commercial interest in the information provided. Indeed, the self-serving character of advertising is perhaps its dominant feature. Although this fact does not necessarily indicate that advertising has little informational content or that it is misleading, it does suggest that consumers would probably be willing to replace a large number of advertising messages by a smaller number of messages from more objective sources of information. Consumer demand for advertising should therefore be influenced by the availability of information from other sources. Where the cost of obtaining consumer information from other sources is relatively low, the demand for advertising will be low, whereas this demand will be high when consumer information derived from other sources is difficult and costly to obtain.

Consumer demand for advertising depends on the relative benefits as well as the relative costs of obtaining information from more objective sources. Where the gains from additional information are large, consumers are likely to allocate substantial resources to additional search, and there should be little demand for advertising. In the opposite case, where the gains from additional information are small, there should be more demand by consumers for advertising. In these circumstances, a greater reliance on the content of advertising messages as opposed to more objective information would be the consumer's equivalent of the "optimally imperfect decision" of the firm.[10] This position is consistent with Katona's view that "the influence of advertising . . . decreases in proportion to the importance the consumer attaches to a matter."[11]

A similar view of the concept of "brand loyalty" has been advanced. It is argued that where "brands are generally considered good substitutes for

9. In this chapter we are concerned with the market for advertising messages and not with advertising as a product attribute, except as it affects the demand by firms for advertising of their products. An examination of the influence of advertising as a product attribute on consumer purchasing decisions is found in the following chapters.

10. William J. Baumol and Richard E. Quandt, "Rules of Thumb and Optimally Imperfect Decisions," *American Economic Review*, 54 (March 1964), 23–46.

11. George Katona, *The Mass Consumption Society* (New York, McGraw-Hill, 1964), p. 58. A similar view is advanced in Peter Doyle, "Advertising Expenditure and Consumer Demand," *Oxford Economic Papers*, 20 (November 1968), 402.

one another, then households which put considerable effort into gathering market information should appear less brand loyal towards all products than those families which search relatively little."[12] Where the optimal volume of information is low, consumers respond by having a high demand for the information content of experience with the product and thereby place greater reliance on repeat purchasing. Therefore, an explanation for "brand loyalty" may be that it is a typical response to the presence of high levels of consumer ignorance in circumstances where the cost of factual information is relatively high.

A salient feature of the market for advertising messages is that the quantity of messages is determined by the firm that produces and sells the advertised product. An individual consumer cannot generally purchase a quantity of advertising that is different from the quantity of messages made available by the firm. Although the number of consumption units may differ from one consumer to another, that number is set by the volume of messages that are produced. On this account, advertising has important aspects of a public good as it pertains to consumers.[13]

We have been discussing various factors that influence the marginal evaluations of advertising by individual consumers. These evaluations determine individual demand schedules for advertising, and it is the vertical sum of these schedules that represents aggregate consumer demand for advertising messages.

## THE PRICE OF ADVERTISING MESSAGES

A major characteristic of the method by which advertising is provided is that typically these messages are not sold at all but rather are given away. In fact, the relevant price for most of these messages is negative, since consumers are paid to consume them.[14] For various reasons, however, these payments are not in cash. Although, in principle, it would be possible for sellers to offer cash payments to consumers willing to read or listen to an advertising message,

12. Farley, "Brand Loyalty," p. 370. Another study which uses the same framework is Ronald E. Frank, Susan P. Douglas, Rolando E. Polli, "Household Correlates of 'Brand Loyalty' for Grocery Products," *Journal of Business*, 41 (April 1968), 237–245.

13. See James M. Buchanan, *The Demand and Supply of Public Goods* (Chicago, Rand McNally, 1968), pp. 49–75.

14. Examples of advertising which is sold to final buyers do exist, but account for a very small portion of total advertising outlays. A larger portion is represented by advertising provided free but unaccompanied by subsidized services; obvious cases are billboard advertising and mail circulars. However, the major share of total outlays is accounted for by advertising in newspapers and magazines and on radio and television. Such advertising, because of the subsidized services provided by the medium, has an effective negative price to the final consumer.

it might be difficult to create institutional arrangements which ensured that payments were made only to those who received the message. Furthermore, the "consumption" of an advertising or promotional message requires not merely that it be read or listened to but also that it be given some element of credence and recognition. It requires that some degree of validity be imputed to the message.

For these reasons, the payments to consumers to receive the messages take the form of subsidies to the information media. Because of these subsidies, consumers receive the content of the medium either at a much reduced price, as in the case of magazines or newspapers, or completely free, as in the case of television or radio. By mixing advertising messages thoroughly with the normal content of the medium, it is made inconvenient to obtain this content without the messages, and the latter are in effect forced on the consumer of the medium. Advertising and the normal content of the medium are not generally separated in time or in space, for this separation would facilitate payment being made without the message being received.

Joint products therefore exist in the provision of advertising messages, but the joint supply is of the message with the content of the medium and not of the message with the advertised product. The same production facilities and other inputs produce both the message and the content of the medium, and there is no fully nonarbitrary way to allocate various categories of cost between the message and the nonadvertising content of the information medium. Not only is this arrangement derived from the nature of the production process but also it provides a mechanism by which the volume of advertising messages provided may exceed the quantity demanded by consumers when price equals zero. It provides the vehicle through which an effective negative price may be established.

Furthermore, there may be significant economies of integration in the production and distribution of advertising messages in conjunction with the nonadvertising content of the media, which can be realized in part by the advertiser. Not only may there be technical economies of joint supply, but, equally important, the cost to the advertiser to provide a message via the media may be far less than the monetary payment that otherwise would be paid to consumers to receive the message, even if the same technology were used. Current charges to large advertisers on network television lie generally between $2.00 and $5.00 per thousand messages provided,[15] and it is not unlikely that

15. Price statistics for evening programs on the NBC television network during March 1966 are given in "Possible Anticompetitive Effects of Sale of Network TV Advertising," *Hearings before the Subcommittee on Antitrust and Monopoly*, Committee on the Judiciary, U.S. Senate, 89:2, Part 2, December 12–14, 1966, pp. 638–639.

consumers would demand higher monetary payments than between 0.2 and 0.5 cents per message to receive the volume of messages currently placed before them.

The volume of advertising messages consumed depends on the nature of the "payment" that is offered to consumers as well as on the inherent utility of the advertising messages. Where the demand curve falls below the horizontal axis, we expect that a different set of factors becomes operative, so that the two portions of the curve may bear little relation to each other. Even though the demand curve may be quite inelastic at positive price levels, it may become relatively elastic when the relevant price becomes negative. Consumer reactions may even diverge so sharply that the curve is discontinuous at the horizontal axis.

At positive price levels, the demand for advertising messages is derived from the consumer's demand for information. The higher the price of alternative sources of information, the greater is the demand for advertising messages. In addition, some advertisements are valued as entertainment as much as for their informational content. Although alternative sources of information generally entail monetary costs and almost always require some outlay of time or effort on the part of the consumer, this is not generally so in the case of advertising. Permitting the demand curve for advertising messages to fall below the horizontal axis explicitly acknowledges this fact. What is implied when the effective price of advertising messages is negative is that consumers receive the content of more advertising messages than they would be willing to pay for or even accept if provided freely. At negative price levels, therefore, the demand for advertising messages is set by the nature of the "payment" made to consumers and by the disutility they impute to receiving an excess volume of messages.

## THE MARKET FOR ADVERTISING

There are two demands in the market for advertising,[16] and as a result two prices are established. In addition to consumer demands for advertising and the price charged to consumers, there is the demand for advertising by individual firms and the price paid by them to the information media for carrying their messages to consumers. Advertising to the firm represents a productive input where the various media are competing suppliers. The firm's demands for these services are derived from the profit calculations of the firm and, like

16. The existence of two demand curves for advertising messages was noted originally in Peter O. Steiner, "Economics of Broadcasting and Advertising: Discussion," *American Economic Review*, 56 (May 1966), 473. The second demand curve below, however, is defined on a different basis from that originally presented by Steiner.

other inputs, are defined by the marginal revenue of advertising messages. In equilibrium, the marginal revenue from advertising must equal the marginal cost of advertising.

Since advertising is typically "sold" to consumers at a negative price, there are generally no revenues that are derived from direct payments by consumers. Instead, the marginal revenue from advertising reflects the marginal profit on the increase in the number of units sold or the increased price at which output can be sold that is due to a unit increase in the number of messages purchased from the media and supplied to consumers. For firms, as opposed to consumers, advertising can be viewed as a private good,[17] and therefore the market demand is the horizontal sum of constituent firm demands. If the market for advertising messages is competitive, the intersection of this demand curve with the relevant supply curve determines the price and quantity of messages provided. If advertising messages are sold in imperfectly competitive markets, different outcomes result, but they depend in any case on the same two functional relations. To simplify the discussion, we therefore deal only with the former case.

In Figure 2.1, demand curve $D$ indicates the aggregate consumer demand

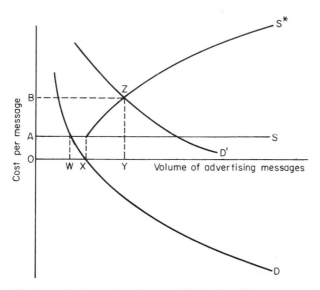

Fig. 2.1.   The market for advertising messages

17. By this we mean simply that a firm can purchase a volume of advertising messages which is independent of the number of messages purchased by other firms. The impact of these messages is generally influenced by the number of messages purchased by other firms. As a result, the market demand curve must reflect these external effects. These external effects are discussed further below and in Chapter 7.

for advertising messages, whereas $D'$ is the demand curve for these messages by sellers of advertised products. The fact that we observe generally negative consumer demand prices for advertising suggests that firms' marginal revenue of advertising exceeds consumers' aggregate marginal willingness to pay for advertising at the current volumes of messages. It is for this reason that curve $D'$ is drawn to the right of curve $D$.

The relevant supply curve in this market is the marginal cost curve of advertising messages. These include both the cost of producing and distributing messages and the "payments" made to consumers in the form of subsidies to the information media. The two are combined as in Fig. 2.1. Curve $S$ indicates the locus of supply prices for the production and distribution of advertising messages as such. Constant costs are assumed here, although this is not required for the analysis. Beyond the point $X$ where $D$ cuts the horizontal axis, the relevant supply price, however, includes the cost of the subsidy to media services, so that at each volume of messages this payment is added to $S$ to obtain $S^*$. Since this subsidy equals the implicit payments to consumers in the form of improved or lower-priced media services, the vertical difference between $S^*$ and $S$ equals the vertical difference between $D$ and the horizontal axis. The portion of $S^*$ to the left of a volume of messages equal to $OX$ is not drawn, since it depends on conflicting considerations. Although $S^*$ might be expected to fall below $S$ at this point, this might not be so if substantial "transaction costs" would result from the collection of fees from receivers of advertising messages.[18] Whatever happens to the left of point $X$, however, this is not generally the relevant range of the supply curve for advertising messages and it can be ignored in this analysis.

In Fig. 2.1., the volume of advertising messages that are provided is $OY$, at a cost per message of $OB$. Of this latter amount, $OA$ refers to the unit cost of producing and distributing the messages and $AB$ indicates the payment that must be paid, in the form of subsidies to the information media, to induce consumers to "consume" this volume of messages. Here $AB$ exceeds $OA$, which may well be the case in most markets for advertising messages. Where joint costs are present, so that the costs of distributing the content of the media are not separable, the division of total cost into these two components may contain a large arbitrary element. In either case, however, the total sum paid by advertisers is given by the rectangle $OBZY$. At the same time, since there are a large number of advertisers in the market, the effective supply price for each individual firm will be constant at $OB$.

The difference between firms' and consumers' demands is accentuated by the fact that, even when more messages are received than would be paid for,

18. Telser, "Demand and Supply of Advertising Messages," p. 458.

the entire volume of messages nonetheless contributes to the consumer's stock of information regarding the advertised product. Even where the marginal utility of advertising messages is negative, they may still contribute to consumer information and influence purchasing decisions. This apparent paradox disappears when it is recognized that a static model is used to describe behavior at different times. The receipt of advertising messages is viewed as taking place prior to the time when purchasing decisions are made, so that consumers are content to use the content of these messages once provided even if they are unwilling to pay for them, since the disutility associated with receiving advertising messages takes place when the messages are received. A negative demand price for a volume of advertising messages may indicate simply that the disutility at the time of their receipt exceeds the positive utility derived from using the information obtained when purchasing decisions are made.

A further consideration provides additional support for this view of the demand and impact of advertising messages. It is often argued that consumers are not free to ignore the content of these messages, either when received or when purchasing decisions are made. Not only is it made difficult for a consumer to dispense with these messages through the manner in which they are intermixed with the content of the media, but also he is frequently not able to ignore, even if he wants to, the fact that advertising has made a product well known. Furthermore, a rational consumer might be willing to pay to avoid advertising messages precisely because he will recognize that he cannot avoid being influenced—perhaps subconsciously—by their blandishments.[19]

## IS ADVERTISING EXCESSIVE?

At this point, we can review the controversy whether the volume of advertising is excessive. As summarized by Telser,[20] the affirmative view rests on two points: first, the price set for advertising messages lies below marginal costs and therefore an inefficiently large volume of messages is provided; and second, the joint supply of advertising and advertised products leads to the provision of more messages than there would be in separate markets. Telser

---

19. The classic popular discussion of the inability of many consumers to ignore the blandishments of advertising messages is Vance Packard, *The Hidden Persuaders* (New York, D. McKay, 1957). Kaldor argues similarly that: "The information supplied in advertisements . . . attempts to influence the behavior of the consumer, not so much by enabling him to plan more intelligently through giving more information, but by forcing a small amount of information, through its sheer prominence to the foreground of consciousness." Nicholas Kaldor, "The Economic Aspects of Advertising," reprinted in *Essays on Value and Distribution* (Glencoe, Ill., Free Press, 1960), p. 103.
20. Telser, "Demand and Supply of Advertising Messages," p. 457.

takes the opposite view by emphasizing the additional transaction costs that may result when a positive price is set for advertising.

The first charge is then rejected, since lower costs are in this case achieved with the larger output attained when price equals zero. Because of the presence of transaction costs, the total costs of providing a volume of messages equal to $OX$ may be less than those required to limit the volume received to $OW$, which is the output where price equals marginal costs and where there is no additional firm demand for advertising. The second charge is similarly rejected by noting that there may be economies in the joint supply of advertising with the product. Not only may costs be lower with this arrangement, but also it may provide a vehicle through which a positive price can be charged for advertising messages, which, Telser argues, is the difference in price between advertised and unadvertised products that are otherwise identical.[21]

Both the criticism of advertising and the defense suffer, however, from an acceptance of the view that advertising is supplied jointly with the product despite the major analytical difficulties that are involved. However, when it is recognized instead that advertising messages are supplied jointly with the information or entertainment content of the carrying media, the controversy changes in important respects. Under these conditions, advertising may be excessive in some sectors but not in others—a possibility not readily encompassed within an analysis based on the assumption that advertising and advertised products are in joint supply.

In the absence of transaction costs, firms would always provide at least the amount of advertising demanded by consumers, since the consumers can be charged directly for the costs of the advertising provided to them. Where the transaction costs of directly charging consumers are large, which may be the situation for most advertising, this conclusion no longer holds. For example, under conditions of pure competition with imperfect information, producers may provide a suboptimal volume of advertising. Because the product is relatively homogeneous, each producer will ignore the positive external effects of his own advertising on the sales of his competitors in the market.

In large-numbers markets with product differentiation (monopolistic competition), the opposite result holds. Now each producer will ignore the negative external effects of his advertising on his competitors' sales. Since price is greater than marginal cost, the firm's demand price for advertising will probably exceed the consumers' demand price. Hence, some advertising in excess of the amount demanded by consumers is another facet of monopolistic competition. However, whether such advertising can be regarded as excessive from a social point of view in large-numbers monopolistically competitive

21. *Ibid.*, pp. 457–462.

markets is difficult to determine, since advertising will affect both the scale of the representative firm and the variety of differentiated products available to consumers within such markets.

In markets where entry is retarded, on the other hand, the volume of advertising contributes to the volume of monopoly profits earned by member firms. This effect is exacerbated where advertising permits firms to establish higher price-cost margins than would otherwise be the case. Where advertising has a strong impact on entry barriers, or where it serves to reduce the elasticity of demand for the major firms' products, the two demand curves for advertising may be far apart. In other words, the gap between $D$ and $D'$ is probably greatest in precisely those markets where the effects of advertising on competition is strongest. It is in such markets that one can infer that advertising is clearly excessive from a social standpoint, since those benefits to the firm that are not benefits to consumers accrue precisely because of the anticompetitive effects of the advertising.

What is important therefore is the extent to which advertising is used to achieve anticompetitive market results. In particular, an important issue is the extent to which heavy advertising constructs barriers to the entry of new firms into a market and thereby protects the positions of established firms. This question lies at the heart of much of the current debate over whether advertising is excessive. It is therefore the subject of many of the remaining chapters.

# CHAPTER 3 Advertising and Consumer Choice

Advertising affects the distribution of sales among competing products or brands of different firms in the same industry as well as the distribution of sales among industries. In this chapter, we examine the role of advertising in influencing consumers' choice of rival brands within a market.

Since the extent of the differential effects of advertising upon the products of large and small firms or of old and new firms within an industry will largely determine its impact on market structure and performance, we develop a model of consumer choice that emphasizes these effects. This model describes some circumstances that might lead to differential effects. Tests of the hypothesis that these differential effects are important are presented in the empirical analysis of subsequent chapters.[1]

The problem of consumer choice may usefully be divided into two distinct decision problems: the choice among alternative commodities and the choice among alternative brands of the same commodity. In this view of the process of consumer choice as one of sequential decision-making, the choice among alternative brands or products is a suboptimization problem that is reached after consumers have already made their decisions regarding the set of commodities to be purchased.

At the first level, we assume that decisions are not made with reference to actual product prices but rather on the basis of a price bracket that represents some notion of the expected price for a commodity. As a result, actual prices

1. As is typical of a result derived from highly restrictive assumptions, other sets of assumptions might well lead to the same testable hypothesis. Hence, such a test does not imply that the particular assumptions used are necessarily valid or invalid.

of brands enter the decision-making process primarily in the choice among alternative brands of the same commodity. There is preliminary empirical evidence that consumers in fact behave this way and do not have an exact price in mind when a decision is made to purchase a commodity,[2] which provides some support for an approach that emphasizes a sequential process

## ADVERTISING AND CONSUMER IGNORANCE

In choosing among alternative brands of the same commodity, consumers face an information problem that may well be more difficult than the one they face when choosing from the menu of commodities. It may be reasonable to assume that specified tastes exist for various commodities and that consumers have prospective quality levels sufficiently well in mind that problems of ignorance and information are not the dominant factors that influence final decisions.[3] In considering the choice among alternative brands of the same commodity, however, the picture is different. Apart from instances where differences in styling or taste play a major role, consumers are unlikely to have strong preferences for one brand over another, so that decisions are likely to be influenced substantially by the consumer's efforts at finding information and coping with his remaining ignorance. In this decision-making process, the choices that are made could diverge significantly from those that would have been made if the consumer had free and perfect information.

Many aspects of consumer behavior can be explained only with reference to the problems of ignorance and information. One such important aspect is that many demand curves may have substantial regions with positive rather than negative slopes, where price is indeed used as a measure of quality.[4]

A separate but related question concerns the existence of brand loyalty and the problem of explaining why this is a dominant feature of consumer behavior. One possible reason is that differences among brands exist and that consumers simply prefer one set of product characteristics to another. This

2. Andre Gabor and C. W. J. Granger, "Price as an Indicator of Quality: A Report on an Inquiry," *Economica*, 33 (February 1966), 43–70.

3. As demonstrated in Chapter 5, however, advertising apparently *does* affect consumer demands for broad classes of products.

4. A survey study recently concluded that "the typical short-run market demand curve for competitive branded products has a substantial backward sloping portion." Gabor and Granger, "Price as an Indicator of Quality," p. 66. Some further evidence is provided by the frequency of the response that "You get what you pay for" in a survey of consumer purchasing decisions among private and national brands of the same commodity. As expected, these responses were given primarily by consumers who used lower prices to indicate lower qualities and therefore were more eager to purchase a high-priced than low-priced brand. John C. Myers, "Determinants of Private Brand Attitude", in Harold H. Kassarjian and Thomas S. Robertson, eds., *Perspectives in Consumer Behavior* (Glenville, Ill., Scott Foresman and Co., 1968), pp. 149–152.

explanation may be true in many instances, but it fails to account for the existence of significant brand loyalty where few major objective differences exist among brands. A different explanation, which does not rest on the existence of differences among brands, is simply that "much brand loyalty is a device for reducing the risks of consumer decisions," and that this loyalty may be "seen as a means of economizing of decision effort by substituting habit for repeated, deliberate decisions."[5] If we accept this argument, it appears that many features of consumer behavior, at least as they refer to the choice among alternative brands of the same commodity, can be explained only with reference to the problems of ignorance and information.

This approach to the problem of consumer decision-making is similar to that emphasized by Katona in various writings.[6] He distinguishes between "habitual behavior" and "genuine decision-making," and suggests that the latter is relatively rare and normally requires strong incentives. In most circumstances, the consumer follows accustomed patterns of behavior that both "reduce uncertainty and help escape from vacillation and conflict by reliance on procedures which have proved themselves in the past."[7] Katona maintains that, rather than indicating irrationality, the cost of more circumspect actions is frequently sufficiently high that this represents a rational mode of behavior. What is important is not "impulse buying, in the sense of whimsical and ununderstandable purchases," but rather "frequent manifestations of habitual behavior."[8]

Where consumer behavior is better characterized by routine decisions than by a careful calculus, consumers are likely to place greater reliance on some sources of information than on others. Not only are some sources more costly in terms of both time and money, but, equally important, they require careful and deliberate actions if they are to influence consumer decisions. For this reason, information sources such as advertising assume a major role precisely because they can be digested with little effort on the part of the consumer. Moreover, as indicated in the previous chapter, consumers are effectively paid to receive the current volume of advertising messages. This source may provide little factual information, but it does have the effect of making a product "well known," a characteristic datum that may influence many

5. Raymond A. Bauer, "Consumer Behavior as Risk Taking," in Perry Bliss, ed., *Marketing and Behavioral Sciences* (Boston, Allyn and Bacon, 1963), p. 90.
6. George Katona, *Psychological Analysis of Economic Behavior* (New York, McGraw-Hill, 1951), pp. 63–69; his "Rational Behavior and Economic Behavior," *Psychological Review*, 60, no. 5 (1953), 307–317; and his *The Powerful Consumer* (New York, McGraw-Hill, 1960), pp. 138–154.
7. Katona, *The Powerful Consumer*, p. 140.
8. *Ibid.*, p. 144.

consumers. This form of consumer information is not so much searched for as reacted to. It therefore can be viewed as an exogenous factor rather than as an additional variable to be manipulated in the course of decision-making.

Where considerable consumer ignorance exists regarding the relative merits of alternative products, and where consumer behavior may be characterized as "routine behavior," advertising outlays are more likely to have a major influence on decisions. This is not because consumers accept this source of information as more objective than it is, but rather because it provides an important distinction among products, which serves as a guide to decision-making: the distinction between advertised and unadvertised products. What becomes important is not so much the content of an advertising message as the simple fact that a product or brand is well advertised; and we can note the common description of a brand as advertised in particular magazines. Furthermore, it appears that in choosing a well-known, highly advertised, but expensive brand over an unknown, little-advertised, but low-priced product, the consumer may simply be doing his best to cope with his lack of objective information concerning relative product quality, and this may represent a reasonable method of minimizing the risk to him that the product will not do the job for which it is being purchased. In other words, consumers may regard advertising as an implied warranty regarding product performance. The model of consumer behavior outlined below emphasizes these considerations, and facilitates an examination of the process by which advertising and promotion may influence consumer choice among competing brands.

## A MODEL OF CONSUMER CHOICE

In this section, we present a model of consumer choice among different brands of the same commodity. We assume that the consumer has already determined how much he will spend on the commodity and therefore approximately how many units he will purchase. As a result, we are concerned with the solution to a suboptimization problem. Since we are dealing with alternative brands of the same commodity, we assume that competing products are highly substitutable for one another. This assumption, which stems from the basic formulation of the problem, enables us to be more definite regarding the form of the preference function, for it implies that it is divisible into parts that refer to individual products. We therefore start with a general utility function given by

$$U = U(q_1, q_2), \tag{1}$$

where $q_1$ and $q_2$ are quantities of two brands of the same commodity.

If we also assume constant marginal utilities for each brand (at least across the relevant range of quantities to be purchased), we can rewrite the preference function for an individual consumer in the form

$$U = q_1 U_1 + q_2 U_2, \tag{2}$$

where $U_1$ and $U_2$ refer to the marginal utility of each unit purchased of the prospective products.

The consumer maximizes his preference function subject to a standard budget constraint, but where the total budget is given by the outcome of the primary optimization problem. The total budget allocated to this commodity need not be spent, although it does place a ceiling on how much may be spent for this commodity. We then write the constraints faced by the consumer as

$$Y \geq p_1 q_1 + p_2 q_2; \; q_1 \geq 0, \; q_2 \geq 0. \tag{3}$$

This is a classical view of consumer decision-making and the outcome is obtained as the solution to a mathematical programming problem. As is well known, this problem is solved by forming the appropriate Lagrangian expression:

$$V = q_1 U_1 + q_2 U_2 + \lambda(Y - p_1 q_1 - p_2 q_2), \tag{4}$$

where the Kuhn-Tucker first-order conditions for a maximum are given by

$$\frac{\partial V}{\partial q_1} = U_1 - \lambda p_1 \leq 0,$$

$$\frac{\partial V}{\partial q_2} = U_2 - \lambda p_2 \leq 0, \tag{5}$$

$$q_1(U_1 - \lambda p_1) > 0,$$

$$q_2(U_2 - \lambda p_2) < 0.$$

Since the products are substitutes, the marginal rate of substitution between the two brands is generally constant, and we expect to reach a "corner solution," where the consumer will purchase only a single brand. He will purchase the first brand if

$$\frac{U_1}{U_2} > \frac{P_1}{P_2} \tag{6}$$

and will purchase the second brand if

$$\frac{U_1}{U_2} < \frac{P_1}{P_2} \tag{7}$$

He is of course indifferent between the two brands if the two ratios are equal. Where there are differences in utility between the two products, we can let

$U_1$ be the utility index attached to the preferred product and $U_2$ be the utility index of the second product. For purposes of the latter analysis, it will be useful to consider the first brand as that of a "representative product" that is sold by established firms in the market whereas the second represents a less well-known brand trying to obtain the consumer's dollar.

For the consumer to purchase the second brand, its price must be sufficiently lower that

$$\frac{P_1 - P_2}{P_2} > \frac{U_1}{U_2} - 1. \tag{8}$$

Let $\beta$ represent the minimum percentage markdown in price for the second brand that is required to induce the consumer to purchase it; $\beta$ therefore equals the right-hand side of expression (8). As expected, $\beta$ is directly related to the utility of the first brand and inversely related to the utility of the second. In these circumstances, the seller of the second brand can hope to reduce $\beta$ only by taking steps to increase $U_2$ relative to $U_1$.

To this point, we have relied on the classical theory of consumer behavior. The interesting questions, of course, concern the factors that determine $U_1$ and $U_2$, and it is only by making some assumptions regarding these quantities that further results may be obtained. As argued before, these assumptions must deal explicitly with the problem of the consumer's ignorance, in terms of his inability to evaluate the merits of competing products, as well as with the impact of various sources of information, in particular that of advertising.

It seems reasonable to assume that the utility of one brand or product relative to another depends on its subjectively perceived performance. Consumer preferences will depend on performance characteristics that are perceived at the time of purchase and therefore are a subjective phenomenon, as contrasted with actual performance which might be determined objectively. Thus, if we let $a_i$ be an index of the perceived performance of the $i$th brand in a commodity class, we can view the utility function as having $a_i$ as its primary argument.

An alternative way of interpreting the index of perceived performance $a_i$ is as a weighted average of expectations on "relevant" product characteristics.[9] Products have various dimensions and the consumer measures perform-

9. These product characteristics are analogous to those used by Lancaster. In this sense, the theory proposed here resembles the one proposed by Lancaster in that utility depends on specific product characteristics. It differs from his, however, in that it is limited to consumer decisions among brands in the same commodity class and also in assuming that utility "weights" exist which may be attached to relevant product characteristics to form a single index of performance. As a result, Lancaster's theory is more general. See Kelvin J. Lancaster, "A New Approach to Consumer Theory," *Journal of Political Economy*, 74 (April 1966), 132–157.

ance separately in each. Aggregate performance of a product then depends both on its rating for each characteristic and on the utility weights that reflect their relative importance to the consumer.

Another important assumption of the model is that consumers are risk averse with regard to perceived product performance so that the marginal-utility function for the $i$th brand is given by

$$U_i = U(Ea_i, Va_i), \tag{9}$$

where $EA_i$ and $Va_i$ are the expectation and the variance of subjectively perceived performance. Then

$$\frac{\partial U_i}{\partial Ea_i} > 0 \text{ and } \frac{\partial U_i}{\partial Va_i} < 0. \tag{10}$$

If we let these partial derivatives be constants that depend on the particular commodity class and do not vary among brands within the class, then expression (9) can be rewritten in the form

$$U_i = \alpha_1 Ea_i - \alpha_2 Va_i, \tag{11}$$

where both $\alpha_1$ and $\alpha_2$ are nonnegative.

The remaining major assumptions deal with the factors likely to determine the expectation and the variance of $a_i$. Both must depend on the degree of consumer information regarding the particular brand as well as on the "true" product characteristics. Where consumer information is "perfect," the subjective expected value would equal the true value of product performance. Where consumer information on the product—beyond that required to identify it as being within the commodity class—is completely absent, expected product performance should be unrelated to its true value.

One shortcoming of this view of consumer information is that it requires that information apply equally to all product characteristics and does not permit consumers to be more knowledgeable about some characteristics than about others. To permit the latter would require that information be of a multidimensional character. Although the restricted definition is used to simplify the analysis, it does serve to limit further the generality of the model.

The expectation of $a_i$ should depend on three factors: the "true" product characteristics of the brand, the typical characteristics of brands in the class, and the degree of consumer information. Moreover, the last can be viewed as a factor determining the weights by which the first two factors should be joined from the point of view of the consumer. Using the simplest formulation of this notion gives a simple linear expression of these determinants:

$$Ea_i = X\bar{a}_i + (1 - X)k\bar{a}, \tag{12}$$

where $\bar{a}_i$ indicates "true" product performance and $\bar{a}$ represents the mean product performance among the leading brands in the commodity class. These represent *ex post* values but not ones that require consumer omniscience. Here $X$ is an index with values between 0 and 1 that denotes the degree of consumer information about the product. Note that this expression implies that the consumer has in mind some concept of typical or average product performance within the commodity class, which is consistent with the view that he has already made a choice among alternative commodities. Not only is an average or typical price required for the solution of the primary optimization problem, but also an average "quality" variable as well. Furthermore, $Ea_i = \bar{a}_i$ when $X = 1$, while $Ea_i = k\bar{a}$ when $X = 0$, which is consistent with the definition of information given above.

The constant $k$ is introduced to recognize explicitly that all consumers may not behave identically when little information is available about a particular brand. For example, when information is wholly absent, some consumers may believe that an unknown product is likely to be better than the average in the class when originally confronted with it, whereas others may view it as likely to be substandard.[10] In the first case, $k$ exceeds unity, and in the second, it is less than unity. When the value of $k$ equals unity, consumers will view an unknown brand as equal in quality to the typical product in the class. In all cases, however, $Ea_i$ should approach $\bar{a}_i$ as the degree of consumer information increases.

Our final assumption concerns the variance of $a_i$. Again assuming linearity, we hypothesize that $Va_i$ is determined by the degree of consumer information in the following manner:

$$Va_i = (1 - X)V\bar{a}, \tag{13}$$

where $V\bar{a}$ is the subjective variance of the distribution of product quality in the absence of information.[11] Where $X = 1$, $Va_i = 0$, and therefore expressions (12) and (13) together imply that $a_i = \bar{a}_i$, which is the definition of "perfect" information. Where $X = 0$, on the other hand, the variance of perceived performance is proportional to $V\bar{a}$.

In this framework, note that $Va_i = 0$ when information is "perfect," or, in other words, that there is no variance in true product quality of a particular brand. This follows from the fact that any *ex post* product variance is a performance characteristic in the Lancastrian sense, which must be included

10. Note that even where $X = 0$, we assume that consumers do know that the brand exists and lies within a certain commodity class.

11. $V\bar{a}$ may be related to the *ex post* distribution of product qualities observed by the consumer. However, even if the *ex post* variance is zero, the subjective variance of an unknown product exceeds zero.

among the various indices of product performance. The only variance that remains, therefore, is that due to the lack of full information regarding the individual product or brand.

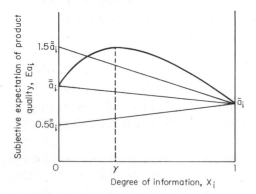

Fig. 3.1.   Dependence of subjective expectation of product quality on degree of information

An important assumption, embodied in expressions (12) and (13), is of course that of linearity. To examine some of its implications, we turn to Fig. 3.1, which describes the assumed relation between $Ea_i$ and $X$. The diagram posits that $\bar{a}_i$ is less than $\bar{a}$, but similar implications would exist if this relation were reversed. Three lines are drawn on the basis of different assumed values of $k$: 1.5, 1.0, and 0.5. Although the linear curves conform to our requirement that $Ea_i$ approaches $\bar{a}_i$ as $X$ approaches unity, there is no flexibility under this assumption for a curve that reflects the adage that "a little information is a dangerous thing." Even where $k$ equals unity, consumers might sometimes move along a curve such as the curved line in Fig. 3.1. To the left of $\gamma$, a little information might indeed be less useful than none at all and $Ea_i$ would be closer to the "true" value where $X = 0$ than where $X = \gamma$. Thus, our assumption of linearity may be misleading if consumers behave in this manner. If advertising and other sources of information create a misleading picture of the true product, a relation such as that indicated by the curved line might be appropriate, for in these instances a small amount of misleading information is provided. As can be seen, the significance of the assumption of linearity depends on the relative position of the point $\gamma$. Beyond that point, linear relations at some value of $k$ might instead provide a reasonable approximation. In assuming linearity, the effects of misleading information are excluded, and the more information, the better.

In Fig. 3.2 an analogous diagram is drawn of the assumed relation between

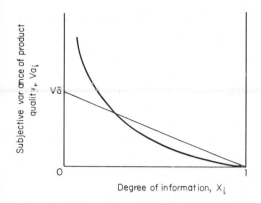

Fig. 3.2.  Dependence of subjective variance of product quality on degree of
information

$Va_i$ and $X$. The straight line represents the assumed relation. A reasonable
alternative hypothesis might be that $Va_i$ expands without limit as $X$ approaches
zero. Under this alternative hypothesis, the appropriate function would
resemble the curved line in Fig. 3.2. Here the assumption of linearity provides
a poor approximation in the region of $X = 0$ but might be a reasonably good
approximation as the degree of information increases.

## CONSUMER BEHAVIOR AND THE REQUIRED DISCOUNT

Since both products or brands belong to the same commodity class, we
assume that $\alpha_1$ and $\alpha_2$ in equation (11) are the same for each brand. On this
basis, we can substitute from equations (12) and (13) into (11) to obtain

$$U_i = X_i(\alpha_1\bar{a}_i - \alpha_1 k \bar{a} + \alpha_2 Va) + [\alpha_1 k \bar{a} - \alpha_2 Va], \tag{14}$$

which can then be substituted into the definition of $\beta$ from expression (8),
to give

$$\beta = \frac{X_1[\alpha_1(\bar{a}_1 - k \bar{a}) + \alpha_2 Va] - X_2[\alpha_1(\bar{a}_2 - k \bar{a}) + \alpha_2 Va]}{X_2[\alpha_1(\bar{a}_2 - k \bar{a}) + \alpha_2 Va] + [\alpha_1 k \bar{a} - \alpha_2 Va]}. \tag{15}$$

This expression is important because it gives the factors that determine, under
the behavioral assumptions of the model, the price discount required for the
consumer to purchase the product with lower expected utility. It emphasizes
that expected utility depends not only on "true" product performance, but
also on consumer information and on the degree of risk aversion in the consumer's preference function. To see this more clearly, we examine some special
cases.

First, consider the case where both products are of average quality, so that

$\bar{a}_1 = \bar{a}_2 = \bar{a}$, and that consumers have a balanced view of information, so that $k = 1$. In these circumstances, equation (15) collapses to

$$\beta = \frac{\alpha_2\ V\bar{a}(X_1 - X_2)}{\alpha_2\ V\bar{a}(X_2 - 1) + \alpha_1\bar{a}}. \tag{16}$$

Note that when $\alpha_2 = 0$, which indicates the absence of risk aversion, $\beta = 0$, and no discount is required. When consumers are not risk averse, no price discount is required to sell an unknown product so long as both brands are in fact of average quality. Where average or standard products are concerned, the required price discount depends completely upon: (1) the element of risk aversion in the consumer's preference function; (2) the variance of quality in related products and how consumers react to this variance; and (3) differences in information. What is suggested is that, regardless of differences in relative information and regardless of the degree of variation in the quality of related products, the required price discount is zero when consumers are not risk averse and when they behave as though an unknown product is drawn from the same distribution as existing products.

A second special case concerns the circumstances in which consumers are not risk averse, so that $\alpha_2 = 0$, and where the products are not necessarily of average quality. Here, equation (15) becomes

$$\beta = \frac{X_1(\bar{a}_1 - k\ \bar{a}) - X_2(\bar{a}_2 - k\ \bar{a})}{X_2\bar{a}_2 + (1 - X_2)\ k\ \bar{a}}. \tag{17}$$

It is apparent again that the price discount is zero when the products are of average quality and consumers behave in neutral fashion with regard to unknown products, *regardless* of the degree of consumer information about the two products. With no risk aversion, consumer information plays a role only when the two product qualities diverge from the average, or when consumers do not behave in a neutral manner toward unknown products. Thus, the existence of a price discount turns on three factors: the degree of risk aversion, the nature of consumers' predictions about the characteristics of unknown products, and differences in "true" product qualities. These three factors, moreover, are precisely those that lead advertising to have a major impact on consumer purchasing decisions.

## THE SOURCES OF INFORMATION

To this point, we have treated the degree of consumer information as exogenous and have examined its probable effects on consumer decisions. We now consider the role played by advertising and other sources of information.

Among the most important of the various sources of information are:

advertising; the consumer's own experience with the product, which depends on his having used it before; word-of-mouth information from other consumers; and sources such as *Consumer Reports* that aim to provide "objective" information regarding the product. Other sources might also be defined but would probably be less important in consumer decision making. The two most important clearly are the messages provided by the firm's selling efforts and the results of the experience of both the particular consumer and other individuals with whom he has some contact.

On these grounds, there must exist a functional relation

$$X_i = f(A_i, E_i, \ldots), \tag{18}$$

where $A_i$ indicates the informational content of advertising messages and other selling efforts regarding the $i$th product in the market and $E_i$ represents the accumulated information that is due to consumer experience with the same product. More will be said later regarding the likely characteristics of this function; we assume here only that the partial derivatives of both $A$ and $E$ are nonnegative.

Substituting from (18) into equation (15) and rearranging terms, we obtain

$$f(A_2, E_2, \ldots) = \frac{X_1[\alpha_1(\bar{a}_1 - k\,\bar{a}) + \alpha_2 V\bar{a}] - \beta[\alpha_1 k\,\bar{a} - \alpha_2 V\bar{a}]}{(\beta + 1)\,[\alpha_1\,(\bar{a}_2 - k\,\bar{a}) + \alpha_2 V\bar{a}]}. \tag{19}$$

If we consider product I as a "representative" product, which is sold by existing firms in the market, and product II as that sold by a new entrant for which information is relatively low, equation (19) defines the trade-off function for the second brand between the required price discount, $\beta$, and the level of selling expenditures required to counter the effect of no consumer experience with the product. A reasonable picture of this relation is given in Fig. 3.3, which reflects the presumption of a sufficiently declining marginal effectiveness of advertising and promotion. These two parameters are the only decision

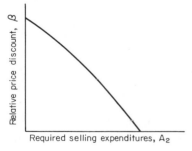

Fig. 3.3.   Relation between relative price discount and volume of selling
            expenditures required for entry

variables open to the seller of brand II. At any point on the frontier that describes some combination of price discount and selling effort, the consumer will purchase his product, whereas for a combination of the two variables inside the frontier, the consumer will purchase product I.

Equation (19) also indicates that a number of shift factors exist which influence the position of the curve. As can be seen, the trade-off function will shift to the right when $X_1$ increases so long as the "true" quality of the first is not substandard, or, algebraically, so long as

$$\bar{a}_1 > k\bar{a} - \frac{\alpha_2}{\alpha_1} V\bar{a} . \tag{20}$$

When $\bar{a}_1 = \bar{a}$, which will be true when the first brand is taken as a "representative" product, then an increase in $X_1$ will generally lead to a rightward shift in the trade-off function for brand II. On the other hand, the trade-off function will shift to the left when the "true" quality of brand II exceeds that of the "representative" product and as the value of $E_2$ increases with use.

The presence of such a trade-off function has important implications for the investment required to introduce a product into an existing market. It represents the situation where new firms face the alternatives of either selling their products at a substantial discount or spending large sums on advertising and promotion. Under the assumptions of this model, the function given in Fig. 3.3 describes the trade-off between these two alternatives that must be faced if the new entrant is to sell to a particular consumer.

It is interesting to consider the nature of the trade-off function when both products are in fact of average quality. In this case, $\bar{a}_1 = \bar{a}_2 = \bar{a}$. Let $k = 1$, so that

$$f(A_2, E_2, \dots ) = \frac{X_1 + \beta}{1 + \beta} - \frac{\beta}{1 + \beta} \frac{\alpha_1 \bar{a}}{\alpha_2 V\bar{a}} . \tag{21}$$

From this equation, it is clear that the trade-off function is likely to be altered significantly by the relative importance of risk aversion in the preference function of the consumer, as measured by the ratio of $\alpha_1$ to $\alpha_2$. As the relative importance of risk aversion declines, that ratio will increase and the trade-off function will shift to the left. As the importance of risk aversion increases, the ratio will decline and the trade-off function will shift to the right. Although these effects exist generally, in equation (21) they are clearly indicated. Thus, the required levels of advertising and promotion, or the required price discount, or both, are likely to increase with the degree of risk aversion in the preference function of the consumer.

As noted above, the trade-off function generally shifts to the right when $X_1$

increases. Since the value of $X_1$ depends, among other things, on the selling expenditures of the firm, this may provide existing firms with some control over the volume of investment in selling expenditures required of a new entrant.

To examine this question more fully, we consider the effect of changes in the selling policies of each firm upon changes in the required price discount. Returning to equation (15), we can regard the terms in brackets as constants and rewrite the equation in the form

$$\beta = \frac{X_1 L - X_2 M}{X_2 M + N} . \tag{22}$$

Then,

$$\frac{\partial \beta}{\partial A_1} = \frac{(\partial X_1/\partial A_1)\,[L(M X_2 + N)] - (\partial X_2/\partial A_1)\,[M(L X_1 + N)]}{(M X_2 + N)^2}, \tag{23}$$

and

$$\frac{\partial \beta}{\partial A_2} = \frac{(\partial X_1/\partial A_2)\,[L(M X_2 + N)] - (\partial X_2/\partial A_2)\,[M(L X_1 + N)]}{(M X_2 + N)^2} . \tag{24}$$

These expressions formally describe the effect of the selling policies of both firms on the required price discount. As expected, they emphasize the importance of the relation between advertising and consumer information. They also indicate that cross-over effects may exist which influence required price discounts. In the absence of cross-over effects, however, the effect of the selling efforts of each firm on the required price discount will depend on the marginal effectiveness of advertising and promotion on consumer information.

## CONSUMER BEHAVIOR AND REQUIRED ADVERTISING INVESTMENT

In this section, we examine the additional outlays on advertising and promotion *required* of a new brand in the market because of increased expenditures on existing brands for a given required price discount. These are given by

$$\frac{dA_2}{dA_1} = \frac{(\partial X_1/\partial A_1)\,[L(M X_2 + N)] - (\partial X_2/\partial A_1)\,[M(L X_1 + N)]}{(\partial X_1/\partial A_2)\,[L(M X_2 + N)] + (\partial X_2/\partial A_2)\,[M(L X_1 + N)]} . \tag{25}$$

The question whether this derivative exceeds or is less than unity is crucial, for it will be likely to have a major impact on the returns from being first in those markets where advertising and promotion significantly affect consumer decisions. Where this expression is less than unity, these gains should decline sharply with the introduction of new brands, whereas a coefficient that exceeds unity may enable the original firms to reap large rewards. A detailed discussion of barriers to entry and monopoly returns is presented in the next chapter. At this point, note only that where this coefficient exceeds unity, the prospect that the returns of established firms will contain a significant element of economic rent is increased.

As already indicated, direct as well as cross-over effects may have a significant impact on the size of this coefficient. We consider the nature of cross-over effects below, but it is useful first to examine the case where they are absent.

For a given utility function, the price discount required for the consumer to purchase an unknown brand depends on the "true" qualities of both products as well as on relative differences in consumer information. Therefore, where both brands are in fact average products, the required price discount is zero only where consumers are equally informed about both products. Where consumers are more knowledgeable about one product than another, and where they are unbiased in their prediction processes, a well-known product can command a price premium even where equal objective performance standards are reached. We have no further to look than the markets for liquid bleach and aspirin for illustrations of such price premiums. For no price discount to be required and full brand acceptance to be gained, on the other hand, selling expenditures for the new brand must be positive even if those for existing products are zero.

The foregoing analysis says little more than that advertising and promotion constitute one source of consumer information while the experience of consumers is another. Since these are alternative sources of information, $A_2$ must exceed $A_1$ when $E_1$ is greater than $E_2$ to achieve full brand acceptance for a new product. Since experience as a source of information must be greater for an established product than for a new brand, expenditures for advertising and promotion for an unknown product must be higher to achieve equal levels of consumer information. This conclusion provides a rationale for the fact that the volume of selling expenditures required for "brand switching" will typically exceed that required to maintain "repeat buying."

If cross-over effects are ignored, the derivative defined in equation (25) depends entirely on the ratio of $\partial X_1/\partial A_1$ to $\partial X_2/\partial A_2$, since full brand acceptance and the reduction of the price discount to zero requires for average products that $X_1 = X_2$. We are therefore concerned with the ratio of the marginal effectiveness of advertising and promotion of one brand to that of another. Although it seems reasonable that the marginal effectiveness of advertising for an established brand is less than the marginal effectiveness for a new and unknown brand, when advertising and promotion are carried on at the same volume for both brands, or where $A_1 = A_2$, this relation may *not* hold at the volumes of advertising required of each brand to achieve the same levels of consumer information.

These relations are more easily examined with the help of Fig. 3.4. Both curves describe information production functions that relate consumer information to the volume of selling and promotional messages provided by the firm. In this diagram, the remaining sources of information, including particularly the extent of consumer experience, represent shift factors. Since we assume that brand II has recently been introduced into the market, whereas brand I is an established brand, we have drawn the curve for the latter above the former. Whether curve II ever reaches curve I is problematical and depends on whether there exists a volume of selling efforts that will substitute fully for a low level of consumer experience. We assume that differences in consumer information between the two brands decline as the volume of selling expenditures on both brands increases, and the curves have been drawn on this assumption. We also posit a declining marginal effectiveness of advertising and promotion.

The functional relations presented in Fig. 3.4 have an additional property which is given for purposes of explanation but which may not be found in all cases. As indicated, there are many points where $\partial X_1/\partial A_1$ is less than $\partial X_2/\partial A_2$ for $A_1 = A_2$ while, at the same time, $\partial X_1/\partial A_1$ is greater than $\partial X_2/\partial A_2$ for $X_1 = X_2$. The former relation holds, for example, where the volume of advertising and promotion on both brands is set equal to $OB$, whereas the latter relation holds where consumer information on both brands is given by $OY$.

As noted above, the important comparison concerns the marginal effects where $X_1 = X_2$. This issue can also be examined through the relative positions of the two curves in the diagram. If the producer of the first brand spends

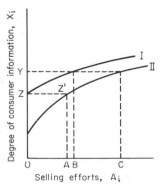

Fig. 3.4.   Production functions relating consumer information to selling efforts of established and new firms

nothing on advertising and promotion, it still reaches a high level of consumer information because of existing consumer experience, and $X_1$ will equal $OZ$. In these circumstances, the seller of the second brand must provide $OA$ advertising and promotional messages to reach the same level of consumer information. Therefore, $OA$ represents the required investment in information to obtain full brand acceptance and reduce the price discount to zero. If, however, some volume of advertising is used to promote the established product, the investment required in brand II increases. If firm I carries out a selling effort equal to $OB$, $X_1$ will equal $OY$, and therefore the seller of the second brand must provide $OC$ messages to reach that level of consumer information. In these circumstances, the additional effort on brand I equals $OB$ and the additional selling effort on brand II, required to obtain full consumer acceptance, equals $AC$. Where $AC$ exceeds $OB$, as indicated in the diagram, an additional volume of selling messages by an established firm will require that more than this quantity be allocated to promoting a new and unknown brand if an equal level of consumer information is to be reached. When $AC$ is less than $OB$, on the other hand, the opposite conclusion is reached. It can be shown, moreover, that where both functions are strictly convex, up to the point where they become horizontal, a sufficient condition for $AC$ to exceed $OB$ in Fig. 3.4 is that the slope of function I at point $Z$ exceed the corresponding slope of function II at point $Z'$.

As indicated, a critical issue rests on the relation between the slopes of the functions drawn in Fig. 3.4. If the decline in the marginal effectiveness of advertising brought about by a mixture of advertising and experience is less than the decline brought about by advertising alone, then $\partial X_1/\partial A_1$ will always exceed $\partial X_2/\partial A_2$ for any point of effective information parity. This circumstance, moreover, is intuitively appealing since it embodies the assumption that experience and selling expenditures are substitutable but not perfectly so in the production function for information. Since experience and advertising provide different kinds of information about consumer products, it is likely that an increase in information brought about by both experience and advertising has less of a depressing effect on $\partial X_i/\partial A_i$ than the same increase in information that results from advertising alone. Indeed, there are probably limits to the level of information that can be obtained from advertising without experience. This can be represented graphically by a difference in the horizontal asymptotes of the two functions. When the asymptote of curve I lies above the asymptote of curve II, there will clearly be some range in the distribution of consumer information where $AC$ exceeds $OB$ in Fig. 3.4. On these grounds, the functional relations described in the diagram may well exist and there may be many instances where $dA_2/dA_1$ exceeds unity.

To this point, we have ignored the possible influence of cross-over effects, and, in effect, have considered the information production functions as independent. From equation (25), however, it can be seen that cross-over effects play an analogous role to direct effects. Since increased advertising outlays on one brand may tend to depress the strength of consumer information regarding another, cross-over effects should be negative. To this extent, a movement along curve I in Fig. 3.4 will cause curve II to shift downward, whereas an increase along curve II will lead to a downward shift in curve I.

There are two reasons for postulating a negative effect of advertising on information regarding a rival product. The first is that conflicting claims may reduce the consumer's confidence that he knows what he is buying and thereby restrict his perceived degree of information. In addition, there is some prospect that advertising and promotion may create a volume of "noise" in the minds of consumers such that it becomes necessary to "shout" to be heard; it becomes necessary to provide even more advertising and promotional messages to a consumer in order to counter the effects of rival outlays. Thus, Marshall argued that an important result "caused by bold displayed advertisements is the relative obscurity into which they are designed to throw, and do throw, the smaller advertisements of less wealthy men."[12] On these grounds, $\partial X_i / \partial A_j$ may be negative in many cases, which will affect the value of $dA_2/dA_1$ evaluated at information levels required for information parity and full brand acceptance.

## CONCLUDING COMMENTS

The impact of advertising by established firms on the effectiveness of new entrants' advertising may have an important influence on rates of return earned by these two types of firms in a market characterized by heavy advertising. This issue has been examined in the context of a specific model of consumer behavior, which indicates that the relative costs and gains are likely to depend substantially on the significance of risk aversion in the preference functions of the consumer. Moreover, these costs and gains are affected by the consumer's degree of ignorance of the qualities of new products.

When consumers purchase a high-priced brand in a commodity class where low-priced brands are frequently available, this can probably be explained by the consumer's degree of risk aversion together with the fact that, in the absence of alternative sources of low-priced information, the degree of consumer ignorance about unadvertised products is likely to be high. Where

12. Alfred Marshall, *Industry and Trade* (London, Macmillan, 1927), p. 307. Negative cross-over effects have also been assumed in other models of advertising expenditures. See Lawrence Friedman, "Game Theory Models in the Allocation of Advertising Expenditures," *Operations Research*, 6 (September–October 1958), 700.

consumers are able to examine a new product and easily recognize its relative quality, advertising and promotion may not play a major role in consumer decisions. Where ignorance is pervasive, however, and the costs of obtaining "objective" information are substantial relative to prospective gains, advertising and promotion may well have a substantial impact on consumer decisions. In markets where this is the situation, heavy advertising may create barriers to the entry of new firms. This issue is examined in some detail in the following chapter.

# CHAPTER 4 Advertising as a Barrier to Entry

In this chapter we consider the circumstances in which a high volume of advertising expenditures by established firms in an industry imposes barriers to the entry of new firms. The question here is not whether heavy advertising serves in all cases to restrict entry but rather whether there are circumstances in which such outlays have this effect. Our second concern is to identify the process through which advertising barriers are created. At this point, we consider only the economic consequences of entry barriers, and postpone discussion of any normative or policy implications until the final chapter.

That heavy advertising expenditures may sometimes serve as a barrier to entry has been denied by some writers.[1] For this reason, it is necessary first to define what is generally meant by this term. In his classic discussion of these issues, Bain writes that "conditions of entry," which may reflect either the presence or the absence of entry barriers, are indicated by the advantages of established sellers in an industry over potential entrant sellers, these advantages being reflected in the extent to which established sellers can persistently raise their prices above a competitive level without attracting new firms to enter the industry."[2]

1. See, for example, Yale Brozen, "An Economist's View," National Industrial Conference Board, *Competition, Efficiency, and Antitrust*, Eighth Conference on Antitrust Issues in Today's Economy, New York, March 6, 1969, p. 25.

2. Joe S. Bain, *Barriers to New Competition* (Cambridge, Mass., Harvard University Press, 1956), p. 3. Stigler gives a slightly different definition, but one consistent with Bain's. He writes that "a barrier to entry may be defined as a cost of producing (at some or every rate of output) which must be borne by a firm which seeks to enter an industry, but is not borne by firms already in the industry." George J. Stigler, *The Organization of Industry* (Homewood, Ill., R. D. Irwin, 1968), p. 67.

Entry restrictions depend on the presence of differential advantages of existing firms over new entrants, and not merely on the cost of entry, which may have been required of established firms in the past. If heavy advertising is required to participate effectively in a market, then the costs or investment required for entry are greater, but not necessarily the differential costs on which entry barriers depend. This issue is important precisely because it is the presence of differential advantages between entrants and their established rivals that permit high prices to be set without attracting new firms into the industry. Thus, the question at issue is whether circumstances may exist in which heavy advertising requirements create differential advantages for existing firms.

Note that the presence of such differential advantages alone will not necessarily exclude all entrants from the market. Entry will be forestalled only where the policies of established firms are to limit their short-run excess profits to the levels permitted by their differential cost advantages. Such policies may take the form of setting prices below the level of maximum short-run returns, as suggested by the theory of limit pricing, or of increasing the aggregate volume of industry advertising expenditures. Differential cost advantages create entry barriers because established firms have the power to exclude entrants—whether or not this power is actually exercised. Indeed, the presence of even substantial barriers to entry is unlikely to exclude firms from entering on the fringes of the market, because the leading established firms are unlikely to react. Firms may be expected, however, to resist a major frontal attack on their market positions.

Where entry barriers are important and persist over time, established firms can reach an *equilibrium* position in which excess profits are earned. These higher returns represent an economic rent, but one associated with the market power of the firm rather than with a scarce input in the production process.

The presence of substantial economies of scale creates barriers to entry, and it is useful to review the factors that lead to this result. Even though the same structure of costs is faced by prospective entrants as was faced originally by established firms, a new entrant can expect higher unit costs precisely because existing firms were there first. Where the minimum size of an efficient firm constitutes a large share of the market, prospective entrants face a dilemma. On the one hand, they may produce at a small volume, thereby adding little to total industry output, so that postentry prices approach preentry prices, although unit costs may be substantially higher. On the other hand, production can be set at a large volume of output so that minimum cost levels are reached, but here industry output is likely to be increased sufficiently that postentry prices are substantially lower than preentry prices.[3]

To the extent that established firms were not forced earlier to face this dilemma, it represents an important gain from being first in the market. Under some circumstances, it can be viewed as a return from innovation. These gains, however, must be distinguished from other returns from innovation in that they are not generally competed away with time but rather represent long-run equilibrium profits. They may be expected to withstand all encroachments except a successful counter-innovation.

## ADVERTISING AND PRODUCT DIFFERENTIATION

The degree of product differentiation in a market is measured by the cross-elasticities of demand and supply that exist among competing products. Low cross-elasticities of demand between these products indicate that buyers prefer the products or brands of particular sellers and will not switch in significant numbers in response to small differences in price. Low cross-elasticities of supply, on the other hand, signify that firms are unable to imitate the products of their rivals sufficiently well to eliminate these consumer preferences. Whereas cross-elasticities between the products of existing producers reflect the character of the rivalry that exists between them, cross-elasticities between the products of established firms and potential entrants indicate the height of entry barriers posed by product differentiation.[4]

Product differentiation reflects two sets of factors: the basic characteristics of products within the market and the present and past policies of established firms with respect to advertising, product design, servicing, and distribution. On the demand side, products are more likely to be differentiable when buyers are relatively uninformed about the relative merits of existing products. As emphasized in the preceding chapter, this may be particularly important

3. This result follows from Bain's assumption that the output of established firms is maintained in the face of entry, and that this is recognized by prospective entrants. Although this assumption may not be valid in all circumstances, there is some prospect that a large addition to industry output which results from new entry will have a significant depressing impact on industry prices. For further discussion of this issue, see F. M. Scherer, *Industrial Market Structure and Economic Performance* (Chicago, Rand McNally, 1971), pp. 219–234. See also Franco Modigliani, "New Developments on the Oligopoly Front", *Journal of Political Economy* (June 1958), pp. 215–232.

4. It is important to distinguish product differentiation from product variety. The steel industry, for example, produces a great variety of products, that are sold to knowledgeable buyers, but product differentiation is minimal. In contrast, the cigarette industry offers a smaller variety of products, but product differentiation—based largely on extensive advertising—is great. Bain, *Barriers to New Competition*, pp. 127–129.

for differentiation achieved via advertising. On the supply side, differentiation is more likely where the products of rivals cannot easily be imitated and where new entrants have difficulties in producing products that are identical to those sold by successfully established firms. In producer-goods industries, successful imitation requires investment in product design and adequate service facilities. In consumer-goods industries, successful imitation may require investment in advertising as well.

It is noteworthy that Bain, in his examination of product differentiation in 20 manufacturing industries, found advertising to be the most important source of product differentiation in the consumer-goods industries in his sample.[5] Distribution policies are also important where forward integration is prevalent, whereas customer services and product design play contributing but relatively minor roles.

The relation between product differentiation and advertising can be clarified with the theoretical results of Dorfman and Steiner.[6] They concluded that the optimal level of advertising is attained where the marginal revenue from advertising equals the ordinary price elasticity of demand for the firm. This result implies that, where product differentiation is high as a result of other factors, the price elasticity of demand will be reduced, and a higher level of advertising is therefore required to equate marginal revenue with the price elasticity of demand. Hence, an increase in product differentiation, other things being equal, will tend to increase advertising.

On the other hand, where the products within a market are heterogeneous, an increase in advertising will also tend to reduce the price elasticity of demand for the firm. As a result, the price elasticity of demand under an optimal advertising policy will be lower in absolute value than the price elasticity of demand without advertising. Hence the level of advertising may be said to affect the degree of product differentiation as measured by the price elasticity of demand for the firm's product.

For typical consumer-goods industries, a persistently high level of advertising expenditures can therefore be viewed in two ways:

(a) If firms behave reasonably, high levels of advertising indicate that the product is differentiated; in this sense, advertising is a symptom of product differentiation.

(b) The high level of advertising is itself an important determinant of the level of differentiation that is attained for established advertised products as

5. Bain, *Barriers to New Competition*, pp. 114–143.
6. Robert Dorfman and Peter O. Steiner, "Optimal Advertising and Optimal Quality," *American Economic Review*, 44 (1954), 826–836.

against unadvertised products and the products of potential entrants; in this sense, advertising is a source of product differentiation.

Provided that firms act reasonably, observed advertising expenditures furnish a useful measure of the extent of product differentiation. We write "reasonably" rather than "rationally" since, in an oligopolistic market, rational policies are not unambiguous. What is rational policy for a group acting in concert is not rational policy for the individual firm expecting to gain a march on its rivals. It is quite possible, moreover, that rivalry via advertising among established firms may be carried to the point of diminishing returns in terms of group profit rates.

Not only may advertising and the accompanying product differentiation raise entry barriers, but also it may have a direct influence on the character of competition among established firms. As has been noted by others, the achievement of product differentiation provides the firm with a measure of freedom from the constraints imposed by the competitive actions of its rivals.[7] In this manner, effective differentiation has an effect on price-cost margins which is analogous to that of a collusive agreement among established firms. In both instances, the firm is insulated to some extent from the competitive efforts of its rivals, and high profits may be gained so long as there is no fear of attracting new firms into the industry. This latter issue, therefore, is particularly important, and it is to this matter that the rest of this chapter is devoted.

## ADVERTISING AND ABSOLUTE COST ADVANTAGES

Product differentiation via advertising may influence the height of entry barriers in three ways, each of which is analogous to the other determinants of overall entry barriers. In this section, we deal with the first of these: whether high prevailing levels of advertising are likely to create additional costs for new entrants above those experienced by existing firms, which exist at all levels of output. Our concern is with the differential advantages of being first in the market, and not merely with the prospect that new firms may be forced to spend more on advertising currently to counter the heavy expenditures of existing firms in the past.

Where such differential advantages do exist, they represent the additional rewards from early entry into the market. Therefore, as in the case of substantial economies of scale, these rewards can be viewed as a portion of the returns from innovation. Here also, these gains must be distinguished from other innovational returns in that they will not be competed away with the entry of new firms, but rather will remain for long periods of time.

7. Bain, *Barriers to New Competition*, pp. 114–115.

It has been observed that advertising leads more readily to repeat purchases than to sales made to consumers who previously had purchased another brand.[8] In these circumstances, more advertising messages per prospective customer must generally be supplied to induce brand switching as compared with repeat buying. This proposition by itself, however, says little as to whether advertising creates absolute cost advantages to existing firms, which concerns the differential advantages of being first. The relation between "brand switching" and "repeat buying" affects the size of the required advertising investment for a new firm, an investment which may have been required in the past of existing firms. Although the volume of advertising messages per customer for new entrants, who must entice purchases from consumers who have previously purchased existing products, will generally be higher than that of existing firms who are content with maintaining established market positions, no entry barriers are created unless these costs exceed those previously encountered by existing firms.

In many circumstances, however, the effectiveness of advertising in a new product area may be greater than where products are well established and where consumers have come to rely on specific brands. Consumer attachments to individual products are often originally weak or absent, so that advertising messages encounter relatively little resistance. Brand loyalty is created specifically to withstand the lower prices of more imitative products. Cross-elasticities of demand are increased and effective product differentiation is achieved. To attract customers, therefore, new entrants frequently must spend even more heavily on advertising than did established firms. Consumer resistance may be encountered that requires a proportionately larger volume of advertising if a substantial market share is to be gained. Indeed, advertising costs may increase more than proportionately as output expands and customers more closely tied to the products of established firms need to be attracted.

This matter can be explored further with the help of the model of consumer choice presented in the previous chapter. This model suggests that the relative volumes of advertising expenditures by established firms and by new entrants depend on the nature of the interaction between the informational value of prior consumer experience and that of advertising messages. As indicated, these considerations determine the relative positions of the two curves presented in Fig. 3.4. A test was proposed which dealt directly with the fact that the relative levels of advertising may depend significantly on the advertising policies of established firms. So long as the conditions indicated in

8. See Nicholas Kaldor, "The Economic Aspects of Advertising," reprinted in *Essays on Value and Distribution* (Glencoe, Ill., Free Press, 1960), p. 125. Some tentative support in the case of one industry is given in Lester G. Telser, "Advertising and Cigarettes", *Journal of Political Economy*, 70 (October 1962), 489.

Fig. 3.4 are present, new entrants must provide more advertising messages to build an allegiance to their products than may have been the case for established firms upon their earlier entry into the market.

Existing firms may have been able to generate a demand for their products, together with the accompanying consumer experience, slowly over a period of time—with a relatively low volume of advertising in the early stages. To the extent that this option is no longer open to prospective entrants into a market, differential costs are higher and entry barriers are created, in much the same manner as in the case of economies of scale in production. Thus, where advertising has a major impact on consumer decisions, there may well be circumstances in which it also has the effect of creating absolute cost advantages for established producers in terms of higher market-penetration costs for new entrants than were borne by established firms.

Moreover, as indicated above, this test ignores the possible role of cross-over effects in which the volume of advertising by one firm in an industry affects the perceived degree of consumer information regarding another. These effects should also influence the volume of advertising messages required of a new entrant. To the extent that the advertising of others creates "noise" in the market, one must "shout" louder to be heard, so that the effectiveness of each advertising message declines as the aggregate volume of industry advertising increases. In this case, it will be necessary for new entrants to spend more today to gain an established market position than existing firms spent yesterday, when aggregate industry advertising was probably far less. From these circumstances also, new entrants may have differentially higher advertising costs than did established firms at their entry into the market.

Consider the likely course of events in the absence of current advertising by the original firms in the market. Their own sales would slowly create a reservoir of consumer experience with their products, since experience is a joint product with consumption itself. Then to enter the market a new firm would need to overcome the experience factor. If advertising were now permitted to new entrants, the existing consumer experience with the products of established firms could be overcome by an extensive advertising campaign, indicated by $OA$ in Fig. 3.4. Alternatively, a substantial price discount could be offered until the required experience was created. Which strategy would be best would depend, of course, on the relative values of the price and advertising elasticities of demand. In either case, the required volume of advertising, price discount, or both for a new entrant would be less than in the presence of advertising by the established firms in circumstances where the test given by Fig. 3.4 is satisfied. In this case, advertising would lead to more restricted conditions for the entry of new firms.

Let us now compare this discussion with the argument made by Brozen.

Rather than serving as a barrier to entry, he argues that advertising outlays promote new entry, and indeed if advertising were limited,

> it would become more expensive to inform prospective customers that a firm new to a given market is prepared to supply them. It would raise the cost of letting the world know that a better mouse trap has been built. It would force firms to invest more heavily in a dealer network or in a distribution system if they were limited in their advertising outlays, thus raising the long-run cost curves of prospective entrants. It would become more expensive to build volume quickly to create a level which would achieve a major part of the available economies of scale. Efficiency would fall because firms would be forced to resort to the inefficient substitutes for advertising they avoid when this method of selling and promotion is open.[9]

In this passage, Brozen emphasizes that advertising affects the extent of consumer information available for new products. There is no dispute on this point. The second curve in Fig. 3.4 has a positive slope, and advertising may indeed be a more effective means of countering the effects of consumer experience with established products than alternative ways of providing information or than price discounts. However, Brozen ignores the impact of advertising by established firms and the prospect that advertising's effectiveness is influenced by consumer experience with the products of established firms. The presence or absence of entry barriers due to advertising depends on the effects of advertising by established firms as well as by prospective entrants, and on the relation between them. It is therefore not sufficient to look only at the effects of advertising by prospective entrants.

Note that entry barriers of this character do not require a prolonged effect of advertising expenditures. Even if dissipated in a year or less, this effect would still exist. What is required is that the informational value of consumer experience have a substantial impact on consumer decisions, that this experience be not easily or quickly gained at low cost to the consumer, and that advertising be not fully substitutable for other types of information. The important issue here is not the length of the period of the advertising effect, but rather the nature of the interaction that exists between experience and advertising messages as alternative sources of consumer information, as well as the period in which consumer experience plays a dominant informational role. Where advertising serves to reinforce the experience that consumers have with established products, current advertising expenditures by existing firms

---

9. Brozen, "An Economist's View," pp. 25–26.

may neutralize a larger volume of advertising by new entrants, and it is in this setting that entry barriers are created.

## ADVERTISING AND ECONOMIES OF SCALE

Entry barriers may be created by the presence of substantial economies of scale, which may be due to advertising and promotion as well as to production. For this reason, we need to consider possible explanations for such economies as well as their probable extent in the consumer-goods sector of the economy.[10]

Scale economies in advertising may result from two sets of relations which are usefully distinguished. First, advertising messages are purchased from the various information media so that advertiser economies are available where the price per comparable message declines as the number purchased increases. Second, messages do not all have identical effects on consumer demands and firm revenues, and their effectiveness may depend on the quantity as well as the quality of the messages purchased. Thus, advertising economies may result from an increasing effectiveness of advertising messages as well as from decreasing costs. In this section, we are concerned with the relation between scale and the effectiveness of advertising and shall postpone until later our discussion of advertising costs. In this discussion, we assume provisionally a constant relation between the price per message and the volume of messages.

The presence of scale economies depends on the relation between the volume of sales and the number of advertising messages provided by the firm. Where the functional relation resembles that given in Fig. 4.1, economies in the form of increased advertising effectiveness exist to a point, and diseconomies thereafter. In this case, the marginal return from an increased volume of messages eventually approaches zero.

Although it is difficult to argue unequivocally that this functional form is appropriate, there are various factors that suggest it. The standard rationale for an *S*-curve is given by Joel Dean. He argues that the early portion of the curve

> is partially explained by economies of specialization. Larger appropriations may make feasible the use of expert services and more economical media. More important than specialization, usually, are economies of repetition. Each advertising attack starts from ground that was taken on previous forays where no single onslaught can overcome the inertia of

10. The likely existence of scale economies in advertising and their effect on competition were noted earlier by Kaldor. He writes that "the shift of the demand curve resulting from advertising cannot be assumed to be strictly proportionate to the amount spent on advertising—the 'pulling power' of the larger expenditure must overshadow that of smaller ones with the consequence that the larger firms are bound to gain at the expense of the smaller ones." Kaldor, "Economic Aspects of Advertising," p. 116.

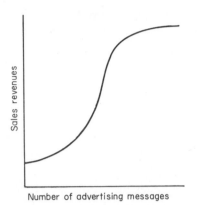

Fig. 4.1.   A typical response function of sales revenue to the number of
advertising messages

existing spending patterns; the hammering of repetition often overcomes
skepticism by attrition.

At some point, however, these advantages are exhausted and another set of
factors becomes significant. Dean writes that diseconomies are encountered

> primarily by tapping successively poorer prospects as the advertising
> effort is intensified. Presumably, the most susceptible prospects are
> picked off first, and progressively stiffer resistance is encountered from
> layers of prospects who are more skeptical, more stodgy about their
> present spending patterns, or more attached to rival sellers. [It] may also
> be caused by progressive exhaustion of the most vulnerable geographic
> areas or the most efficient advertising media. Promotional channels that
> are ideally adapted to the scale and market of the firm are used first.[11]

According to Dean, the increased effectiveness of a larger volume of advertising
messages throughout the early range in the distribution is due primarily to the
effects of repetition.[12] Many exposures to the advertisement seem required to
build product awareness or familiarity, which is a major function of advertising.[13]

11. Joel Dean, *Managerial Economics* (New York, Prentice-Hall, 1951), pp. 357–358.

12. Empirical support for increasing returns due to repetition is found in John B. Stewart,
*Repetitive Advertising in Newspapers* (Boston, Harvard Business School, 1964).

13. Similar arguments are found in Joe S. Bain, "Advantages of a Large Firm: Production, Distribution, and Sales Promotion," *Journal of Marketing* (April 1956), pp. 339–343;
Neil H. Borden, *The Economic Effects of Advertising* (Chicago, R. D. Irwin, 1942), pp. 426–
427; and, Edward H. Chamberlain, *The Theory of Monopolistic Competition*, 8th ed.,
(Cambridge, Mass., Harvard University Press, 1962), pp. 133–134. However, it should be
noted that a recent writer, after reviewing the evidence, finds that "increasing returns to
repetition and size constitutes a monstrous myth." Julian L. Simon, *Issues in the Economics
of Advertising*, (Urbana, Ill., University of Illinois Press, 1970), p. 22.

A related functional form exists where a threshold level of advertising must be reached before any significant benefits are realized. In this case, the schedule in Fig. 4.1 is a discontinuous step function where the threshold determines the point of discontinuity. The importance of scale economies thereby depends on the volume of advertising required to reach the threshold. Although the evidence is far from conclusive, some empirical support for this type of relation is given in a study of various advertising campaigns. The authors conclude that

> there is a threshold value of advertising of a not inconsiderable quantity below which there is no applicable response and that there is eventually a state of near saturation in the sense of inordinate increase in advertising is required to achieve any increase in response.[14]

A threshold effect of this sort is particularly likely when buyers react to different brands in the market as either familiar or unfamiliar. Where this classification is made in terms of product familiarity, where familiarity or awareness is due primarily to advertising, and where a substantial volume of messages must be received before the consumer recognizes the product as "well known," the appropriate schedule may indeed be discontinuous. That this type of functional relation may be common is indicated by the large number of consumer-goods markets in which brands are divided into two classes, frequently called "major brands" and "independent brands." These are distinguished generally on the basis of consumer familiarity and acceptance. In these cases, we typically find high cross-elasticities of demand among brands in either group but lower cross-elasticities of demand between brands in different groups.

The presence of advertising scale economies in general, and of a threshold level of advertising in particular, creates a degree of asymmetry in the market between old firms and new, which may be the source of restricted conditions of entry. When existing firms entered the market, their entry was probably associated with an innovation of some sort or with a period of rapid growth of demand. In either case, there was the prospect of rapidly increasing sales which would permit an increased volume of advertising with a corresponding increase in effectiveness per message. In effect, these firms faced a probability distribution of prospective returns that included some states of the world in which competitive entry lagged sufficiently that expected profits were positive.

Prospective entrants in the present, unaccompanied by innovation, face different contingencies. To reach the advertising effectiveness of their established rivals, they must either spend more on advertising per unit of output or

14. B. Benjamin and J. Maitland, "Operational Research and Advertising: Some Experiments in the Use of Analogies," *Operational Research Quarterly*, 9 (September 1958), 209–210.

expand their output sufficiently to support the required level of expenditures with comparable unit advertising costs. Neither alternative is attractive to the entrant. If the latter is chosen, and if existing firms maintain their levels of output and advertising expenditures, aggregate industry output will expand substantially.[15] The market becomes more competitive than before and price-cost margins decline. Entrants will recognize that they must go into an industry with "too competitive" a structure—made so by the fact of their own entry.

If, on the other hand, the former alternative is chosen, the entrant must bear higher unit advertising costs. With a smaller output than established firms, the need to spend similar amounts on advertising to reach comparable levels of advertising effectiveness leads to higher advertising:sales ratios. In the absence of scale economies in advertising, smaller firms and new entrants could simply purchase fewer messages but achieve the same sales effectiveness per message. In the presence of scale economies, this option is not available, and new entrants must be prepared to bear higher unit advertising costs than established firms. These higher costs, moreover, may place new entrants at a strong competitive disadvantage.[16]

Where scale economies take the form of a required threshold volume of advertising, the competitive disadvantages of new entrants may be even more severe. Entrants who wish their products viewed as "major brands" must reach this threshold. In this case, leading firms, which are invariably larger, can spread this fixed cost over more units of output. Higher output levels are therefore associated with lower unit advertising costs, and smaller firms, including most potential entrants, are placed at a substantial disadvantage.

Many examples of this phenomenon can be found in the consumer-goods sector of the economy; the case of the automobile industry during the 1950's is well documented. During this period, the two smaller firms were forced to spend more than twice as much on advertising per car sold than did either Ford or General Motors. Despite this fact, their products were not generally viewed as equal in quality to those of the leaders and frequently sold at a discount. As an annual average between 1954 and 1957, Studebaker and American Motors spent on national advertising, respectively, $64.04 and

15. Whether or not established firms will maintain output levels in the face of impending entry has been the subject of much discussion. See again Scherer, *Industrial Market Structure and Economic Performance*, pp. 219–234.

16. Some supporting evidence for the hypothesis that new brands require disproportionate advertising expenditures to obtain substantial market shares is presented in James O. Peckham, "Can We Relate Advertising Dollars to Market Share Objectives?" *Proceedings of the Advertising Research Foundation Annual Meeting*, 1966, pp. 53–57, reprinted in Malcolm A. McGiven, *How Much to Spend for Advertising* (1969), pp. 23–30.

$57.89 per automobile sold, whereas General Motors spent $26.56 and Ford spent $27.22 per unit. Chrysler assumed an intermediate position, spending $47.76 per unit sold.[17] These figures can be explained by the presence of a threshold volume of advertising expenditures which was never quite reached by the smaller firms. But whether a discernable threshold existed or not, it is apparent that the existence of scale economies in advertising was an important factor which permitted the leading firms to spend far less per unit sold than their smaller rivals.[18]

There is an important qualification to this result. It applies only to the relation between selling expenditures and firm size within the relevant market. When a firm in a regionally segmented market expands its national market share by moving into new geographical areas, unit advertising costs are not likely to decline. In these circumstances, larger firms have less of an advantage relative to their smaller rivals.

## THE ADVERTISING PRICE STRUCTURE AND ECONOMIES OF SCALE

Economies of scale in advertising may also result when the cost per advertising message declines as the number of messages purchased increases. In the previous section, we assumed that prices were fixed regardless of the number of messages purchased, but here we relax this assumption and ask whether the price structure in the market for advertising messages creates an additional source of economies of scale.

The question is whether quantity discounts are a major component of the advertising price structure. To the extent that large advertisers have more elastic demands for advertising messages than their smaller rivals, and where cost differences among various buyers are small, we would expect to find a negative relation between average prices charged and the volume of messages purchased; a positive relation would result if larger advertisers had less elastic demand curves. The necessary conditions for effective price discrimination appear to exist—products cannot be resold and sellers frequently have substantial market power—so that the issue is likely to rest on the relative demand elasticities of large and small advertisers. Although little direct evidence is

17. Leonard W. Weiss, *Economics and American Industry* (New York, Wiley, 1961), p. 342. Further empirical evidence on the pattern of advertising:sales ratios within industries is presented in Chapter 9 below.

18. A similar form of economy of scale appears to be associated with style change costs in this industry. A threshold ratio of output is given by the volume at which the special dies required for new models deteriorate divided by the time period associated with style obsolescence. Before this threshold is reached, but not beyond, style changes lead to higher costs. See John A. Menge, "Style Change Costs as a Market Weapon," *Quarterly Journal of Economics* (November 1962), pp. 632–647.

available on relative elasticities, large advertisers should have more elastic demand schedules if a greater choice of media is available to them on account of their size. In these circumstances, price discrimination should lead to quantity discounts. Our concern here is whether lower prices are charged for larger quantities of messages of the same quality and not merely with whether different prices are charged for messages of different qualities so long as price differences are proportional to differences in quality.[19]

Since advertising messages are supplied via various information media, a full analysis of this question should deal separately with each. For advertising messages provided by manufacturers of consumer goods, however, a most important medium in recent years is television. Whether substantial quantity discounts are offered on network television has been the subject of active debate in recent years. The presence of substantial discounts on network rate cards was noted in an article published in 1965.[20] The authors suggested a few months later that large advertisers could benefit from discounts not available to smaller advertisers by as much as 75 percent of the basic time charge.[21]

These claims brought forth a flood of replies. Not only was it announced that most quantity discounts had been eliminated on more recent rate cards,[22] but also that most sales were now made on the basis of "participating minutes" to which the published rate cards did not apply.[23] Even more important, published rate cards did not reflect prices set on off-list sales, which, it was suggested, cover a substantial portion of advertising on network television.[24]

An interesting feature of actual prices paid for network television advertising is the striking difference in the composition of messages purchased by large

19. It is generally believed that quantity discounts are offered by most media. Thus, the authors of a current text in marketing write that "it is not uncommon for volume cumulative discounts to be granted to customers after a given size of purchase in a medium is made." David L. Montgomery and Glen L. Urban, *Management Science in Marketing* (New York, Prentice-Hall, 1969), p. 151. Note that these discounts generally apply to the entire corporation rather than to individual products. Smaller brands of large advertisers may therefore enjoy the same media rates as larger brands.

20. Harlan M. Blake and Jack A. Blum, "Network Television Rate Practices: A Case Study in the Failure of Social Control of Price Discrimination," *Yale Law Journal*, 74 (July 1965), 1339–1401. A similar article which covered much the same ground appeared soon thereafter. Note, "Antitrust Implications of Network Television Quantity Advertising Discounts," *Columbia Law Review*, 65 (November 1965).

21. This figure is contained in Blake's statement before a Congressional subcommittee. Statement of Harlan M. Blake, "Possible Anticompetitive Effects of Sale of Network TV Advertising," *Hearings before the Subcommittee on Antitrust and Monopoly*, Committee on the Judiciary, U.S. Senate, 89:2, Part 1, June 3, 1966, p. 174.

22. Statement on Don Durgin, President of NBC Television, *Hearings*, Part 2, p. 633.

23. David M. Blank, "Television Advertising: The Great Discount Illusion or Tony Pandy Revisited," *Journal of Business*, 41 (January 1968), 22.

24. *Hearings*, Part 2, pp. 600, 620–622.

and by small advertisers. On CBS, for which data are reported, the largest advertisers spend about 85 percent of their budget on conventional purchases, whereas the smaller advertisers spend much less—between 11 and 27 percent— on conventional purchases, the rest being used for participating minutes.[25] An important question with regard to the advertising price structure therefore is what factors may have given rise to this discrepancy.

An empirical analysis of the relation between actual prices and advertising volume has been carried out by Peterman.[26] He estimates a large number of regression equations in which the dependent variable is the average price per commercial minute for each buyer of advertising messages on individual television programs. His primary independent variables are alternative measures of advertiser size: either the firm's total yearly expenditure on network television or a dummy variable to indicate the largest advertisers. Additional independent variables include the number of minutes purchased by any buyer on a particular program, and either the average number of homes in which the program is received or the average number of viewers per commercial minute on the program series. Regression equations are estimated separately for each of the three networks in 1965 and 1966. Peterman's equations, however, are not particularly useful for our purposes since they take the form

$$P = a + b\,PQ \tag{1}$$

rather than

$$P = \alpha + \beta\,Q, \tag{2}$$

and there is no necessary reason for the signs of $b$ and $\beta$ to agree.[27] This point is important because a test for the presence of price discrimination must necessarily focus on the relation between prices and quantities rather than that between prices and total receipts.

This objection does not apply to the estimated coefficients for minutes purchased on particular programs, however, since this is a measure of quantity

25. Blank, "Television Advertising," p. 32.
26. John L. Peterman, "The Clorox Case and Television Rate Structures," *Journal of Law and Economics*, 11 (October 1968), 376–389, 404–412.
27. This is readily demonstrated. If the true relationship is $P = \alpha + \beta Q + u$, where $u$ is a random variable independent of $Q$, then $PQ = \alpha Q + \beta Q^2 + uQ$. The covariance between $P$ and $PQ$ is:

$$cov\,(P, PQ) = \alpha\beta\,var\,Q + \beta^2\,cov\,(Q, Q^2) + \bar{Q}\,var\,u$$

If there are quantity discounts in the pricing structure, $\alpha > 0$ and $\beta < 0$. In this case, however, the sign of $cov\,(P, PQ)$ (and hence the sign of $b$ in a regression of $P$ on $PQ$) may be either positive or negative, since the first term in the above expression will be negative and the last two terms positive.

rather than of value. It is interesting to note that of the 48 coefficients estimated for this variable, 38 are negative and 10 positive. These results indicate that lower prices are typically obtained through the purchase of a greater number of messages on a single program, which represents one form of quantity discount.

A further analysis of these data was carried out.[28] Before we proceed with this analysis, however, it is necessary to consider the types of discounts that might be offered. Do large advertisers receive lower rates for messages provided on the same programs as compared with smaller advertisers, or are lower rates set for messages reserved by some means or other for large advertisers? The importance of this question can be seen by asking whether program dummy variables should be included in the regression equations. To the extent that differences among advertisers are attributable to differences *among* programs as well as to differences *within* programs, to correct for differences among programs would remove a large part of the relevant variation in advertiser rates. Since including dummy variables for individual programs might remove a substantial portion of the relevant variation in advertising rates, they are not included in the regression equations.[29]

In this analysis, we are concerned with the prices and quantities of advertising messages purchased by different firms from a television network. A message in this context is received by a single viewer for a minute. Two definitions of an advertising message are used. The first is the total number of viewer-minutes during which adults receive a given commercial message; the second includes both adult and teenage viewers. In this analysis, we do not count messages received by younger children even though they may have an impact on purchasing decisions. Total advertising outlay refers to total expenditures by the firm on the programs included in the study: a sample of 14 programs in 1965 and 16 in 1966.

Various regression equations are estimated where firm expenditure on advertising in a given network and year is the dependent variable, and the number of viewer-minutes purchased, the independent variable. Both variables are measured in logarithmic form. When the estimated elasticity exceeds unity, increases in the number of messages purchased are associated with

28. The authors are grateful to Professor Peterman for providing his statistics on computer cards for all three networks in 1965 and for ABC and NBC for 1966. Information was obtained on the average prices paid by individual advertisers for commercial messages purchased on network television for a sample of program series. These series include evening programs only. They are also limited to messages solely through participations and thereby do not include program sales which are made via rate cards. For further discussion of these data, see Peterman, "The Clorox Case," pp. 402–412.

29. This contrasts with the approach taken by Professor Peterman where program dummy variables are included in the regression equations.

proportionately greater outlays, which suggests higher rather than lower prices as quantities increase—contrary to the hypothesis of quantity discounts. When this coefficient is less than unity, on the other hand, increased purchases are associated with proportionately lower outlays, which supports the presence of quantity discounts [30]

Some empirical findings are given in Table 4.1. As can be seen, the results are mixed. In three network-years out of five, the coefficients fall below unity, but they exceed unity in the remaining two cases. Moreover, only with regard to the NBC television network is the presence of quantity discounts fairly apparent. For that network in 1966, the two estimated coefficients are both significantly less than unity at the 5-percent level; in 1965, they are both

TABLE 4.1.   Coefficients for regression equations explaining firm expenditures on network television (variables measured in logarithmic form)[a]

| Network and Year | Intercept | Viewer-minutes | | $R^2$ | N |
|---|---|---|---|---|---|
| | | Adult | Adult and teenager | | |
| I.  ABC, 1965 | 1.  −11.5 | 1.12 (0.135) | | 0.41 | 101 |
| | 2.  −11.6 | | 1.11 (0.132) | .42 | 101 |
| II.  NBC, 1965 | 3.  −6.15 | 0.816 (0.141) | | .24 | 108 |
| | 4.  −5.92 | | 0.796 (0.140) | .23 | 108 |
| III.  CBS, 1965 | 5.  −11.8 | 1.13 (0.142) | | .44 | 81 |
| | 6.  −12.2 | | 1.14 (0.142) | .45 | 81 |
| IV.  ABC, 1966 | 7.  −4.51 | 0.856 (0.130) | | .30 | 104 |
| | 8.  −5.46 | | 0.899 (0.134) | .31 | 104 |
| V.  NBC, 1966 | 9.  −2.61 | 0.757 (0.111) | | .29 | 113 |
| | 10.  −2.56 | | 0.748 (0.114) | .28 | 113 |

[a]Total expenditures are limited to selected programs. Figures in parentheses are standard errors of the coefficients.

30. Comparable results would be obtained if the dependent variable were the logarithm of price per message and the resulting coefficient tested against zero rather than unity.

significantly below 1 at the 10-percent level. In the remaining cases, the coefficients are all nonsignificant, even at the 10-percent level.

An alternative approach to interpreting these statistical results rests on the view that they provide independent estimates of the same underlying parameter. If we were willing to assume that the ten estimated elasticities given in Table 4.1 represent the same experience, so that we posit no differences in pricing practices among the three networks, we can test the null hypothesis that the mean coefficient is not less than unity. The mean of the ten coefficients is 0.937, with a standard error of 0.0418.[31] The appropriate $t$ statistic is 1.507, which is significant at the 10-percent but not at the 5-percent confidence level.

A second set of equations are estimated on the basis of program rather than

TABLE 4.2.  Coefficients for regression equations explaining firm expenditures on individual programs on network television (variables measured in logarithmic form)[a]

| Network and Year | Intercept | Viewer-minutes | | $R^2$ | N |
| | | Adult | Adult and teenager | | |
| --- | --- | --- | --- | --- | --- |
| I. ABC, 1965 | 1. $-7.90$ | 0.899 (0.164) | | 0.07 | 431 |
| | 2. $-11.3$ | | 1.09 (0.189) | .07 | 431 |
| II. NBC, 1965 | 3. $-3.56$ | 0.625 (0.237) | | .01 | 485 |
| | 4. $-1.75$ | | 0.511 (0.225) | .01 | 485 |
| III. CBS, 1965 | 5. $-3.85$ | 0.648 (0.140) | | .06 | 333 |
| | 6. $-2.88$ | | 0.583 (0.144) | .05 | 333 |
| IV. ABC, 1966 | 7. $-0.592$ | 0.592 (0.102) | | .06 | 531 |
| | 8. $-3.98$ | | 0.789 (0.124) | .07 | 531 |
| V. NBC, 1966 | 9. $-3.12$ | 0.746 (0.104) | | .08 | 597 |
| | 10. $-4.01$ | | 0.792 (0.114) | .07 | 597 |

[a]The number of viewer-minutes purchased refers to the firm total for the individual program. Figures in parentheses are the standard errors of the coefficients.

31. This variance is computed from the estimated standard errors given in Table 4.1. It equals $(1/100) \sum_i (var \ b_i)$.

firm observations, and are reported in Table 4.2.[32] Here, the dependent variable is total outlays by a firm on a specific program and the independent variable is the quantity of messages purchased on that program. The results obtained suggest strongly that quantity discounts are offered within programs. In nine cases out of ten, the estimated coefficients are less than unity and are significantly less than unity at the 5-percent confidence level in seven cases out of nine. Thus, increased purchases on individual programs are generally associated with lower average prices.

Given the prevalence of this form of quantity discount, it seemed useful to carry out a combined analysis to examine whether any advantages to a large volume of purchases are generally realized in addition to those obtained via discounts on individual programs. This is done by adding a second independent variable to the above equations, which is total purchases by the firm on all programs. The coefficient of the added variable then represents the *additional* effect of total firm purchases—beyond the effect of the volume of purchases on individual programs.

The empirical results are given in Table 4.3. As can be seen, the presence of quantity discounts on individual programs is again indicated. Nine of the ten coefficients of the quantity of messages purchased on individual programs are less than unity, and seven of these coefficients are again significantly below 1. Of the coefficients of the total volume of messages purchased by the firm, however, only four of ten are negative—all on the NBC television network —and only those for 1966 are statistically significant. On this network, quantity discounts appear to be related to aggregate firm purchases as well as to the volume of purchases on individual programs. For the other networks, however, there appear to be no important discounts available beyond those provided from large purchases on individual program series.

On the basis of these results, we conclude that the principal source of any cost advantage to large-scale television advertisers is quantity discounts on programs. The average of the coefficients of program costs given in Table 4.2 is 0.728, indicating that a 10 percent increase in the number of messages purchased on a typical program series is associated with an increase in total costs of about 7.5 percent. With such large program discounts, large advertisers could take advantage of these savings more effectively than small advertisers

32. In two instances, the number of program observations given by the data received from Professor Peterman, and on which this analysis is based, differs from the number published in his article. For the ABC television network in 1966, 531 observations are available, one less than the number given by Peterman of 532. For the NBC network in 1966, data were received on 597 observations, again one less than the figure published by Peterman. However these discrepancies may be resolved, it seems unlikely indeed that they have any appreciable effect on the empirical results.

TABLE 4.3.   Coefficients for regression equations explaining firm expenditures on individual programs on network television (variables expressed in logarithmic form)[a]

| Network and Year | Intercept | Viewer-minutes | | | | R² | N |
| | | Adult | | Adult and teenager | | | |
| | | Firm's total | On particular program | Firm's total | On particular program | | |
| I. ABC, 1965 | 1. −9.78 | 0.083 (0.092) | 0.921 (0.166) | | | 0.07 | 431 |
| | 2. −13.4 | | | 0.090 (0.091) | 1.121 (0.191) | .07 | 431 |
| II. NBC, 1965 | 3. −1.96 | −.096 (.089) | .635 (.237) | | | .02 | 485 |
| | 4. −0.039 | | | −.103 (.089) | .524 (.225) | .01 | 485 |
| III. CBS, 1965 | 5. −5.61 | .096 (.087) | .649 (.140) | | | .06 | 333 |
| | 6. −4.51 | | | .089 (.087) | .583 (.144) | .05 | 333 |
| IV. ABC, 1966 | 7. −370 | .200 (.080) | .558 (.103) | | | .07 | 531 |
| | 8. −7.41 | | | .209 (.081) | .763 (.124) | .08 | 531 |
| V. NBC, 1966 | 9. 0.642 | −.209 (.076) | .753 (.104) | | | .09 | 597 |
| | 10. 0.006 | | | −.220 (.077) | .796 (.113) | .09 | 597 |

[a]Figures in parentheses are standard errors of the coefficient.

by concentrating their budgets on a small number of programs. That they have chosen not to do so may be due to a decline in the marginal effectiveness of advertising through individual programs and resulting gains from message diversification across programs. Because of large program discounts, small advertisers are forced to choose between higher costs, by not taking advantage of these discounts, and foregoing the gains from program diversification. Our previous finding that small advertisers do not generally pay more than large advertisers—with the apparent exception of the NBC television network—therefore indicates that they have chosen to relinquish the possible advantages of diversification. Unfortunately, how important such advantages are cannot be inferred from these results.[33]

Although the evidence presented and discussed above is suggestive rather than conclusive, it appears that quantity discounts may contribute to economies of scale in advertising. Moreover, since messages distributed in certain media are probably not perfect substitutes for those distributed in others because of differences in the audiences reached, the disadvantage created by the failure to realize discounts in some media may not be easily avoided through a greater reliance on others. Therefore, scale economies may result from price discrimination practiced by some media even if not all.

## OVERALL IMPACT ON ENTRY BARRIERS

Before discussing the general effect of advertising on entry barriers, it is useful to consider one other source of entry barriers due to advertising. If economies of scale exist either in production or in advertising, the need to obtain funds for advertising will give rise to capital requirements over and above those needed for physical plant and equipment. Furthermore, this investment in market penetration will involve a particularly risky use of funds, since it does not create tangible assets that can be resold in the event of failure.[34] The required rate of return on such capital should therefore be relatively high.

Furthermore, new entrants are often unable to obtain the requisite volume of funds, because of either imperfections or high transaction costs in the relevant capital markets.[35] Established and well-known firms have generally lower average costs of capital than new entrants to a market, perhaps owing to the higher costs of obtaining information on prospective profitability for the latter than for the former. In these circumstances as well, entry barriers are created and existing firms are able to raise prices to some level over costs without attracting the entry of new firms.[36]

33. For further discussion of quantity discounts on television advertising as well as other media see Leo Bogart, *Strategy in Advertising* (New York, Harcourt Brace Jovanovich, 1967), pp. 250–254.

34. On this point, it is argued that "perhaps the real barrier [to entry] is that financial institutions, though willing to accept plant and equipment as loan collateral, are reluctant to finance marketing investments. This, in turn, is related to the standard accounting practice of treating even introductory advertising as a 'current expense,' rather than as a depreciable asset," Kenneth A. Longman, *Advertising* (New York, Harcourt Brace Jovanovich, 1971), p. 76.

35. For a discussion of the relationship between these two considerations, see George J. Stigler, "Imperfections in the Capital Market," *Journal of Political Economy*, 75 (June 1967), 287–292.

36. See Bain, *Barriers to New Competition*, pp. 156–165.

These various effects of advertising are illustrated diagrammatically in Fig. 4.2. Curve *APC* represents average production costs for established and prospective firms, and *MESP* is minimum efficient scale in production. Curve *AAC* describes average advertising costs for existing firms as well as for new entrants after they have become established. It denotes unit advertising costs that are required in order to maintain a firm's market position and to preserve a given volume of sales once it has been established. These costs will depend on both the total level of advertising outlays and their distribution among established firms. The curve therefore describes prospective advertising costs for entrants only if existing firms do not react to any loss of market share. To the extent that they do respond, required advertising outlays will be higher. Curve *ATC*, the vertical sum of these two curves, represents average total costs for established firms,[37] and *MES* denotes the minimum efficient scale

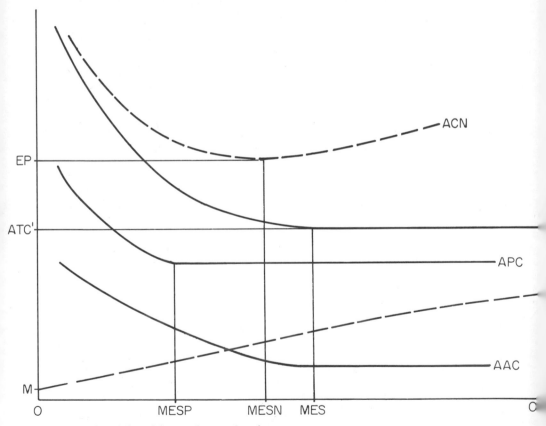

Fig. 4.2.   Advertising and entry barriers

37. For simplicity, we assume here that advertising constitutes the only form of selling expense.

in both production and advertising for an established firm with a given share of the market.

In addition, curve *AMPC* describes average market penetration costs for new entrants. Penetration costs represent an investment in establishing a market position and therefore depend on the opportunity cost of capital as well as on total penetration expenditures.[38] This schedule therefore denotes the required rate of return on capital invested in market penetration multiplied by the total expenditure required to establish a given volume of sales and divided by the number of units sold. The figure illustrates the case where average penetration costs rise throughout the relevant range of output. This assumes that the growing difficulty involved in winning over customers with stronger preferences for the products of established firms, reinforced by rising required rates of return as the absolute amount of capital required for penetration increases with the scale of entry, is not fully offset by economies of scale of advertising or by bandwagon effects for the new entrant's products.

Curve *ACN* represents average costs, including penetration costs, for new entrants, and *MESN* is the most efficient scale for entry if the reactions of established products are neglected. From this, it follows that *EP* is the *minimum* price at which entry will occur. If *MESN* is a negligible fraction of the market, *EP* is an entry-inducing price. If, however, *MESN* is a significant fraction of the market, entry is unlikely to occur even at price *EP* because the entrant will expect established producers to contest the encroachment on their market position through an increase in advertising outlays or by a reduction in price. The gap between *EP* and *ATC'* represents, therefore, the minimum price-cost margin that may induce entry.

Figure 4.2 demonstrates, moreover, that the interaction between rising market penetration costs and economies of scale at the firm level is important even if no allowance is made for the reactions of existing producers. If economies of scale in both production and advertising were absent, the relevant price-cost margin would be simply *OM*, which is less than *EP − ATC'*.

The analysis presented in this chapter provides a basis for the hypothesis that advertising expenditures may create barriers to new competition, thereby permitting established firms to set prices above long-run average costs (including normal profit). Chapters 6–8 present empirical evidence designed to test this hypothesis. Chapter 5 examines the impact of advertising on market demand.

---

38. Penetration costs include extra advertising outlays which are required for entry. These outlays will represent total penetration costs if the price charged by the entrant is the same as that set by established producers. If the entrant is forced to set a price below that of existing firms, there are additional penetration costs which equal the price differential times the amount of output sold by the entrant at the lower price. In this analysis, we assume that existing firms did not need to incur penetration costs to establish their market positions.

# CHAPTER 5 Advertising and Market Demand

The theoretical analysis of previous chapters suggests that advertising by existing firms in an industry could affect the character of competition among firms in a market and could have an impact on entry barriers. Since such effects are likely to be structural, in the sense of changing only slowly over time, it is appropriate to examine them in a cross-sectional context. Further consideration of these effects and the presentation of cross-sectional empirical results is contained in subsequent chapters.

In the present chapter we examine a third possible effect of advertising: its impact on market demand. Although the literature has tended to emphasize the importance of advertising in affecting the distribution of demand between brands within a market, the impact of advertising upon the total demand for the group of products produced by an industry is important in a number of respects. First, it is interesting to determine the extent to which advertising has a resource allocation function and to examine how its importance in this respect compares with that of relative prices, the variable emphasized in traditional microeconomic theory. Second, as will be discussed further in Chapter 8, it is important to measure the time pattern of effects of advertising in an industry in order to determine whether there are biases in the cross-sectional analyses and to make appropriate adjustments to the data to compensate for these biases. Where the effects of advertising do not occur instantaneously but are spread over time, it may be useful to consider advertising as generating a "goodwill stock" which in turn influences sales.

Our purpose in this chapter is therefore twofold: to develop estimates of the time pattern of response of sales to advertising outlays, in order to use these to construct estimates of goodwill stocks created by advertising, and to test some hypotheses about the effects of advertising on consumer behavior. To fulfill these objectives we need to estimate models that incorporate the effects of advertising on market demand and that (a) allow for sufficient variety in the time pattern of consumer responses and (b) are compatible with an under-lying theory of consumer behavior.

A model that meets these requirements for consumer-demand models without advertising is that developed and extensively tested by Houthakker and Taylor.[1] In the remainder of this section we extend the Houthakker-Taylor model to include advertising as an additional determinant of consumer expenditures.

The basic Houthakker-Taylor model is developed from two equations. These are a relation between consumer expenditures $C_t$ on a commodity, its underlying determinants—relative prices $P_t$ and total expenditure $Y_t$—and a state (or stock, in the case of durable goods) variable $S_t$:

$$C_t = \alpha + \beta S_t + \gamma Y_t + \eta P_t, \tag{1}$$

and an equation expressing the relation of the state variable to the flow of consumer purchases:

$$\dot{S}_t = C_t - \delta S_t. \tag{2}$$

The state variable in this model represents the cumulative impact of past purchases. In the case of durable goods, this variable represents the value of the stock of the particular commodity held, and may be expected to have a negative impact upon current sales. In the case of nondurable goods or of services, this variable represents the strength of habit formation, and may be expected to have a positive impact on sales.

The derivation of the estimating equations from these structural relations is rather tedious and need not be repeated here.[2] The estimating equation in discrete time is

$$C_t = a_0 + a_1 \Delta Y_t + a_1 \lambda Y_{t-1} + a_2 \Delta P_t + a_2 \lambda P_{t-1} + a_3 C_{t-1}. \tag{3}$$

As Houthakker and Taylor have shown,[3] estimates of the structural para-meters $\alpha$, $\beta$, $\gamma$, $\eta$, and $\delta$ may be derived from the $a_i$ and $\lambda$.

Advertising may be introduced into this model as another determinant of consumer expenditures in the first equation. In this form, the treatment of

1. H. S. Houthakker and L. D. Taylor, *Consumer Demand in the United States*, 2d ed. (Cambridge, Mass., Harvard University Press, 1970).
2. *Ibid.*, pp. 10–17.
3. *Ibid.*, p. 17.

advertising is parallel to that of prices and incomes.[4] Equation (1) is modified to include advertising as follows:

$$C_t = \alpha + \beta S_t + \zeta A_t + \gamma Y_t + \eta P_t, \tag{1a}$$

where $A_t$ is advertising. The equation for the state-flow relation (2) is unchanged. From these two equations, the following estimating equation may be derived:[5]

$$
\begin{aligned}
C_t = a_0 &+ a_1 \Delta A_t + a_1 \lambda A_{t-1} + a_2 \Delta Y_t + a_2 \lambda Y_{t-1} \\
&+ a_3 \Delta P_t + a_3 \lambda P_{t-1} + a_4 C_{t-1}.
\end{aligned} \tag{4}
$$

Note that, as is the case with the original Houthakker-Taylor model, the ratios of the coefficient of each lagged independent variable to the coefficient of the corresponding first difference of that variable are constrained to be equal.

Estimates of the structural parameters may be derived from the $a_i$ and $\lambda$.[6] However, this estimating equation may also be interpreted more simply as a generalization of the distributed-lag model developed by Koyck.[7] We therefore refer to this model henceforth as the Generalized Koyck (or GK) model.

Another model, which corresponds to the Flow-Adjustment model (FA model) used by Houthakker and Taylor, was also estimated.[8] This model is a special case of the Houthakker-Taylor model in which target consumption

4. An alternative approach involved introducing advertising into the state flow relationship by postulating that the state variable is composed of two elements, the effects of past purchases and the effects of past advertising expenditures:
$$\dot{S}_t = W_1 C_t + W_2 A_t - \delta S_t. \tag{2a}$$
An estimating equation was derived from (2a) and (1), using a finite period approximation (see Appendix 5-A). The results of estimating this model, however, were generally inferior to that of the GK model presented in this chapter, although the pattern of results obtained was similar.

5. The details of the derivation of this model are provided in Appendix 5-A.

6. These formulae are as follows:

$$\delta = \frac{\lambda}{1 - \lambda/2}$$

$$\beta = \frac{2(a_4 - 1)}{a_4 + 1} + \frac{\lambda}{1 - \lambda/2}$$

$$\gamma = \frac{2a_2(1 - \lambda/2)}{a_4 + 1}$$

$$\zeta = \frac{2a_1(1 - \lambda/2)}{a_4 + 1}$$

$$\eta = \frac{2a_3(1 - \lambda/2)}{a_4 + 1}.$$

7. L. M. Koyck, *Distributed Lags and Investment Analysis* (Amsterdam, North-Holland Publishing Co., 1954).

8. Houthakker and Taylor, *Consumer Demand in the United States,* pp. 26–27.

flows depend on the underlying determinants, and actual flows are adjusted to the gap between actual and target flows. An FA model which includes the effect of advertising may be specified as follows:

$$\hat{C}_t = \xi + \omega A_t + \mu Y_t + \eta P_t , \tag{5}$$

where $\hat{C}_t$ is the desired or target level of purchases, and

$$\dot{C}_t = \theta(\hat{C}_t - C_t) . \tag{6}$$

The estimating equation for this model in discrete time is

$$C_t = b_0 + b_1\bar{A}_t + b_2\bar{Y}_t + b_3\bar{P}_t + b_4C_{t-1} , \tag{7}$$

where bars over the variables indicate that they are averages of current and last year's values. Estimates of the structural parameters may be derived from the $b_i$.[9] Note that this model is a special case of the first model derived above.

Estimates of the theoretical parameters of either of these models, which are derived from the empirical coefficients of the estimating equations, may be unreliable for two reasons. First, the sales of many of the industries include intermediate as well as final products and investment as well as consumer goods. For example, some of the output of the confectionery industry is used by the bakery industry, and the automobile industry produces trucks and parts as well as cars. Hence some part of the demand for an industry is a derived demand from the final demands for other products, and some portion is explained by the investment decisions of firms rather than the consumption decisions of households. This problem does not, of course, cloud the empirical results of Houthakker and Taylor, since their equations were applied to categories of final consumer demand in the national accounts, whereas ours apply to the sales of manufacturing industries.

Second, the sales of manufacturers are not typically made directly to consumers, but pass through the hands of wholesale and retail distributors. This means that a buffer of inventories held by wholesalers and retailers stands

9. These formulae are as follows:

$$\xi = \frac{b_0}{1 - b_4}$$

$$\omega = \frac{b_1}{1 - b_4}$$

$$\mu = \frac{b_2}{1 - b_4}$$

$$\eta = \frac{b_3}{1 - b_4}$$

$$\theta = \frac{2(1 - b_4)}{1 + b_4}$$

The details of the derivation of this model are provided in Appendix 5-A.

between the manufacturer and the final consumer. Although in the long run the demands of the consumer for a product should be translated into the derived demands for the products of manufacturers, the short-run dynamics of manufacturing sales adjustment and consumer expenditure adjustment could differ because of adjustments in the inventories held by distributors. The estimates of the underlying structural parameters in the GK model will be quite sensitive to errors in the estimate of $a_4$, the coefficient of the lagged dependent variable, and $\lambda$, the constraint coefficient. Similarly, estimates of the structural parameters in the FA model will be sensitive to errors in the measurement of $b_4$. Estimates of both sets of coefficients will in turn be quite sensitive to differences in dynamic-adjustment patterns. Hence it may be misleading to use equations that adequately capture the dynamic adjustment of manufacturers' sales to draw inferences about the underlying parameters of the consumer model.

Because of these problems, our equations are more useful for estimating manufacturers' investment in goodwill, our primary objective, than they are for drawing precise inferences about the dynamics of consumer behavior. However, certain effects of interest from the standpoint of the theory of consumer behavior may nevertheless be estimated—those that are not particularly sensitive to errors in the estimates of the dynamic structure, such as estimates of the equilibrium rates of adjustment of sales to advertising, price, and income—and tests of the direction and estimates of the magnitude of the immediate effects of advertising and price and income upon manufacturers' sales may be provided.

## SPECIFICATION AND PRESENTATION OF SINGLE-EQUATION ESTIMATES

As is the case with the original Houthakker-Taylor model without advertising, the first model developed above is nonlinear in the coefficients, and is overdetermined. In the case of the GK model, equation (4), ordinary least squares would yield eight coefficients from which to estimate six parameters. Hence we develop single-equation estimates of these models by an iterative nonlinear estimation procedure,[10] using as initial conditions approximate estimates of the parameters derived from the ordinary least-squares coef-

10. The nonlinear estimation routine used is part of the MASSAGER econometric estimation program developed by M. C. McCracken, as modified by programmers at the Bank of Canada. A manual describing this program (MASSAGER '70) may be obtained from Computel Systems, Ltd., Ottawa, Ontario.

The computing algorithm used in this program is from D. W. Marquandt, "An Algorithm for Least Squares Estimation of Nonlinear Parameters," *Journal of the Society for Industrial and Applied Mathematics*, II, no. 2 (June 1963), 431–441.

ficients.[11] The Flow-Adjustment model is not overidentified, and hence equation (7) is estimated by ordinary least squares.

As discussed further in subsequent sections and appendices to this chapter, there are three important additional econometric estimation problems. Any autocorrelation in the errors of these models will in general yield inconsistent as well as inefficient estimates, because of the presence of a lagged dependent variable on the right-hand side of the equation for each model. Since the Durbin-Watson statistic becomes a somewhat unreliable indicator of autocorrelation in such a situation,[12] another technique has been used to examine whether this problem is important.

Since there is reason to believe that sales, profits, or both could influence advertising as well as being influenced by it—particularly in the short run— there could exist simultaneous-equations bias in the single-equation estimates. Since the Generalized Koyck model is nonlinear in the coefficients, standard simultaneous estimation techniques cannot be used. An approximate two-stage least-squares procedure was therefore developed.

Errors of observation in the different series will probably be positively and negatively correlated with one another, hence introducing biases in the estimates (in addition to the usual bias toward zero that arises from errors of measurement in the independent variables of the model). Two sources of measurement error may be particularly important in this connection.

First, errors of measurement in the absolute price index for the industry will affect both the independent variable (relative price) and the dependent variable (deflated per capita sales). Since the absolute price is the numerator of the relative price variable and enters the denominator of the dependent variable, this will introduce a negative bias to the correlation between prices and deflated sales.

Second, industry-classification errors may affect both the dependent variable and the alternative measures of advertising intensity used. If a firm is classified incorrectly into a particular industry, errors of measurement are introduced in both sales and advertising. Since these errors will be in the same direction, they will introduce a positive bias to the correlation between advertising and sales.

Whether and in what direction the partial regression coefficients for prices and advertising in these models are biased cannot be readily determined,

11. For the GK model, the initial conditions for $a_j$ were the least squares estimates of the coefficients of the unconstrained model. The initial condition for $\lambda$ is an average of the relevant ratios of the coefficients for the lagged exogenous variables to the respective coefficients for the first differences of these variables.

12. Z. Griliches, "A Note on Serial Correlation Bias in Estimates of Distributed Lags," *Econometrica* (January 1961), pp. 65–73.

because of nonzero correlations among the explanatory variables.[13] There are, of course, other sources of measurement error in the independent variables that will bias the estimated coefficients toward zero. We therefore feel that, on balance, the biases resulting from errors of measurement are unlikely to distort the results in favor of the rejection of the null hypothesis.

The next section is devoted to the presentation of single-equation specifications and results. Appendix 5-B to this chapter contains an analysis of the importance of autocorrelation problems. In the following section we present estimates based on simultaneous-equation models. In the penultimate section, we present estimates of certain special case models for those industries for which none of the general models seems appropriate, and select the final equations to be used in the construction of estimates of goodwill stock and in the cross-section analyses of subsequent chapters. An overview of the results obtained is presented in the final section of this chapter.

## SPECIFICATION OF OLS EQUATIONS

For convenience, we rewrite the equations developed above for the two general models to be fitted to the data:

GK model:

$$
\begin{aligned}
C_t = a_0 &+ a_1\Delta A_t + a_1\lambda A_{t-1} + a_2\Delta Y_t \\
&+ a_2\lambda Y_{t-1} + a_3\Delta P_t + a_3\lambda P_{t-1} + a_4 C_{t-1} ;
\end{aligned}
\tag{4}
$$

FA model:

$$
C_t = b_0 + b_1\bar{A}_t + b_2\bar{Y}_t + b_3\bar{P}_t + b_4 C_{t-1} .
\tag{7}
$$

All variables are either annual totals or annual averages. Their precise definition and sources are described in Appendix 5-D.

Following Houthakker and Taylor, we define the dependent variable $C_t$ to be real per-capita sales and the price variable $P_t$ to be the price of the product relative to the price of all consumer goods. For the "income" variable, $Y_t$, we examined three alternative measures: per-capita constant-dollar consumer expenditure (the variable used by Houthakker and Taylor in their work), per-capita constant-dollar disposable income, and an index of per-capita production of consumer goods. The last variable was examined because it might be a more adequate representation of the general demand for manufactured consumer products. In particular, it might mitigate some of the timing problems arising from fluctuations in trade inventories discussed above.

Two alternative specifications of the level of advertising intensity were

13. H. Theil, *Economic Forecasts and Policy* (Amsterdam, North-Holland Publishing Co., 1958), pp. 327–329.

examined: advertising expenditures of the industry expressed in constant dollars per capita and industry advertising expenditures relative to total advertising expenditures by all manufacturers.

The former specification appears somewhat inadequate in retrospect. When used in models with total consumer expenditure as the income variable, it involves the assumption that equal relative increases in advertising in all industries in our sample increase the sales of these industries relative to the sales of other consumer products. If this model were extended to include all consumer goods and services—hence exhausting consumer purchases—such a model would of course become internally inconsistent. When used in models with disposable income as the income variable, the use of absolute advertising expenditures would imply that an increase in total advertising will either increase the sales of the industries that happen to be in our sample as above or else expand total consumer expenditures at the expense of consumer savings. Although there is evidence to support the latter view,[14] such an assumption is unnecessary for our present task.

In addition to these conceptual difficulties, the use of absolute advertising expenditure poses two measurement problems. The first is the selection of a price deflator. Although it proved possible to construct a price deflator for advertising expenditures,[15] the accuracy and coverage of the price indices used are not perfect.

The second problem is whether to deflate real advertising expenditures by population. Since the effective audience for some forms of advertising messages —particularly those broadcast over wide areas—grows with population, such expenditures should not be expressed in per-capita terms. On the other hand, advertising messages in printed media do not have these "public-good" characteristics to the same degree and should be expressed in per-capita terms. Because the improved quality of messages (in terms of audience units) for TV advertising in constructing the price indices was taken into account, we decided to deflate real advertising expenditures by population for the models using absolute advertising expenditures.

Since the use of relative advertising expenditures eliminates all of these conceptual and measurement problems, we have focused our work on models that use this variable. It is important to note that the use of relative advertising expenditures in models with per-capita consumer expenditures as the activity variable is consistent with either a positive or a zero (or indeed a negative) impact of aggregate advertising outlays on aggregate consumer expenditures.

14. L. D. Taylor and D. Weiserbs, "Advertising and the Aggregate Consumption Function," *American Economic Review*, 62 (September 1972).
15. See Appendix 5-D for a description of this price deflator.

This specification makes it clear that our equations are relevant for the *inter-industry* impact of advertising on sales.

Of the 41 industries included in the sample, comparable data for the postwar period up to 1964 could be obtained for only 27. Comparable data for three groupings of industries could be developed by aggregating pairs of the original industries. For the remaining industries, comparable data could be obtained only for the postwar period up to 1957, since changes in the standard industrial classification affected data in subsequent years. Because of the fewness of observations for the latter group, we emphasize the results obtained for the 30 industries and aggregated groups for which longer time series could be obtained. However, with two exceptions, satisfactory demand equations were estimated for each industry in the sample.

Before we proceed to the results, it is useful to present an overview of our approach to these empirical models. There are, of course, a large number of alternative models when both model options and all six of the measurement options are taken into account—not to mention the examination of "special-case" models, which are required in certain industries. In order to reduce the magnitude of this empirical task, we confined much of the necessary experimentation to an unconstrained version of the first model, which could be readily estimated by ordinary least squares.

We estimated an unconstrained version of the GK model using the absolute advertising variable as an alternative to the relative advertising variable, and using the three alternative measures of income. The results indicated that there was little difference between the alternative variables in terms of the statistical performance of the models. Given the small differences in statistical performance, and given that there are conceptual advantages to using relative advertising and per-capita consumer expenditures respectively, we decided to abandon further experimentation with the alternative measures. Relative advertising and per-capita consumer expenditures were therefore selected as the appropriate measures of advertising and income respectively.

## CORE ORDINARY LEAST-SQUARES RESULTS

The results of fitting the two models to the 30 industries or groupings for which reasonably long time series could be assembled are presented in Tables 5.1 and 5.2.

The highlights of these results are as follows:

1. The coefficients of multiple determination $R^2$ are generally high, as would be expected for time-series demand equations. In two industries, however—sugar and paints—neither of the $R^2$'s is satisfactory. For this reason, these industries are deleted from the subsequent cross-section analyses. A significant

TABLE 5.1. Coefficients for demand equations for 30 industries and groupings: Generalized Koyck (GK) model, 1947–1964

| Industry | Constant | Regression coefficients[a] | | | | | $R^2$ |
| --- | --- | --- | --- | --- | --- | --- | --- |
| | | $\Delta A$ | $\lambda$ | $\Delta Y$ | $\Delta P$ | $C_{t-1}$ | $DW$ |
| Soft drinks | −0.011 | 1.854 | 1.556 | 5867 | −0.455 | −0.493 | 0.982 |
| | | (9.15) | (4.56) | (3.73) | (4.44) | (1.33) | 2.05 |
| Malt liquor | .312 | 0.020 | 1.849 | −1632 | −0.628 | 0.205 | 0.857 |
| | | (0.07) | (1.07) | (1.05) | (0.94) | (0.73) | 2.22 |
| Wines | .001 | 5.707 | 0.996 | 307.7 | −0.095 | 0.195 | 0.918 |
| | | (5.99) | (4.30) | (0.71) | (2.77) | (0.87) | 1.85 |
| Distilled liquor | .045 | 7.365 | 0.801 | 1837 | −0.418 | 0.311 | 0.931 |
| | | (7.81) | (2.43) | (0.30) | (0.47) | (1.14) | 1.56 |
| Meat | .984 | 6.063 | 1.356 | 28940 | −3.956 | −0.358 | 0.926 |
| | | (1.18) | (3.65) | (1.66) | (3.91) | (1.33) | 2.40 |
| Dairy products | .227 | 16.87 | 0.285 | 40150 | 0.546 | 0.695 | 0.926 |
| | | (4.74) | (0.72) | (1.26) | (0.22) | (2.71) | 1.26 |
| Canning | .124 | 5.118 | 1.048 | 4942 | −1.661 | 0.332 | 0.929 |
| | | (2.39) | (1.88) | (0.85) | (1.22) | (1.07) | 2.15 |
| Bakery products | .037 | 1.730 | 1.364 | 8630 | −0.402 | −0.145 | 0.862 |
| | | (1.34) | (1.75) | (2.19) | (0.57) | (0.44) | 1.89 |
| Sugar | .121 | 3.425 | −0.370 | 3916 | 0.210 | −0.069 | 0.375 |
| | | (0.86) | (1.21) | (1.35) | (1.48) | (0.34) | 1.51 |
| Confectionery | .183 | 2.385 | 1.256 | −1595 | −0.390 | −0.606 | 0.973 |
| | | (5.85) | (3.84) | (4.01) | (3.65) | (2.15) | 1.66 |
| Knit goods | −.492 | 2.970 | 1.452 | 28690 | 0.061 | −0.319 | 0.981 |
| | | (0.96) | (3.78) | (4.06) | (0.29) | (0.88) | 2.10 |
| Men's clothing | .024 | 10.44 | 0.339 | 26510 | −1.160 | 0.169 | 0.932 |
| | | (3.76) | (1.67) | (4.08) | (1.43) | (0.72) | 1.60 |
| Women's clothing | −.023 | 18.05 | 0.340 | 8640 | −2.842 | 1.034 | 0.921 |
| | | (3.07) | (1.04) | (0.53) | (1.34) | (4.34) | 2.64 |
| Periodicals | .037 | 2.762 | 0.301 | 9318 | −0.811 | 0.386 | 0.834 |
| | | (2.13) | (1.03) | (2.03) | (1.21) | (1.26) | 1.78 |
| Books | −.095 | 2.793 | 1.499 | 8751 | −0.540 | −0.076 | 0.941 |
| | | (2.12) | (2.07) | (2.23) | (0.88) | (0.17) | 1.65 |
| Drugs[b] | .067 | 1.768 | 1.251 | 6178 | −1.543 | 0.204 | 0.943 |
| | | (1.18) | (1.27) | (0.41) | (0.68) | (0.61) | 1.94 |
| Soaps | −.032 | 0.777 | 1.191 | 12930 | −0.919 | −0.151 | 0.931 |
| | | (4.66) | (2.71) | (5.20) | (2.82) | (0.50) | 2.25 |
| Paints | .078 | 5.322 | 0.279 | 1548 | 0.156 | 0.124 | 0.190 |
| | | (1.40) | (0.48) | (0.21) | (0.12) | (0.27) | 1.73 |
| Perfumes[b] | −.064 | 1.392 | 0.641 | 5714 | 0.088 | 0.472 | 0.975 |
| | | (3.14) | (2.04) | (2.34) | (0.37) | (1.72) | 1.83 |

Table 5.1. (continued)

| Industry | Constant | Regression coefficients[a] | | | | | $R^2$ |
|---|---|---|---|---|---|---|---|
| | | $\Delta A$ | $\lambda$ | $\Delta Y$ | $\Delta P$ | $C_{t-1}$ | $DW$ |
| Tires and tubes | .060 | 1.422 (0.84) | 0.008 (0.14) | 34410 (4.28) | −0.009 (0.03) | 0.591 (2.91) | 0.704 1.31 |
| Footwear | .032 | 8.352 (2.86) | 0.660 (1.94) | 4623 (1.89) | −0.343 (0.88) | 0.117 (0.54) | 0.631 1.76 |
| Hand tools | .092 | 2.175 (1.70) | 0.848 (1.61) | 3636 (2.01) | −0.783 (1.83) | −0.146 (0.44) | 0.543 2.06 |
| Motor vehicles | .698 | 10.15 (3.72) | −0.077 (2.03) | 350700 (7.21) | −12.49 (3.01) | 0.516 (4.28) | 0.872 (2.68) |
| Instruments[b] | .317 | 11.02 (4.43) | 1.013 (12.13) | −462.9 (0.08) | −3.134 (1.45) | 0.227 (1.59) | 0.983 2.52 |
| Clocks and watches | .163 | 0.441 (0.87) | 3.186 (0.90) | −688.4 (0.63) | −0.330 (0.84) | 0.351 (1.48) | 0.615 2.72 |
| Jewelry (precious metal) | −.125 | 0.694 (0.90) | 3.675 (1.03) | 1943 (1.04) | 0.122 (0.80) | −0.506 (1.83) | 0.644 2.25 |
| Costume jewelry[b] | .060 | 3.351 (2.27) | 1.017 (22.35) | −1005 (2.38) | −0.335 (2.26) | 0.066 (0.26) | 0.803 2.25 |
| Tobacco[b] | .476 | 1.709 (2.01) | 1.166 (7.37) | 8.9 (0.004) | −2.698 (2.93) | 0.172 (1.10) | 0.624 2.27 |
| Grains and cereals | .445 | 2.134 (1.64) | 0.935 (2.51) | 2888 (0.83) | −3.212 (2.00) | 0.346 (1.86) | 0.820 2.09 |
| Furniture and fixtures | −.672 | 3.954 (2.59) | 1.356 (4.02) | 26550 (4.44) | 2.123 (1.85) | −0.687 (2.20) | 0.920 2.34 |

[a]Values of $t$ in parentheses.
[b]The period of observation is 1948–1964.

part of the output of these industries is sold as intermediate products to other manufacturers, which may account for the weak performance of demand equations based on a theory of consumer demand alone.

2. The relative-price variable typically enters with the expected sign. For two industries where this is not the case—jewelry (precious metal) and perfumes —Veblen goods[16] may account for a significant portion of the output. For one durable-goods industry—furniture and fixtures—the estimated positive price elasticity may reflect a mixture of negative price and positive quality effects.

3. The advertising coefficient typically has the expected sign. More signifi-

16. Veblen goods are defined as goods for which consumers' preferences are an increasing function of price. See H. Leibenstein, "Bandwagon, Snob and Veblen Effects in the Theory of Consumer Demand," *Quarterly Journal of Economics* (May 1950), pp. 183–207.

TABLE 5.2.  Coefficients for demand equations for 30 industries and groupings: Flow-Adjustment model, 1947–1964

| Industry | Constant | Regression coefficients[a] $\overline{A}$ | $\overline{P}$ | $\overline{Y}$ | $C_{t-1}$ | $R^2$ $DW$ |
|---|---|---|---|---|---|---|
| Soft drinks | −0.624 | 3.633 (9.0) | −0.838 (4.7) | 10520 (3.9) | −0.883 (4.3) | 0.979 1.75 |
| Malt liquor | .316 | 0.222 (0.52) | −1.165 (2.3) | −3109 (1.6) | 0.192 (0.76) | 0.858 2.21 |
| Wines | .178 | 8.073 (3.2) | −0.183 (2.8) | 949 (1.6) | −0.439 (1.9) | 0.815 1.61 |
| Distilled liquor | −.155 | 12.831 (5.6) | 0.246 (0.19) | 11285 (1.3) | −0.394 (1.6) | 0.850 1.80 |
| Meat | 1.267 | 7.855 (1.0) | −6.396 (4.2) | 41255 (1.6) | −0.578 (2.6) | 0.912 2.22 |
| Dairy products | −0.299 | 11.536 (0.81) | −3.330 (0.68) | 21282 (0.91) | 0.371 (0.86) | 0.790 1.69 |
| Canning | .901 | 6.728 (3.1) | −1.694 (0.92) | 6408 (0.91) | 0.223 (0.88) | 0.919 2.19 |
| Bakery products | .276 | 2.390 (1.7) | −0.457 (0.52) | 12790 (4.5) | −0.243 (0.94) | 0.858 1.83 |
| Sugar | .119 | −0.537 (0.47) | −0.133 (0.30) | −968 (1.2) | −0.541 (0.19) | 0.105 1.47 |
| Confectionery | .285 | 3.939 (9.2) | −0.880 (7.5) | −3383 (6.5) | −1.171 (7.9) | 0.962 1.73 |
| Knit goods | −.594 | 4.791 (1.1) | 0.233 (0.73) | 48379 (3.9) | −0.451 (1.3) | 0.978 1.96 |
| Men's clothing | .158 | 12.908 (2.4) | −2.363 (1.4) | 14350 (2.1) | −0.232 (0.84) | 0.855 1.87 |
| Women's clothing | −.725 | 17.864 (1.3) | 0.437 (0.26) | 37548 (1.7) | 0.482 (1.6) | 0.854 1.88 |
| Periodicals | −.906 | −0.346 (0.33) | −0.429 (0.54) | 7962 (1.8) | 0.227 (0.84) | 0.814 1.76 |
| Books | −.104 | 4.302 (2.6) | −1.125 (1.3) | 15995 (3.1) | −0.208 (0.57) | 0.939 1.72 |
| Drugs[b] | .021 | 2.361 (1.8) | −1.854 (0.8) | 10231 (0.5) | 0.152 (0.52) | 0.941 1.75 |
| Soaps | −.658 | 1.243 (4.8) | −1.271 (4.0) | 20099 (6.2) | −0.451 (2.0) | 0.913 1.77 |
| Paints | .166 | −0.234 (0.57) | −0.127 (0.11) | −1427 (0.36) | −0.420 (0.14) | 0.065 2.04 |
| Perfumes[b] | .784 | 1.193 (1.7) | −1.216 (2.0) | 3576 (1.3) | 0.744 (0.27) | 0.971 2.10 |

TABLE 5.2  (continued)

| Industry | Constant | Regression coefficients[a] | | | | $\dfrac{R^2}{DW}$ |
| | | $\bar{A}$ | $\bar{P}$ | $\bar{Y}$ | $C_{t-1}$ | |
| --- | --- | --- | --- | --- | --- | --- |
| Tires and tubes | .172 | −2.871 | −0.548 | 6947 | 0.968 | 0.426 |
| | | (1.4) | (1.8) | (2.2) | (0.35) | 2.17 |
| Footwear | .345 | 6.524 | −0.365 | 4103 | 0.246 | 0.482 |
| | | (2.0) | (0.67) | (1.4) | (0.10) | 1.96 |
| Hand tools | .103 | 2.203 | −0.739 | 3466 | −0.322 | 0.452 |
| | | (2.7) | (1.4) | (1.4) | (1.2) | 2.18 |
| Motor vehicles | .241 | −27.777 | 9.689 | 24084 | −0.117 | 0.454 |
| | | (2.4) | (0.89) | (0.87) | (0.47) | 2.39 |
| Instruments[b] | .710 | 18.746 | −7.475 | 4398 | −0.312 | 0.985 |
| | | (6.1) | (5.7) | (0.63) | (1.8) | 2.34 |
| Clocks and watches | .154 | 1.373 | −1.003 | −2062 | 0.402 | 0.599 |
| | | (1.2) | (3.0) | (1.3) | (2.0) | 2.72 |
| Jewelry (precious metal) | −.112 | 2.695 | 0.381 | 6617 | −0.459 | 0.616 |
| | | (1.6) | (1.2) | (3.8) | (1.7) | 2.22 |
| Costume jewelry[b] | .681 | 4.020 | −0.364 | −1320 | −0.375 | 0.800 |
| | | (2.5) | (2.6) | (2.6) | (0.13) | 2.33 |
| Tobacco | .642 | 2.200 | −4.134 | 307 | −0.963 | 0.621 |
| | | (2.0) | (3.7) | (0.98) | (0.41) | 2.00 |
| Grains and cereals | .399 | 1.364 | −2.859 | 3458 | 0.471 | 0.788 |
| | | (1.1) | (1.9) | (1.2) | (2.2) | 1.97 |
| Furniture and fixtures | −.711 | 5.489 | 3.007 | 39015 | −0.819 | 0.905 |
| | | (2.8) | (1.7) | (4.9) | (2.6) | 2.20 |

[a]Values of $t$ in parentheses.
[b]The period of observation is 1948–1964.

cant—from the standpoint of the theory of consumer behavior—more of the advertising coefficients are significant or marginally significant than are the price coefficients, and fewer unexpected signs are observed for advertising than for prices.

4. The income variable is typically positive in its effect, but typically much weaker in statistical significance than one would expect on the basis of previous studies of consumer demand. This probably reflects the timing problem created by inventory adjustments, together with the absence of variables measuring the demands for intermediate uses, which may be an important source of sales in some of these industries.

5. Of the two models, the performance of the GK model is generally superior, although there are some exceptions in particular industries.

6. For the GK model, the coefficients of the lagged dependent variable typically are not significant, and about one-third of the coefficients are negative.

7. The Durbin-Watson coefficients typically do not suggest the presence of either positive or negative autocorrelation of the residuals. However, as noted above, these results are not definite. More stringent tests were applied in the case of the GK model, and are reported in Appendix 5-B.

8. In a number of cases, the performance of the general model suggests that special-case models should be fitted. In two instances—motor vehicles and tires and tubes—the special case for the GK model[17] with $\lambda = 0$ is suggested. In one industry—women's clothing—the coefficient of the lagged dependent variable slightly exceeds unity, suggesting the special case of the GK model with with $a_4 = 1.00$. In two cases—dairy products and furniture—persistent positive price elasticities suggest that estimation of models with prices omitted would be appropriate.[18] Estimates of these special-case models are included in Table 5.7 below.

## RESULTS FOR INDUSTRIES WITH DATA ENDING IN 1957

As noted above, the changes in industrial classification that took place between 1957 and 1958 made it impossible to develop consistent series for each of the 41 industries. In three industries—tobacco products, grain and cereals, and furniture and fixtures—a consistent series could be developed by aggregating two IRS industries. In other cases, this proved impossible. Consistent series could be developed only for the period prior to 1958 for the remaining industries (and for the component parts of aggregated industries). Equations for each of the two general models were fitted; the results for the GK model are presented in Table 5.3.

The reader must be cautioned that these results are based on fewer degrees of freedom than the results already discussed. The findings for these industries are, however, in line with the findings for the industries with more complete data. The advertising variable has the expected sign in all but two industries, cigarettes and grain mill products. With the exception of furs (for which Veblen goods may be the explanation) and furniture and radio, TV and phonograph (for which inadequate measures of quality change may be the explanation), the relative price variable also has the expected sign. $R^2$'s are also generally high. Special-case models were estimated for the grain mill products and radio, TV and phonograph industries; these are reported in Table 5.7 below.

17. For a discussion of the various special cases of the original Houthakker-Taylor model, see Houthakker and Taylor, *Consumer Demand in the United States*, pp. 24–25.

18. As noted above, in the case of furniture, the estimated positive price elasticity may reflect a mixture of quality and price effects.

TABLE 5.3. Coefficients for demand equations for industries with data ending in 1957: GK model, 1947–1957

| Industry | Constant | Regression coefficients[a] | | | | | $R^2$ |
| | | $\Delta A$ | $\lambda$ | $\Delta Y$ | $\Delta P$ | $C_{t-1}$ | $\overline{DW}$ |
|---|---|---|---|---|---|---|---|
| Grain mill products | 0.593 | −1.645 (0.99) | 1.488 (0.81) | −8894 (0.79) | −0.663 (0.31) | 0.171 (0.43) | 0.808 1.77 |
| Cereals | −.023 | 0.370 (1.84) | 1.505 (2.12) | 2017 (2.27) | −0.081 (0.71) | 0.424 (2.10) | 0.952 2.31 |
| Cigars[b] | .027 | 3.102 (2.70) | 1.550 (3.32) | 515 (1.53) | −0.178 (3.36) | −0.050 (0.24) | 0.877 2.02 |
| Cigarettes[b] | .475 | −1.613 (0.91) | 1.696 (6.97) | 9518 (1.34) | −2.121 (4.87) | 0.174 (0.61) | 0.956 1.98 |
| Carpets | −.194 | 13.51 (7.74) | 0.823 (11.92) | 16220 (7.85) | −0.212 (3.64) | −0.255 (1.87) | 0.966 2.55 |
| Hats | −.009 | 0.659 (1.35) | 0.671 (1.27) | 1202 (0.90) | −0.030 (0.13) | 0.211 (0.32) | 0.895 1.85 |
| Millinery | .037 | 10.13 (2.89) | 1.104 (2.09) | −625 (1.50) | −0.106 (2.95) | −0.104 (0.21) | 0.902 2.45 |
| Furs[c] | .005 | 4.231 (1.49) | 1.500 (1.27) | −166 (1.12) | 0.012 (0.34) | −0.231 (0.55) | 0.877 2.54 |
| Furniture[c] | −.494 | 2.861 (0.40) | 1.096 (18.90) | 24540 (3.46) | 2.071 (1.64) | −0.552 (1.90) | 0.918 2.16 |
| Screens and blinds[b] | .002 | 2.544 (1.59) | 0.513 (1.41) | 1140 (1.85) | −0.020 (0.70) | −0.306 (0.92) | 0.867 1.20 |
| Household and service machinery (not electrical) | −.045 | 11.47 (6.78) | 0.815 (4.78) | 13840 (2.40) | −1.618 (1.74) | 0.269 (1.11) | 0.983 2.66 |
| Electrical appliances[b] | .055 | 5.271 (2.14) | 0.487 (0.74) | 1172 (0.17) | −0.880 (1.02) | 0.135 (0.23) | 0.839 2.15 |
| Radio, TV and phonograph | −.060 | 15.73 (2.68) | 0.280 (2.98) | −74250 (1.22) | 5.717 (1.68) | 0.166 (0.41) | 0.974 2.09 |
| Motorcycles and bicycles[b] | .016 | 2.636 (1.43) | 0.263 (1.32) | −1476 (1.79) | −0.074 (1.35) | −0.582 (1.16) | 0.926 1.85 |

[a]Values of $t$ in parentheses.
[b]The period of observation is 1948–1957.
[c]The period of observation is 1946–1957.

## THE PROBLEM OF AUTOCORRELATION

The statistical results presented so far do not suggest that there is auto-correlation of the residuals of these equations. However, since autocorrelation would lead not only to biased but to inconsistent estimates of the coefficients in such models, and since the Durbin-Watson statistic is a less reliable indicator of the presence of autocorrelation in these equations, a more stringent test was carried out.

On the basis of the various tests and estimates involving models with auto-correlated errors discussed in Appendix 5-B, we decided to select the original least-squares estimates in all industries. Although a case could be made for using alternative equations that presume a first-order Markov or moving-average process in the error terms for a few of the industries, we chose not to do so, for reasons discussed in that appendix. This also has the advantage of preserving a consistent treatment across the industries. After all, one could expect to find a few cases of significant autocorrelation in a sample of 30 industries simply by chance.

Because of the very small sample sizes involved, and because of the general absence of significant serial correlation in the 30 industries already discussed, further experimentation with autoregressive models for the remaining industries with data ending in 1957 was unwarranted. Direct least-squares estimates are therefore used in all cases.

## SPECIFICATION AND ESTIMATION OF
## SIMULTANEOUS-EQUATION MODELS

So far we have presented estimates based on single-equation estimation techniques. However, there are reasons to believe that advertising not only influences sales but is influenced by sales as well. There are three arguments to support the hypothesis of this additional causal relation. First, it may be argued that advertising expenditure guidelines are related to sales. To the extent that such a decision rule relating advertising expenditures to sales is followed in the short run, there will be a simultaneous-equations problem.

Second, theoretical considerations suggest that optimal advertising outlays by a firm are related directly to the price elasticity of the firm's demand curve.[19] If the effective price elasticity of the representative firm's demand curve varies with the level of industry sales, firms influenced by short-run profit-maximization considerations will tend to increase their advertising when industry sales increase.

Finally, there exists the possibility of economies of scale at the firm level in advertising. Such economies could lead to either increases or decreases in observed advertising outlays per dollar of sales as sales increase, since the advantages of scale may be reaped in terms of a more effective but larger advertising program.[20]

19. R. Dorfman and P. Steiner, "Optimal Advertising and Optimal Quality," *American Economic Review*, 44 (1954), 826–836.

20. For a discussion of possible economics of scale in advertising see Chapters 9 and 10 below.

To make allowance for such possible feedback effects[21] of sales on advertising, we specify a simple equation relating advertising to sales and other variables. This equation is as follows:

$$AC_t = b_0 + b_1 SC_t + b_2 SC_{t-1} + b_3 RPA_t + b_4 RPA_{t-1} + b_5 AC_{t-1}, \qquad (8)$$

where $AC$ is advertising expenditures, $SC$ is sales, and $RPA$ is the price of the industry's product relative to the price of advertising. Note that the advertising and sales variables in this equation are not deflated by either population or price indices. This specification is to be preferred to one involving deflated variables, since (a) any short-run decision rules would be expressed in current dollar terms, and (b) an increase in constant-dollar sales resulting from a price reduction cannot be presumed to have the same impact on advertising as an increase resulting from a shift in consumer demand.

The price of the final product relative to the price of advertising is introduced for two reasons: (a) to allow for the possibility that advertising is substituted for other marketing outlays or for production inputs when its real price is reduced, and (b) to take into account that a higher level of advertising may be required to market products after product prices are increased. The latter point serves to recall that the price of the product should also be treated as an endogenous variable in our system of equations. However, the estimation of pricing models would itself be a major undertaking. In line with most previous attempts to estimate demand functions, we ignore this element of the simultaneity problem.

The dynamic specification of equation (8) is a flexible form of distributed lag function which allows for a variety of possible relations between short- and long-run effects. The linear form of the equation allows for advertising to either increase or decrease relative to sales as sales increases, thus making allowance for the possible effects of scale economies (or diseconomies).

Since equation (8) determines absolute advertising outlays as a function of absolute sales and other variables, whereas the basic demand model relates per-capita sales in constant dollars to relative advertising outlays and other variables, two identities are required to complete the system of simultaneous equations. For the GK demand model, the complete system of equations is as follows:

$$\begin{aligned} C_t = \ &a_0 + a_1 \Delta A_t + a_1 \lambda A_{t-1} + a_2 \Delta Y_t + a_2 \lambda Y_{t-1} \\ &+ a_3 \Delta P_t + a_3 \lambda P_{t-1} + a_4 C_{t-1}, \end{aligned} \qquad (4)$$

21. The use of the term feedback is appropriate, since we have no doubt that for very short time periods—such as months or even perhaps quarters—the relationship is recursive. The simultaneous equation problem here hence results from aggregation over time—an aggregation we are forced to make because of the unavailability of the basic data for shorter time periods.

$$AC_t = b_0 + b_1 SC_t + b_2 SC_{t-1} + b_3 RPA_t + b_4 RPA_{t-1} + b_5 AC_{t-1}, \quad (8)$$

$$A_t \equiv \frac{AC_t}{ATOT_t}, \quad (9)$$

where $ATOT$, is advertising by all manufacturers, and

$$C_t \equiv \frac{SC_t}{POP_t \cdot P_t \cdot PCE_t}, \quad (10)$$

where $POP_t$ is population and $P_t \cdot PCE_t$ is the absolute price index for the industry's products, $P_t$ being the relative price and $PCE_t$ the consumer expenditure deflator.

Since the demand equation is nonlinear in the coefficients, and since the identities are nonlinear in the variables, standard simultaneous-equation techniques cannot be applied to this system of equations. The details of the procedure used to obtain the simultaneous-equation estimates are provided in Appendix 5-C. Table 5.4 presents two-stage estimates of the GK model for the 30 industries for which time-series data over the period 1948–1964 were available. Table 5.5 presents two-stage estimates of the flow-adjustment model for the three industries for which it was selected as the preferred model.

Table 5.6 highlights the estimates in relation to the single-equation results. The summary statistics in this table show that there is indeed a modest upward bias of about 20 percent in the single-equation estimates of the parameter $a_1$ and related short-run sales elasticities for advertising. The relative biases in the single-equation estimates of the short-run price and income elasticities are much smaller.

The long-run elasticities depend, of course, on the estimates of $\lambda$ (the constraint coefficient) and $a_4$ (the coefficient of the lagged dependent variable) as well as upon the corresponding short-run elasticities. The relative bias in the long-run elasticity for advertising is somewhat less than the short-run bias. The relative biases of the long-run income and price elasticities tend to be somewhat greater than the biases in the short-run counterparts. In all instances, the single-equation bias in the long-run price and income elasticities is toward zero.

Estimates of $\lambda$ and of $a_4$ are of critical importance for the derivation of the goodwill stock estimates used in Chapter 8. Table 5.6 also includes a comparison of the single- and multiequation estimates of these important coefficients. The results indicate that the single-equation estimates of $\lambda$ and of $a_4$ are lower on the average than those of the corresponding multiequation estimates. Since an increase in either $\lambda$ or $a_4$ will increase the long-run elasticity relative to the short-run elasticity, the difference between the single- and multiequation estimates of these coefficients explains the pattern of the long-run elasticities already discussed.

TABLE 5.4.   Coefficients for two-stage estimates for 30 industries and groupings: GK model

| Industry | Constant | Regression coefficients[a] | | | | | $R^2$ |
|---|---|---|---|---|---|---|---|
| | | $\Delta A$ | $\lambda$ | $\Delta Y$ | $\Delta P$ | $C_{t-1}$ | $DW$ |
| Soft drinks | −0.019 | 1.916 | 1.330 | 7626 | −0.565 | −0.418 | 0.905 |
| | | (2.53) | (1.98) | (1.99) | (2.18) | (0.50) | 1.74 |
| Malt liquor | .313 | 0.122 | 2.003 | −1284 | −0.647 | 0.198 | 0.860 |
| | | (0.39) | (1.31) | (0.99) | (1.19) | (0.73) | 2.23 |
| Wines | −.002 | 5.648 | 0.933 | 240 | −0.093 | 0.266 | 0.850 |
| | | (3.87) | (2.96) | (0.36) | (1.87) | (0.89) | 2.19 |
| Distilled liquor | .085 | 6.836 | 0.369 | −2875 | −1.159 | 0.662 | 0.814 |
| | | (2.48) | (0.55) | (0.22) | (0.49) | (1.25) | 1.79 |
| Meat | 1.089 | 4.474 | 1.332 | 24670 | −4.026 | −0.312 | 0.921 |
| | | (0.83) | (3.33) | (1.36) | (3.77) | (1.13) | 2.42 |
| Dairy products | −0.385 | 17.61 | 0.357 | 44540 | 2.200 | 0.616 | 0.905 |
| | | (3.44) | (0.74) | (1.35) | (0.77) | (1.89) | 1.81 |
| Canning | .097 | 3.712 | 1.443 | 3617 | −1.061 | 0.349 | 0.900 |
| | | (1.26) | (1.24) | (0.55) | (0.73) | (0.92) | 1.92 |
| Bakery | .033 | 1.652 | 1.326 | 8740 | −0.372 | −0.124 | 0.851 |
| | | (0.88) | (1.31) | (1.64) | (0.49) | (0.32) | 1.95 |
| Sugar | .116 | −2.895 | −0.327 | 4668 | 0.159 | −0.058 | 0.352 |
| | | (0.56) | (1.37) | (1.63) | (1.05) | (0.28) | 1.50 |
| Confectionery | .138 | 1.001 | 0.594 | −2830 | −0.793 | 0.242 | 0.901 |
| | | (1.47) | (1.56) | (2.39) | (3.96) | (0.75) | 2.68 |
| Knit goods | −.516 | 5.460 | 1.439 | 29200 | 0.018 | −0.301 | 0.983 |
| | | (1.60) | (4.42) | (4.40) | (0.09) | (0.91) | 2.33 |
| Men's clothing | .017 | 9.391 | 0.369 | 26420 | −0.909 | 0.124 | 0.893 |
| | | (2.23) | (1.41) | (3.30) | (0.87) | (0.43) | 2.34 |
| Women's clothing | −.028 | 17.44 | 0.287 | 992 | −2.275 | 1.144 | 0.901 |
| | | (2.36) | (0.70) | (0.05) | (0.87) | (3.94) | 2.45 |
| Periodicals | −.020 | −0.860 | 1.468 | 6061 | −0.416 | 0.377 | 0.833 |
| | | (0.78) | (1.47) | (1.72) | (0.82) | (1.08) | 1.68 |
| Books | −.112 | 1.765 | 2.108 | 8235 | −0.592 | −0.212 | 0.930 |
| | | (1.84) | (1.90) | (1.91) | (1.07) | (0.42) | 1.90 |
| Drugs | .085 | 1.369 | 1.558 | 4590 | −1.276 | 0.221 | 0.935 |
| | | (0.63) | (0.78) | (0.26) | (3.18) | (0.38) | 1.89 |
| Soaps | −.016 | 0.716 | 1.098 | 13060 | −0.955 | −0.123 | 0.875 |
| | | (2.65) | (1.88) | (3.48) | (2.04) | (0.31) | 2.26 |
| Paints | .049 | 8.349 | 0.250 | 3817 | 0.044 | 0.286 | 0.326 |
| | | (2.14) | (0.73) | (0.57) | (0.04) | (0.67) | 1.54 |
| Perfumes | .102 | −0.610 | 0.995 | 3377 | −1.191 | 0.570 | 0.966 |
| | | (1.20) | (14.4) | (1.18) | (1.57) | (2.31) | 1.98 |

Table 5.4. (continued)

| Industry | Constant | Regression coefficients[a] | | | | | R² |
| | | ΔA | λ | ΔY | ΔP | $C_{t-1}$ | DW |
| --- | --- | --- | --- | --- | --- | --- | --- |
| Tires and tubes | .065 | 1.631 (0.91) | 0.004 (0.07) | 34940 (4.33) | −0.037 (0.12) | 0.575 (2.89) | 0.707 1.29 |
| Footwear | .042 | 8.725 (2.34) | 0.747 (2.12) | 4563 (1.72) | −0.416 (0.99) | 0.006 (0.03) | 0.570 1.80 |
| Hand tools | .045 | 3.363 (1.55) | 0.703 (1.50) | 2725 (1.49) | −0.380 (0.57) | −0.048 (0.12) | 0.634 1.74 |
| Motor vehicles | .702 | 10.37 (3.52) | −0.077 (2.03) | 362300 (7.19) | −14.61 (3.31) | 0.503 (4.08) | 0.865 2.69 |
| Instruments | .093 | 0.555 (0.10) | 11.22 (0.10) | 154 (0.07) | −0.083 (0.09) | 0.419 (1.24) | 0.950 2.15 |
| Clocks and watches | .166 | 0.422 (0.84) | 3.364 (0.87) | −664 (0.62) | −0.317 (0.82) | 0.347 (1.46) | 0.612 2.71) |
| Jewelry (precious metal) | −.125 | 0.598 (0.77) | 4.154 (0.90) | 1712 (0.89) | 0.109 (0.74) | −0.501 (1.79) | 0.636 2.28 |
| Costume jewelry | .029 | 1.542 (0.97) | 1.057 (6.50) | −611 (1.07) | −0.117 (0.78) | 0.390 (1.66) | 0.727 2.25 |
| Tobacco | .393 | −0.886 (0.80) | 0.978 (4.73) | 5481 (1.73) | −2.075 (1.90) | 0.114 (0.55) | 0.500 1.61 |
| Grains and cereals | .416 | 0.116 (0.11) | 1.447 (1.46) | 3537 (1.01) | −0.223 (1.08) | 0.607 (2.32) | 0.770 2.16 |
| Furniture and fixtures | −.464 | 5.678 (3.53) | 1.026 (4.33) | 30010 (6.28) | 1.459 (1.40) | −0.483 (1.96) | 0.947 2.15 |

[a]Values of $t$ in parentheses.

Although a case can be made—on asymptotic grounds—for selecting the multi-equation estimates for the subsequent cross-section work, it is worth remembering that the improvement in asymptotic unbiasedness is gained at the cost of increased variance of the estimates of the coefficients. Furthermore, both the single-equation and the multi-equation estimates will in general be biased for small samples.

If we ignore the latter problem by assuming that there is no bias in the multi-equation estimates, and assume further that the mean difference observed for the sample as a whole between the single- and multi-equation estimates represents the bias for each industry in the single-equation estimates, we can readily compare the single- and multiequation estimates by the criterion of estimated mean-square error. Table 5.6 includes a summary tabulation of the estimated mean-square error of single- and multiequation coefficients on the

TABLE 5.5. Coefficients for Flow-Adjustment models for three industries: single-equation and two-stage estimates

| Industry | Constant | Regression coefficients[a] | | | | $R^2$ |
| | | $\bar{A}$ | $\bar{Y}$ | $\bar{P}$ | $C_{t-1}$ | $DW$ |
|---|---|---|---|---|---|---|
| | | A. *Direct estimates* | | | | |
| Malt liquor | 0.316 | 0.022 | −3109 | −1.165 | 0.192 | 0.858 |
| | | (0.05) | (1.6) | (2.3) | (0.76) | 2.21 |
| Clocks and | .154 | 1.373 | −2061 | −1.003 | 0.402 | 0.599 |
| watches | | (1.2) | (1.3) | (3.0) | (2.0) | 2.72 |
| Jewelry (precious | −.112 | 2.695 | 6617 | 0.381 | −0.459 | 0.616 |
| metal) | | (1.6) | (3.8) | (1.2) | (1.7) | 2.22 |
| | | B. *Two-stage estimates* | | | | |
| Malt liquor | .313 | 0.239 | −2583 | −1.292 | 0.198 | 0.860 |
| | | (0.48) | (1.3) | (2.6) | (0.79) | 2.23 |
| Clocks and | .158 | 1.351 | −2151 | −1.021 | 0.405 | 0.592 |
| watches | | (1.1) | (1.4) | (3.0) | (2.0) | 2.71 |
| Jewelry (precious | −.110 | 2.715 | 6586 | 0.372 | −0.457 | 0.600 |
| metal) | | (1.4) | (3.6) | (1.1) | (1.6) | 2.28 |

[a]Value of $t$ in parentheses.

TABLE 5.6. Comparison of the reliability of single-equation and two-stage estimates (Generalized Koyck model)

| Parameters of GK model | Averages for 30 industries | | |
| | Single-equation estimates | | Two-stage estimates |
| | Bias[a] | RMSE[b] | RMSE[c] |
|---|---|---|---|
| $a_1$ (relative advertising) | 0.900 | 2.182 | 2.441 |
| $a_2$ (total expenditure) | −127. | 6948 | 7979 |
| $a_3$ (relative price) | −.175 | 0.964 | 0.997 |
| $a_4$ (lagged sales) | −.083 | .283 | .324 |
| $\lambda$ (constraint) | −.411 | .810 | 4.538 |

[a]The bias of the single-equation estimates is the average of the single-equation estimates less the average of the two-stage estimates. The bias of the two-stage estimates is assumed to be zero.

[b]The root-mean-square error of each coefficient is obtained from the formula:
$$RMSE_i = [(Bias)^2 + (StdError_i)^2]^{1/2}.$$
These statistics are then averaged across the 30 industries.

[c]The average root-mean-square error for the two-stage estimates is simply the average standard error for the relevant coefficients.

basis of these assumptions. As is clear in this table, the estimated reduction in the bias is typically offset by the increase in the variance of the estimates. This is not surprising in view of the small sample sizes.

It is also worth emphasizing that the elimination of a bias that is constant across industries is of no consequence for our subsequent cross-section work, since such a bias will affect only the intercept term and not the slopes in any cross-section regressions. Although the interindustry analysis of goodwill stocks may be affected by such common biases in the estimates of $\lambda$ and $a_4$, increases in the variance of the estimates of these coefficients are likely to cause more severe distortions.

For both analyses, therefore, our variance aversion should be at least as strong as our bias aversion. Since the estimated biases are not large enough to affect the substantive conclusions drawn earlier, and since the estimated mean-square error is typically smaller with the single-equation estimates, we use the single-equation coefficients in the subsequent cross-section work with price and advertising elasticities, and base the goodwill-stock estimates and adjustments upon these coefficients.

## SPECIAL-CASE MODELS AND THE
## SELECTION OF THE FINAL MODELS

We have now completed the presentation of the results from two general models of consumer demand, together with a discussion of alternative estimates based on multi-equation models and on models that allow for the effects of autocorrelation in the residuals. Our remaining tasks in this chapter are to select the most satisfactory models for each industry and, for those industries for which the general models are not satisfactory, to estimate certain special-case models (the latter are shown in Table 5.7).

Of the two general models presented, the Generalized Koyck model yielded the most satisfactory results, on the average, both in terms of goodness of fit and in terms of the signs and significance of the partial regression coefficients. Although the Flow-Adjustment model's performance was generally inferior to that of the other model, it was the model selected for three industries —malt liquors, clocks and watches, and jewelry (precious metal)—where its performance was adequate and where the coefficients for the GK model indicated the special case of the FA model might be appropriate.

There were, as already noted, two industries—sugar and paints—for which neither model proved satisfactory. These industries were therefore deleted from the subsequent cross-section work. There were several other industries for which the general version of the GK (or FA) model presented difficulties. In seven industries, positive price elasticities were obtained. For three of

TABLE 5.7. Coefficients for various special case models for certain industries

| Industry | Constant | Regression coefficients[a] | | | | | $R^2$ |
|---|---|---|---|---|---|---|---|
| | | $\Delta A$ | $\lambda$ | $\Delta Y$ | $\Delta P$ | $C_{t-1}$ | $DW$ |
| Dairy products | −0.208 | 16.74 (4.89) | 0.297 (0.80) | 37500 (1.45) | — | 0.698 (2.86) | 0.925 1.27 |
| Grain mill products[b] | .571 | — | 1.174 (1.37) | −10490 (0.91) | −1.196 (0.75) | 0.185 (0.50) | 0.760 1.84 |
| Sugar | .103 | 2.454 (0.57) | −0.275 (1.05) | 3945 (1.26) | — | −0.047 (0.21) | 0.255 1.45 |
| Knit goods | −.454 | 3.255 (1.11) | 1.394 (4.16) | 28200 (4.32) | — | −0.287 (0.86) | 0.980 2.09 |
| Women's clothing | −.036 | 17.99 (3.42) | 0.372 (1.16) | 10520 (1.09) | −2.721 (1.40) | 1.00 (constr.) | 0.920 2.57 |
| Paints | .128 | 6.003 (1.98) | −0.305 (0.94) | 12400 (1.39) | — | 0.562 (1.39) | 0.328 1.80 |
| Paints | .063 | 5.674 (11.6) | — | 8929 (0.89) | 0.035 (0.04) | 0.457 (0.92) | 0.188 1.61 |
| Paints | .062 | 5.688 (1.7) | — | 9606 (0.93) | — | 0.443 (1.0) | 0.188 1.61 |
| Perfumes | −.055 | 1.308 (3.03) | 0.698 (2.04) | 4972 (2.04) | — | 0.459 (1.71) | 0.975 1.85 |
| Tires and tubes | .063 | 1.494 (1.0) | — | 34814 (4.8) | −0.022 (.08) | 0.598 (3.2) | 0.704 1.31 |
| Radio, TV, and phonograph[c] | −.440 | 4.902 (2.25) | 0.798 (1.38) | 36720 (1.47) | — | 0.570 (1.14) | 0.954 2.23 |
| Motor vehicles | .439 | 10.18 (3.2) | — | 325104 (6.1) | −9.793 (2.1) | 0.439 (3.4) | 0.822 1.83 |
| Furniture and fixtures | −.204 | 3.662 (2.03) | 1.162 (2.79) | 22640 (3.46) | — | −0.386 (1.33) | 0.897 2.09 |

[a]Values of $t$ in parentheses.
[b]For 1947–1957.
[c]For 1948–1957.

these—furs, perfumes, and jewelry (precious metal)—we felt that it was not unreasonable to obtain positive price elasticities because of the possible importance of Veblen goods in those industries. We therefore retain the general models for those industries.

In two durable-goods industries—furniture and radio, TV, and phonograph —the positive price elasticities may reflect inadequate allowance for quality changes in the price measures used. The price elasticity could consequently represent a mixture of price and quality elasticities. For both of these industries, we assumed a price elasticity of zero for the cross-section work, and, in order to be consistent, reestimated the GK equations with the price variables omitted. The resulting equations were selected as the final equations for the two industries.

For two nondurable-goods industries—dairy products and knit goods—positive price elasticities were obtained for the general version of the GK model. We again suppressed the price variable in estimating the final equations for these industries. The general results also suggested the possibility of another special case model for two important durable-goods industries—tires and tubes and motor vehicles. For both of these industries, the estimate of λ was either negative or very close to zero, suggesting the special case where λ = 0. The final equation for each of these industries was therefore obtained by setting λ = 0 and estimating the resulting equation by ordinary least squares. Note that the effect of this constraint is to force the static long-run elasticities to be equal to zero.

Finally, for the women's clothing industry, the coefficient of $C_{t-1}$ is slightly greater than unity, indicating that the equation is unstable. We therefore re-estimated the model with the constraint that $a_4 = 1$ to obtain the final equation for this industry. Note that this constraint implies that the static long-run elasticities are not defined.[22]

As noted earlier, for some industries the time series do not extend beyond 1957. In some of these we have no choice but to use equations based on ten or eleven observations. For others, however, estimates based on an aggregation with another industry for a longer period were available as an alternative. In the latter cases, the choice made was based on the statistical and theoretical performance of the two alternatives, taking into account the weight of the original industry in the aggregation.

The final advertising, income, and price elasticities are presented in Table 5.8. This table includes the details about the models selected and the estimation period used for each industry.

---

22. While either of these special cases may appear somewhat unreasonable when assessed in a static content, it is interesting to point out that finite long-run multipliers exist when evaluated under conditions of equilibrium growth in both instances.

Consider the general model:

$$Y_t = a\Delta X_t + a\lambda X_{t-1} + bY_{t-1}.$$

Along a stable equilibrium growth path:

$$\Delta X_t = gX_{t-1} \text{ and}$$

$$Y_t = \frac{a(g + \lambda)}{1 + g - b} X_t.$$

Consider now each of the special cases.

(1) λ = 0. In this case, the long-run multiplier is $\dfrac{ag}{1 + g - b}$.

(2) $b$ = 1. In this case, the long-run multiplier is $\dfrac{a(g + \lambda)}{g}$.

## OVERVIEW AND SUMMARY OF DEMAND EQUATIONS

At this point it is worth pausing to consider what we have accomplished in this chapter. Despite various data problems, we have obtained reasonable estimates of demand functions for 28 of the 30 industries or groupings of industries for which complete postwar time-series data could be obtained. Additional reasonable equations were obtained for the remaining industries, although the quality of the statistical estimates necessarily suffers from the fewness of degrees of freedom.

Although many of the individual coefficients are not significant by the usual statistical criteria, the set of equations is satisfactory in a number of respects. First, the signs of the price coefficient are generally negative, which is consistent with the conventional theory of consumer behavior. For three of the industries for which positive price coefficients were obtained, it is reasonable to suppose that Veblen goods may have been important. For two other industries, we suspect that the positive effect of measured prices may in fact reflect a mixture of negative true price effects and positive quality effects.

These results could be interpreted as a victory of sorts for conventional neoclassical price theory; nevertheless, the results for the advertising variable suggest that a variable neglected in the conventional theory may be an even more important determinant of consumer expenditures than are relative prices. In virtually no instance was a negative advertising effect found. Advertising is more frequently significant than relative prices. Although the elasticity of sales response to changes in advertising is typically less than the elasticity with respect to price changes, the magnitude of the effect of an increase of one percentage point in the advertising:sales ratio is typically much greater than the magnitude of the effect of a one percent reduction in price. The latter comparison is the relevant one, since the two changes have equivalent effects upon profit margins at a given sales volume.

This result reflects the effects of advertising upon the interindustry distribution of sales. Hence the argument that advertising serves merely to allocate spending between brands within broad groupings of products is called into question by these results. If anything, advertising comes through as a more important determinant of the interindustry allocation of sales than are relative prices.

The coefficients of the total expenditure variable, though statistically weak in a number of instances, nevertheless have the desirable property of adding up to a net elasticity of consumer spending on manufacturing products that looks very reasonable. The overall short-run elasticity of consumer spending on the products of these industries with respect to changes in total consumer

TABLE 5.8. Advertising, income, and price elasticities based on final equations selected

| Industry | Model | Advertising | | Income | | Price | | Mean sales $\bar{S}$ |
|---|---|---|---|---|---|---|---|---|
| | | SR | LR | SR | LR | SR | LR | |
| Soft drinks | GK 48-64 | 0.567 | 0.591 | 2.008 | 2.093 | -1.478 | -1.540 | 0.0480 |
| Malt liquor | FA 48-64 | .004 | .010 | -0.184 | -0.456 | -0.562 | -1.392 | .1387 |
| Wine | GK 48-64 | .972 | 1.202 | .407 | .503 | -.680 | -0.842 | .0124 |
| Distilled liquor | GK 48-64 | .641 | 0.745 | .179 | .208 | -.253 | -.295 | .1682 |
| Meat | GK 48-64 | .130 | .130 | .489 | .489 | -.365 | -.364 | .9709 |
| Dairy products ($a_3 = 0$) | GK 48-64 | 1.521 | 1.650 | 2.378 | 2.581 | .0 | .0 | .2372 |
| Canning | GK 48-64 | 0.614 | 0.963 | 0.359 | 0.563 | -.820 | -1.287 | .2263 |
| Grain mill products } | GK 48-64 | .224 | .320 | .177 | .253 | -1.469 | -2.099 } | .2418 |
| Cereals | | | | | | | | .0255 |
| Bakery products | GK 48-64 | .223 | .265 | .757 | .902 | -0.263 | -0.313 | .1872 |
| Sugar[a] | – | – | – | – | – | – | – | – |
| Confectionery | GK 48-64 | .367 | .287 | -.327 | -.256 | -.576 | -.450 | .0801 |
| Cigars } | GK 49-64 | .408 | .575 | .001 | .001 | -1.809 | -2.547 } | .0184 |
| Cigarettes | | | | | | | | .1726 |
| Knit goods ($a_3 = 0$) | GK 48-64 | .114 | .124 | 2.813 | 3.047 | .0 | .0 | .1644 |
| Carpets | GK 48-57 | 1.516 | .994 | 5.838 | 3.829 | -.658 | -.431 | .0456 |
| Hats | GK 48-57 | 0.734 | .624 | 2.732 | 2.323 | -.451 | -.384 | .0072 |
| Men's clothing | GK 48-64 | .431 | .178 | 2.350 | 0.959 | -.676 | -.276 | .1852 |
| Women's clothing ($a_4 = 1$) | GK 48-68 | .849 | b | 0.676 | b | -1.117 | b | .2553 |
| Millinery | GK 47-57 | .245 | .245 | -2.213 | -2.214 | -4.164 | -4.165 | .0046 |
| Furs | GK 47-57 | .200 | .244 | -0.557 | -0.678 | 0.452 | 0.551 | .0049 |

[a]No satisfactory model.
[b]Long-run elasticities are not defined for Women's clothing.

Table 5.8. (continued)

| Industry | Model | Advertising | | Income | | Price | | Mean sales |
|---|---|---|---|---|---|---|---|---|
| | | SR | LR | SR | LR | SR | LR | $\bar{S}$ |
| Furniture (including screens and blinds) ($a_3 = 0$) | GK 48-64 | .396 | .276 | 2.223 | 1.548 | .0 | .0 | .1712 |
| Screens and blinds | GK 47-57 | .353 | .139 | 2.262 | 0.889 | -.537 | -.211 | .0083 |
| Periodicals | GK 48-64 | .026 | .013 | 1.498 | 0.733 | -.743 | -.363 | .1021 |
| Books | GK 48-64 | .250 | .348 | 2.205 | 3.071 | -.774 | -1.078 | .0652 |
| Drugs | GK 49-64 | .663 | 1.042 | 0.719 | 1.129 | -1.079 | -1.695 | .1410 |
| Soaps | GK 48-64 | .284 | 0.294 | 1.684 | 1.742 | -0.758 | -0.784 | .1261 |
| Paints[a] | — | — | — | — | — | — | — | — |
| Perfumes | GK 49-64 | .026 | .013 | 2.438 | 2.959 | .237 | .287 | .0385 |
| Tires and tubes ($\lambda = 0$) | GK 48-64 | .125 | .0 | 3.329 | 0.0 | -.020 | .0 | .1715 |
| Footwear | GK 48-64 | .563 | .421 | 0.704 | .527 | -.392 | -.293 | .1078 |
| Hand tools | GK 48-64 | .434 | .321 | 0.890 | .659 | -1.578 | -1.168 | .0671 |
| Household and service machinery (not electrical) | GK 48-57 | .963 | 1.073 | 1.374 | 1.532 | -1.108 | -1.235 | .1653 |
| Electrical appliances | GK 49-57 | .804 | 0.453 | 0.537 | 0.303 | -2.781 | -1.567 | .0358 |
| Radio, TV, and phonograph ($a_3 = 0$) | GK 48-57 | .412 | .764 | 2.088 | 3.874 | 0.0 | 0.0 | .2848 |
| Motorcycles and bicycles | GK 49-57 | .172 | .028 | -5.687 | -0.944 | -2.321 | -.385 | .0003 |
| Motor vehicles ($\lambda = 0$) | GK 48-64 | .346 | .0 | 5.477 | .0 | -1.350 | .0 | .9734 |
| Instruments | GK 49-64 | .979 | 1.283 | -0.032 | -.042 | -1.493 | -1.958 | .2377 |
| Clocks and watches | FA 48-64 | .174 | 0.583 | -0.844 | -2.821 | -2.933 | -9.802 | .0201 |
| Jewelry (precious metal) | FA 48-64 | .147 | .201 | 1.792 | 2.456 | 0.661 | 0.906 | .0303 |
| Costume jewelry | GK 49-64 | .282 | .307 | -1.407 | -1.532 | -3.007 | -3.275 | .0117 |

expenditure is 1.852; the long-run response is 0.854.[23] Since all of the durable goods purchased by consumers are provided by the manufacturing sector, the relatively high short-run income elasticity is to be expected.

Negative "income effects" were found in five industries—malt liquor, confectionery, instruments, clocks and watches, and costume jewelry. The hypothesis that the malt liquor, confectionery, and costume jewelry industries produce products with negative income effects would not appear unreasonable. In the case of clocks and watches, we suspect that the negative total-expenditure effect is a proxy for negative trends reflecting the operation of other factors, such as the penetration of imports into the domestic market. For instruments, the otherwise inexplicable negative income response may reflect the fact that this industry produces investment goods and intermediate products as well as consumer goods.

Let us now turn briefly to the implied dynamics of manufacturers' sales adjustment. As already noted, we have selected the Generalized Koyck model in all but three industries, for which the Flow-Adjustment model was used. In preliminary work, we also experimented with the simpler lag structure of the Koyck model,[24] which yielded inferior results. Hence this set of equations provides additional evidence supporting the conclusion drawn by Houthakker and Taylor that the dynamic specification of demand models is of great importance.

Looking at the final equations selected for 39 of our original 41 industries, we find that the long-run sales response exceeds the short-run sales response for 22 of the industries and the short-run effects exceed the long-run effects in the other 17. For most of the durable-goods industries—motor vehicles, tires and tubes, hand tools, electrical appliances, furniture, screens and blinds, and motorcycles and bicycles—the short-run effects exceed the long-run effects, which is what one would expect where stock adjustment predominates over habit formation. For the remaining durable-goods industries—radio, TV and phonograph, household and service machinery, and books—the long-run

23. These total expenditure elasticities were weighted averages of elasticities for 38 industries (sugar, paints, and women's clothing excluded), the weights being average sales in the 1954–1957 period. If tires and tubes and motor vehicles are also excluded from the calculations (the model for both of these industries is the special case where $\lambda = 0$), the results are as follows:

Short-run expenditure elasticity       1.022,
Long-run expenditure elasticity        1.068.

Hence these two industries account for the high short-run expenditure elasticity.

24. This model is specified as follows:

$$C_t = b_0 + b_1 A_t + b_2 Y_t + b_3 P_t + b_4 C_{t-1}.$$

effect slightly exceeds the short-run effects, indicating that habit-formation effects had offset stock adjustment.[25]

Most of the other industries for which the short-run effects exceed the long-run effects were semi-durables—footwear, carpets, and men's clothing. Among the nondurable industries, only periodicals showed a dynamic response pattern opposite to what we should expect.

Two uses are made of these equations in later chapters. First, estimates of the price elasticity of demand are introduced as an explanatory variable in the cross-section equations predicting profit rates. Although the price elasticity of demand has been a frequently cited variable of importance in the analysis of market behavior, it typically has not been included in formal statistical studies because of the general absence of estimates. Since we have developed estimates of this variable for 38 of the original 41 industries,[26] and since the presumption is that this variable could affect both advertising and profits, we estimate the cross-section models with the price elasticity of demand included as one of the explanatory variables.

It is also possible to use these dynamic demand equations to construct estimates of the stock of "goodwill" generated by advertising in 39 industries. In Chapter 8, adjusted rates of return and net profit margins based on these goodwill-stock estimates are used in interindustry regression analyses.

25. Note that Houthakker and Taylor found that habit formation dominates stock adjustment in some of the durable goods they examined. See Houthakker and Taylor, *Consumer Demand in the United States*, pp. 72, 82, 96, 110, and 126.

26. As noted above, no satisfactory models were obtained for the sugar and paints industries. Women's clothing was also omitted because the long-run price elasticity for this industry is undefined.

# APPENDIX 5-A. DERIVATION OF ALTERNATIVE DEMAND MODELS THAT INCLUDE ADVERTISING

In the Generalized Koyck model, advertising is introduced as a direct determinant of consumer expenditures. The estimating equations are derived by extending the first equation in the original Houthakker-Taylor model to include advertising, as follows:

$$C_t = \alpha + \beta S_t + \zeta A_t + \gamma Y_t + \eta P_t . \tag{1}$$

The equation for the state-flow relation remains unchanged:

$$\dot{S}_t = C_t - \delta S_t . \tag{2}$$

Now substitute for $S_t$ from (1) in (2), obtaining

$$\dot{S}_t = C_t - (\delta/\beta)(C_t - \alpha - \zeta A_t - \gamma Y_t - \eta P_t) . \tag{3}$$

Differentiate (1) with respect to time:

$$\dot{C}_t = \beta \dot{S}_t + \zeta \dot{A}_t + \gamma \dot{Y}_t + \eta \dot{P}_t . \tag{4}$$

Substitute from (3) into (4), obtaining:

$$\dot{C}_t = (\beta - \delta)C_t + \delta(\alpha + \zeta A_t + \gamma Y_t + \eta P_t)$$
$$+ \zeta \dot{A}_t + \gamma \dot{Y}_t + \eta \dot{P}_t ,$$

or

$$\dot{C}_t = \alpha\delta + (\beta - \delta)C_t + \zeta \dot{A}_t + \delta\zeta A_t + \gamma \dot{Y}_t + \gamma\delta Y_t \tag{5}$$
$$+ \eta \dot{P}_t + \eta\delta P_t .$$

Now let us derive a finite approximation for (5), defining:

$$\Delta C_t = C_t - C_{t-1}, \qquad \bar{C}_t = (C_t + C_{t-1})/2,$$

and so on. Then

$$\Delta C_t \approx \alpha\delta + (\beta - \delta)\bar{C}_t + \zeta\Delta A_t + \delta\zeta\bar{A}_t + \gamma\Delta Y_t \qquad (6)$$
$$+ \gamma\delta\bar{Y}_t + \eta\Delta P_t + \eta\delta\bar{P}_t.$$

After rearrangement this becomes

$$C_t = \frac{\alpha\delta}{1 + \delta/2 - \beta/2} + \frac{\zeta(1 + \delta/2)}{1 + \delta/2 - \beta/2}\Delta A_t + \frac{\delta\zeta}{1 + \delta/2 - \beta/2}A_{t-1} \quad (7)$$

$$+ \frac{\gamma(1 + \delta/2)}{1 + \delta/2 - \beta/2}\Delta Y_t + \frac{\delta\gamma}{1 + \delta/2 - \beta/2}Y_{t-1}$$

$$+ \frac{\eta(1 + \delta/2)}{1 + \delta/2 - \beta/2}\Delta P_t + \frac{\delta\eta}{1 + \delta/2 - \beta/2}P_{t-1}$$

$$+ \frac{1 - \delta/2 + \beta/2}{1 + \delta/2 - \beta/2}C_{t-1}.$$

The estimating equation for the Flow-Adjustment model is derived in a straightforward manner:

$$\hat{C}_t = \xi + \omega A_t + \mu Y_t + \eta P_t, \qquad (8)$$

$$\dot{C}_t = \theta(\hat{C}_t - C_t). \qquad (9)$$

Substituting from (8) in (9) we obtain

$$\dot{C}_t = \theta\xi + \theta\omega A_t + \theta\mu Y_t + \theta\eta P_t - \theta C_t. \qquad (10)$$

A finite approximation of this equation is

$$\Delta C_t \approx \theta\xi + \theta\omega\bar{A}_t + \theta\mu\bar{Y}_t + \theta\eta\bar{P}_t - \theta\bar{C}_t, \qquad (11)$$

which, after rearrangement, becomes

$$C_t = \frac{\theta\xi}{1 + \theta/2} + \frac{\theta\omega}{1 + \theta/2}\bar{A}_t + \frac{\theta\mu}{1 + \theta/2}\bar{Y}_t + \frac{\theta\eta}{1 + \theta/2}\bar{P}_t \qquad (12)$$

$$+ \frac{1 - \theta/2}{1 + \theta/2}C_{t-1},$$

which is the estimating equation used.

The derivation of the estimating equation for the model referred to in note 4 is as follows. Substitute for $S_t$ from equation (1) in equation (2a), obtaining

$$\dot{S}_t = W_1 A_t + W_2 C_t - (\delta/\beta)(C_t - \alpha - \gamma Y_t - \eta P_t). \qquad (13)$$

Differentiate (1) with respect to time:

$$\dot{C}_t = \beta\dot{S}_t + \gamma\dot{Y}_t + \eta\dot{P}_t. \qquad (14)$$

Substitute for $\dot{S}_t$ from (13) in (14):

$$\dot{C}_t = \beta W_1 A_t + \beta W_2 C_t - \delta(C_t - \alpha - \gamma Y_t - \eta P_t) + \gamma \dot{Y}_t + \eta \dot{P}_t. \qquad (15)$$

Now we simplify (15):

$$\dot{C}_t = \alpha\delta + \beta W_1 A_t + \gamma \dot{Y}_t + \delta\gamma Y_t + \eta \dot{P}_t \qquad (16)$$
$$+ \delta\eta P_t + (\beta W_2 - \delta)C_t.$$

Let us derive a finite approximation for (16) as follows:

$$C_t \approx \alpha\delta + \beta W_1 \bar{A}_t + \gamma\Delta Y_t + \delta\gamma \bar{Y}_t + \eta\Delta P_t \qquad (17)$$
$$+ \delta\eta \bar{P}_t + (\beta W_2 - \delta)\bar{C}_t.$$

After rearrangement this becomes

$$C_t = \frac{\alpha\delta}{1 - \beta W_1/2 + \delta/2} + \frac{\beta W_2}{1 - \beta W_1/2 + \delta/2}\bar{A}_t \qquad (18)$$

$$+ \frac{(1 + \delta/2)}{1 - \beta W_1/2 + \delta/2}\Delta Y_t + \frac{\gamma\delta}{1 - \beta W_1/2 + \delta/2}Y_{t-1}$$

$$+ \frac{\eta(1 + \delta/2)}{1 - \beta W_1/2 + \delta/2}\Delta P_t + \frac{\eta\delta}{1 - \beta W_1/2 + \delta/2}P_{t-1}$$

$$+ \frac{1 + \beta W_1/2 - \delta/2}{1 - \beta W_1/2 + \delta/2}C_{t-1}.$$

Note that the original Houthakker-Taylor model in which advertising does not enter the state variable may be derived as a special case of equation (18) with $W_1 = 1$:

$$C_t = \frac{\alpha\delta}{1 - \beta/2 + \delta/2} + \frac{\gamma(1 + \delta/2)}{1 - \beta/2 + \delta/2}\Delta Y_t + \frac{\gamma\delta}{1 - \beta/2 + \delta/2}Y_{t-1}$$

$$+ \frac{\eta(1 + \delta/2)}{1 - \beta/2 + \delta/2}\Delta P_t + \frac{\eta\delta}{1 - \beta/2 + \delta/2}P_{t-1}$$

$$+ \frac{1 + \beta/2 - \delta/2}{1 - \beta/2 + \delta/2}C_{t-1}.$$

# APPENDIX 5-B. TESTS FOR AUTOCORRELATION

The test devised for the GK model is specifically for the purpose of testing for first-order serial correlation in the true errors. The derivation of the test is straightforward.

Consider the GK model:

$$C_t = a_0 + a_1 \Delta A_t + a_1 \lambda A_{t-1} + a_2 \Delta Y_t$$
$$+ a_2 \lambda Y_{t-1} + a_3 \Delta P_t + a_3 \lambda P_{t-1} + a_4 C_{t-1} + U_t. \tag{1}$$

Now assume that $U_t$ is generated by the first-order Markov process:

$$U_t = \rho U_{t-1} - e_t, \tag{2}$$

where $e_t$ is a nonautocorrelated random variable. Substituting for $U_t$ in the H-T model, we obtain

$$C_t = a_0 + a_1 \Delta A_t + a_1 \lambda A_{t-1} + a_2 \Delta Y_t + a_2 \lambda Y_{t-1} + a_3 \Delta P_t \tag{3}$$
$$+ a_3 \lambda P_{t-1} + a_4 C_{t-1} + \rho U_{t-1} + e_t.$$

Lagging this equation one period, multiplying by $\rho$, subtracting from equation (3) and rearranging, we obtain

$$C_t = a_0(1 - \rho) + a_1 \Delta A_t + a_1(\lambda - \rho)\Delta A_{t-1} + a_1 \lambda(1 - \rho)A_{t-2} \tag{4}$$
$$+ a_2 \Delta Y_t + a_2(\lambda - \rho)\Delta Y_{t-1} + a_2 \lambda(1 - \rho)Y_{t-2}$$
$$+ a_3 \Delta P_t + a_3(\lambda - \rho)\Delta P_{t-1} + a_3 \lambda(1 - \rho)P_{t-2}$$
$$+ (a_4 + \rho)C_{t-1} - a_4 \rho C_{t-2} + e_t.$$

This equation is nonlinear in the coefficients and overdetermined, but it can be estimated by means of nonlinear iterative techniques. A test for serial correlation in the GK model is provided by testing whether $\hat{\rho}$ in this equation differs significantly from zero.

Test results for each of the 30 industries for the GK model are presented in
Table 5-B.1. With the exception of four industries, the null hypothesis cannot

TABLE 5–B.1.   Coefficients for GK model with a first-order autoregressive process

| Industry | Regression coefficients[a] | | |
|---|---|---|---|
| | $\lambda$ | $C_{t-1}$ | $\hat{\rho}$ |
| *I. Selected statistics for 30 industries and groupings* | | | |
| Soft drinks | 1.476 | −0.388 | −0.155 |
| | | | (0.14) |
| Malt liquor | 2.544 | .092 | −.084 |
| | | | (.12) |
| Wines | 1.315 | −.079 | .319 |
| | | | (.73) |
| Distilled liquor | 0.821 | .285 | .271 |
| | | | (.23) |
| Meat | 1.264 | −.267 | −.290 |
| | | | (.02) |
| Dairy products | 0.550 | .402 | .432 |
| | | | (.15) |
| Canning | .985 | .780 | −.638 |
| | | | (2.08) |
| Bakery products | 1.770 | −.472 | 0.412 |
| | | | (1.21) |
| Sugar | −0.409 | .118 | .071 |
| | | | (0.12) |
| Confectionery | 1.437 | −.871 | .582 |
| | | | (1.31) |
| Knit goods | 1.102 | .124 | −0.470 |
| | | | (0.70) |
| Men's clothing | 0.319 | .114 | .402 |
| | | | (.73) |
| Women's clothing | .216 | 1.093 | −.730 |
| | | | (3.31) |
| Periodicals | .375 | 0.292 | 0.187 |
| | | | (0.09) |
| Books | 1.673 | .028 | −.127 |
| | | | (0.12) |
| Drugs | 3.419 | −.866 | .804 |
| | | | (8.90) |
| Soaps | 1.292 | −.221 | −0.113 |
| | | | (0.06) |

TABLE 5–B.1.  (continued)

| Industry | Regression coefficients[a] | | |
|---|---|---|---|
| | $\lambda$ | $C_{t-1}$ | $\hat{\rho}$ |
| I. *Selected statistics for 30 industries and groupings* | | | |
| Paints | 0.405 | .055 | .507 |
| | | | (.60) |
| Perfumes | .818 | .289 | .138 |
| | | | (.06) |
| Tires and tubes | .050 | .454 | .439 |
| | | | (.56) |
| Footwear | .660 | .117 | .121 |
| | | | (.05) |
| Hand tools | .939 | −.245 | .055 |
| | | | (.05) |
| Motor vehicles | −.078 | .572 | −.485 |
| | | | (1.51) |
| Instruments | 1.699 | −.311 | −0.425 |
| | | | (0.47) |
| Clocks and watches | 4.649 | .453 | −0.522 |
| | | | (1.56) |
| Jewelry (precious metal) | 3.277 | .288 | −1.087 |
| | | | (4.94) |
| Costume jewelry | 1.357 | .051 | 0.156 |
| | | | (0.13) |
| Tobacco | 1.343 | .186 | −.254 |
| | | | (.32) |
| Grain mill products and cereals | 1.236 | .065 | −.107 |
| | | | (.07) |
| Furniture and fixtures | 1.062 | −.473 | −.692 |
| | | | (.82) |

| Industry | Regression coefficients[a] | | | | | | $R^2$ |
|---|---|---|---|---|---|---|---|
| | $\Delta A$ | $\lambda$ | $\Delta Y$ | $\Delta P$ | $C_{t-1}$ | $\hat{\rho}$ | $DW$ |
| II. *Complete equations for 4 industries* | | | | | | | |
| Canning | 4.742 | 0.985 | 3366 | 0.331 | 0.780 | −0.638 | 0.926 |
| | (2.76) | (2.08) | (0.81) | (0.21) | (2.82) | (2.08) | 1.92 |
| Women's clothing | 22.18 | 0.216 | 16220 | −5.365 | 1.093 | −0.730 | 0.965 |
| | (6.45) | (2.27) | (1.05) | (3.19) | (8.43) | (3.31) | 2.70 |
| Drugs | 0.876 | 3.419 | 10130 | −2.332 | −0.866 | 0.804 | 0.967 |
| | (1.26) | (2.02) | (1.34) | (1.67) | (3.19) | (8.90) | 2.28 |
| Jewelry (precious metal) | 6.807 | 3.277 | 1335 | 0.017 | 0.288 | −1.087 | 0.840 |
| | (1.08) | (1.15) | (1.23) | (0.41) | (1.52) | (4.94) | 2.67 |

[a]Values of $t$ in parentheses.

be rejected. In these four industries significant serial correlation of the first order was found. Complete equations for these industries are presented in Part II of the table. It is noteworthy that in three of these four cases the Durbin-Watson coefficient for the autoregressive equation suggested the presence of negative serial correlation in the transformed errors. This would imply either that there was serial correlation of order higher than the first in the original model, or that the original errors were generated by a moving-average process rather than a Markov process. For reasons we now present, we feel that a moving-average process is a likely possibility. We refer the reader back to the derivation of the estimating equation in the GK model from the behavioral equation and the stock-flow relation. It is readily demonstrated that the existence of nonautocorrelated errors in the behavioral equation gives rise to a moving-average process in the errors of the estimating equation.

If the behavioral equation for the GK model is modified by introducing a random term $U$, the final estimating equation becomes:

$$C_t = a_0 + a_1 \Delta A_t + a_1 \lambda A_{t-1} + a_2 \Delta Y_t + a_2 \lambda Y_{t-1} \qquad (5)$$
$$+ a_3 \Delta P_t + a_3 \lambda P_{t-1} + a_4 C_{t-1} + V_t,$$

where

$$V_t = \frac{1 + \delta/2}{1 + \delta/2 - \beta/2} U_t - \frac{(1 - \delta/2)}{1 + \delta/2 - \beta/2} U_{t-1}.$$

This demonstrates that, if $U_t$ is random, the errors in the estimating equation are generated from a moving-average process rather than a Markov process.

Note that the coefficients of the moving-average process are related directly to $\lambda$, one of the coefficients in the model. We therefore develop a technique based on the ordinary least-squares estimates of $\lambda$ which is analogous to applying generalized least squares to the nonlinear estimating equation. To simplify the exposition we write

$$V_t = \epsilon_t - K \epsilon_{t-1},$$

where

$$\epsilon_t = \frac{1 + \delta/2}{1 + \delta/2 - \beta/2} U_t$$

and

$$K = \frac{(1 - \delta/2)}{(1 + \delta/2)} = 1 - \lambda.$$

From the unadjusted nonlinear estimates, we obtain an estimate of $\lambda$ from which we may derive an estimate of $K$. Denoting the estimate so derived as $\hat{K}$, we apply the following sequence of transformations to the observations:

| Observation No. | Transformation | Error in transformed observation |
|---|---|---|
| 1 | None | $\epsilon_1 - \hat{K}\epsilon_0$ |
| 2 | $V_2 + \hat{K}V_1$ | $\epsilon_2 - \hat{K}^2\epsilon_0$ |
| 3 | $V_3 + \hat{K}V_2 + \hat{K}^2V_1$ | $\epsilon_3 - \hat{K}^3\epsilon_0$ |
| . | . | . |
| . | . | . |
| . | . | . |
| $N$ | $V_N + \hat{K}V_{N-1} + \hat{K}^2V_{N-2} \ldots \hat{K}^{N-1}V_1$ | $\epsilon_N + \hat{K}^N\epsilon_0$ |

After applying these transformations to the set of observations, we now estimate the following equation:

$$C_t^* = a_0 + a_1\Delta A_t^* + a_1\lambda A_{t-1}^* + a_2\Delta Y_t^* + a_2\lambda Y_{t-1}^* \qquad (6)$$
$$+ a_3\Delta P_t^* + a_3\lambda P_{t-1}^* + a_4 C_{t-1}^* + a_5 K^n ,$$

where * indicates that the variables have been transformed as above, and the exponent $n$ on $K$ is the observation number: $n = 1, \ldots, N$. The coefficient $a_5$ provides an estimate of the unknown initial error term $\epsilon_0$.

Since, for other reasons, we have decided to select the Flow-Adjustment model for the jewelry (precious metal) industry, this technique was applied only to the remaining three industries for which first-order autocorrelation was found to be important, the previous approach being used. For each of these industries we calculated the $\hat{K}$ implied by the equation fitted to the transformed data in order to determine whether additional iterations would be required.

TABLE 5-B.2. Coefficients for GK model with a moving-average error process

| Industry | $\dfrac{\hat{K}_D^a}{\hat{K}_I^b}$ | Regression coefficients[c] | | | | | | $\dfrac{R^2}{DW}$ |
|---|---|---|---|---|---|---|---|---|
| | | $\hat{e}_0$ | $\Delta A$ | $\lambda$ | $\Delta Y$ | $\Delta P$ | $C_{t-1}$ | |
| Canning | −0.048 | −0.26 | 5.312 | 1.122 | 5238 | −0.168 | 0.288 | 0.920 |
| | −.122 | (0.62) | (2.37) | (1.93) | (0.87) | (1.20) | (0.88) | 2.12 |
| Women's | .659 | −.023 | 19.60 | 0.362 | 9548 | −4.926 | 1.062 | 0.998 |
| clothing | .638 | (.09) | (4.95) | (2.44) | (0.85) | (3.37) | (10.50) | 2.80 |
| Drugs | −.251 | −.111 | 1.351 | 2.104 | 5172 | −1.289 | −0.088 | 0.914 |
| | −1.104 | (.16) | (0.84) | (1.02) | (0.42) | (0.66) | (0.25) | 1.66 |

[a]Specified value of $\hat{K}$ used in transforming the data.
[b]Value of $\hat{K}$ implied by the resulting equation.
[c]Values of $t$ in parentheses.

Results are presented in Table 5-B.2. For two of the industries—canning and women's clothing—the values of $\lambda$ (and hence of $\hat{K}$) do not change much;

we therefore decided not to attempt further iteration. However, for neither of these industries did the results obtained differ significantly from the results obtained with direct least squares. We therefore used the direct least-squares estimates for the canning industry, and used a constrained equation (with $a_4 = 1.00$) for the women's clothing industry.

For the drug industry, the value of $\hat{K}$ changed by a larger amount, so we decided to iterate using this technique across a range of values for $\hat{K}$. The results of this iteration did not indicate a clear convergence, however. Estimates of the dynamic coefficients $\lambda$ and $a_4$ were sensitive to the initial specification of $\hat{K}$, but the standard error of estimate was not. The Durbin-Watson statistic signaled the appearance of positive serial correlation when $K$ assumed large negative values and negative serial correlation when $K$ assumed large positive values. Since the ordinary least-squares estimates were about as good as any other set on the basis of three criteria—standard error of estimate, Durbin-Watson coefficient, and the consistency of the preliminary and final estimates of $K$—these estimates were used.

For the three industries where the Flow-Adjustment model was selected as the final model, tests for first-order autocorrelation were carried out by means of nonlinear iterative techniques. The results are reported in Table 5-B.3. In one of these industries—jewelry (precious metal)—serial correlation was significant. However, the autoregressive equation for this industry was unsatisfactory in other respects: it implied a very low income elasticity and a very rapid flow adjustment, neither of which appeared reasonable for this industry. We therefore used the ordinary least-squares estimates for this industry.

On the basis of the various tests and estimates involving models with autocorrelated errors, we decided to remain with the original least-squares estimates in all industries.

TABLE 5–B.3. Coefficients for Flow-Adjustment model with a first-order autoregressive process: selected industries

| Industry | Constant | $\bar{A}$ | $\bar{Y}$ | $\bar{P}$ | $C_{t-1}$ | $\hat{\rho}$ | $R^2$ $DW$ |
|---|---|---|---|---|---|---|---|
| | | | Regression coefficients[a] | | | | |
| Malt liquor | 0.041 | 0.533 | 8177 | −1.109 | 0.765 | −0.281 | 0.711 |
| | | (0.42) | (0.93) | (0.81) | (4.14) | (0.83) | 2.04 |
| Clocks and watches | .008 | 2.804 | 5478 | −0.062 | 0.450 | .234 | 0.430 |
| | | (1.02) | (1.19) | (.05) | (0.69) | (.32) | 1.80 |
| Jewelry (precious metal) | .003 | 2.964 | 373 | −0.863 | −0.591 | 0.945 | 0.420 |
| | | (0.71) | (0.09) | (1.83) | (2.07) | (3.79) | 1.88 |

[a]Values of $t$ in parentheses.

# APPENDIX 5-C SIMULTANEOUS ESTIMATION PROCEDURES

A four-equation model including two stochastic equations (4) and (8) and two identities (9) and (10) is presented in this chapter. We may derive a reduced-form equation for advertising as follows. First we substitute for $SC_t$ from identity (10) in equation (8), obtaining

$$AC_t = b_0 + b_1 (POP_t \cdot P_t \cdot PCE_t) C_t \qquad (1)$$
$$+ b_2 SC_{t-1} + b_3 RPA_t + b_4 RPA_{t-1} + b_5 AC_{t-1}.$$

Now substitute for $C_t$ from the demand equation (4):

$$AC_t = b_0 + b_1 (POP_t \cdot P_t \cdot PCE_t)(a_1 \Delta A_t + a_1 \lambda A_{t-1} \qquad (2)$$
$$+ a_2 \Delta Y_t + a_2 \lambda Y_{t-1} + a_3 \Delta P_t + a_3 \lambda P_{t-1} + a_4 C_{t-1})$$
$$+ b_2 SC_{t-1} + b_3 RPA_t + b_4 RPA_{t-1} + b_5 AC_{t-1}.$$

Next substitute for $A_t$ from the identity (10):

$$AC_t = b_0 + b_1 (POP_t \cdot P_t \cdot PCE_t) [a_1 AC_t / ATOT_t + a_1 (\lambda - 1) A_{t-1} \qquad (3)$$
$$+ a_2 \Delta Y_t + a_2 \lambda Y_{t-1} + a_3 \Delta P_t + a_3 \lambda P_{t-1} + a_4 C_{t-1}]$$
$$+ b_2 SC_{t-1} + b_3 RPA_t + b_4 RPA_{t-1} + b_5 AC_{t-1},$$

which after rearrangement becomes the following nonlinear equation:

$$AC_t = \frac{1}{1 - \{a_1 b_1 (POP_t \cdot P_t \cdot PCE_t) / ATOT_t\}} \Big\{ b_0 + b_1 (POP_t \cdot P_t \cdot$$
$$PCE_t) [a_1 (\lambda - 1) A_{t-1} + a_2 \Delta Y_t + a_2 \lambda Y_{t-1} + a_3 \Delta P_t + a_3 \lambda P_{t-1} \qquad (4)$$
$$+ a_4 C_{t-1}] + b_2 SC_{t-1} + b_3 RPA_t + b_4 RPA_{t-1} + b_5 AC_{t-1} \Big\}.$$

This is a highly nonlinear reduced-form equation with thirteen variables on the right-hand side. Although these variables are not exactly linearly dependent, multicollinearity will be extremely high. In view of this high multicollinearity between some of the variables, it is advisable to delete variables in order to gain scarce degrees of freedom.[1] The variables deleted are the following:

$A_{t-1}$, deleted because of probable extreme collinearity with $AC_{t-1}$, $RPA_t$, and $RPA_{t-1}$;

$\Delta P_t$, deleted because of probable collinearity with $RPA_t$ and $RPA_{t-1}$;

$C_{t-1}$, deleted because of probable collinearity with $SC_{t-1}$, $POP_t$, $PCE_t$, and $RPA_{t-1}$;

$P_{t-1}$, deleted because of probable collinearity with $RPA_{t-1}$ and $PCE_t$; and

$ATOT_t$, deleted because of probable collinearity with $POP_t$, $\Delta Y_t$, $Y_{t-1}$, and $PCE_t$, and because of simultaneity with $AC_t$, since $AC_t$ is a component of $ATOT_t$.

We therefore assume that appendix equation (4) may be adequately approximated by the following linear reduced-form equation:

$$AC_t = r_0 + r_1 SC_{t-1} + r_2 RPA_t + r_3 AC_{t-1} \qquad (5)$$
$$+ r_4 \Delta Y_t + r_5 Y_{t-1} + r_6 POP_t + r_7 PCE_t + r_8 RPA_{t-1}.$$

The procedure from here on is analogous to that of two-stage least squares. Equation (5) is estimated and predicted values of $AC_t$, denoted by $\widehat{AC}_t$, are calculated from the equation. Predicted values $\hat{A}_t$ are then calculated from $\widehat{AC}_t$ from identity (9):

$$\hat{A}_t = \frac{\widehat{AC}_t}{ATOT_t}.$$

Next we calculated an adjusted version of the jointly dependent variable $\Delta A_t$:

$$\Delta A_t^* = \hat{A}_t - A_{t-1},$$

which is presumably purged of simultaneous-equations effects. We then proceed to estimate the demand equation (4), using the same nonlinear iterative technique as before, but replacing $\Delta A_t$ with $\Delta A_t^*$.

For the three industries for which the Flow-Adjustment model was selected, a similar procedure was used. In the estimating equation (7) for this model, $\bar{A}_t$ was replaced by

$$\hat{\bar{A}}_t = \frac{\hat{A}_t + A_{t-1}}{2},$$

where $\hat{A}_t$ is obtained from regression equation (5) and the relevant identity. We then reestimated equation (7) using least squares.

1. If a linearized version of equation (4) were estimated without deleting variables, only four or five degrees of freedom would remain.

# APPENDIX 5-D.  DEMAND-EQUATION DATA

Data on industry sales[1] and advertising expenditures were gathered from the Internal Revenue Service publication, *Statistics of Income*, and the IRS *Source Book* microfilms for the industries in the sample for as many years as are available from 1946 to 1964. In some industries, statistics for each of these years could be obtained. In other industries, data were available only for a smaller number of years, and therefore a shorter time series was used in the estimation of the demand equations. The length of the series used for the final equations selected is shown in Table 5.8.

As a result of the changes made in industry classifications following 1957, there were a number of industries for which data series were available only for the years up to 1957. It was possible to aggregate some industries into broader groupings that were consistent over time. For example, although cigars were distinguished from cigarettes for the years through 1957, and thus were distinguished in our basic cross-section results which referred to the four years from 1954 to 1957, they were combined in succeeding years into tobacco products. A combined demand equation for tobacco was estimated for the entire postwar period, and the same demand parameters were used for each constituent industry. This approach was used also for grain mill products and cereals and for furniture and fixtures (which combines furniture and screens and blinds). For the remaining industries demand equations were estimated on the basis of data up to 1957.

Missing data for 1952 posed an additional problem. Although the IRS reported statistics on industry sales, no data on industry advertising were

1. The sales variable used is "total compiled receipts."

published for that year. Because of the lags in the model, the missing observation would cost two degrees of freedom. The following method of estimating advertising expenditures for 1952 was therefore used. Advertising:sales ratios for both the preceding and the succeeding year were computed and the mean value was obtained. This ratio was then applied to the reported sales figure for 1952 to obtain the estimate of advertising expenditures in that year used in the regression analysis.

In addition to the IRS statistics on advertising and sales, the demand analysis required data on industry prices. The sources of the price indices obtained for each industry are shown in Table 5-D.1. For the most part, the price indices used are constituent series of the wholesale-price index. Only where appropriate WPI series were not available were other price indices used.

TABLE 5–D.1.  Sources of industry price indices

| Industry | Source |
|---|---|
| Soft drinks | WPI series no. 145 |
| Malt beverages | WPI series no. 1441 |
| Wines | WPI series no. 1443 |
| Distilled liquor | WPI series no. 1442 |
| Meat | Weighted average of WPI series nos. 0221 and 0222 using the relative-importance weights from the general WPI |
| Dairy products | WPI series no. 023 |
| Canning | WPI series no. 024 |
| Grain mill products | WPI series no. 021 |
| Cereals | WPI series no. 021 |
| Bakery products | WPI series no. 021 |
| Sugar | WPI series no. 025 |
| Confectionery | WPI series no. 025 |
| Tobacco products | Weighted average of WPI series nos. 141, 142, and 143 using the relative-importance weights from the general WPI |
| Knit goods | WPI series no. 0334 |
| Carpets | WPI series no. 1231 |
| Hats | WPI series no. 352 (series for men's clothing) |
| Men's clothing | WPI series no. 352 |
| Women's clothing | WPI series no. 351 |
| Millinery | BLS department-store inventory price index for "Ladies' accessories" |

Table 5–D.1.   (continued)

| Industry | Source |
|---|---|
| Furs | BLS department-store inventory price index for "Ladies' outerwear and girls' wear" |
| Furniture | WPI series no. 121 |
| Screens and blinds | BLS department-store inventory price index for "Home furnishings/Housewares" |
| Periodicals | OBE implicit price deflators for "Newspapers and magazines" used in H. S. Houthakker and L. D. Taylor, *Consumer Demand in the United States* |
| Books | OBE implicit price deflator for "Books and maps" used in H. S. Houthakker and L. D. Taylor, *Consumer Demand in the United States* |
| Drugs | WPI series no. 063 |
| Soaps | WPI series no. 671 |
| Paints | WPI series no. 621 |
| Perfumes | OBE implicit price deflator for "Toilet articles and preparations" used in H. S. Houthakker and L. D. Taylor, *Consumer Demand in the United States*; observation for 1964 from WPI series no. 675 |
| Tires and tubes | WPI series no. 072 |
| Footwear | WPI series no. 043 |
| Handtools | Weighted average of W.P.I. series nos. 1267 and 1134 using the relative-importance weights from the general W.P.I. |
| Household and service machinery | WPI series no. 124 (Electrical appliances) |
| Electrical appliances | WPI series no. 124 |
| Radio, TV, and phonograph | WPI series no. 125 (observations for 1953 and 1954 are not available; since the reported index for 1952 is 92.9 and that for 1955 is 93.0, the indices for 1953 and 1954 were set at the latter value) |
| Motorcycles and bicycles | WPI series no. 118 (Motor vehicles) |
| Motor vehicles | WPI series no. 118 |
| Instruments | WPI series no. 1544 |
| Clocks and watches | WPI series no. 1543 |
| Jewelry (precious metal) | WPI unpublished price index for "Jewelry" |
| Costume jewelry | WPI unpublished price index for "Jewelry" |

TABLE 5–D.2.   Advertising price index

| Year | Index |
| --- | --- |
| 1946 | 68.8 |
| 1947 | 71.5 |
| 1948 | 75.0 |
| 1949 | 76.9 |
| 1950 | 80.2 |
| 1951 | 85.1 |
| 1952 | 94.6 |
| 1953 | 92.8 |
| 1954 | 96.3 |
| 1955 | 99.6 |
| 1956 | 100.0 |
| 1957 | 102.4 |
| 1958 | 105.3 |
| 1959 | 108.9 |
| 1960 | 111.6 |
| 1961 | 115.2 |
| 1962 | 118.6 |
| 1963 | 119.9 |
| 1964 | 120.0 |
| 1965 | 121.5 |
| 1966 | 123.7 |

Since the cost per advertising message has increased during the postwar period with the general inflation, it is necessary to deflate the raw advertising-expenditure figures by an index of advertising costs. A price index for advertising expenditures was therefore required for the estimation of models with absolute advertising as an independent variable.

Advertising costs per message must necessarily reflect not only price changes in the cost per minute or per column inch or per page that is paid by the advertiser, but also changes in the number of listeners or viewers or readers of the message. Increased costs per unit of medium space may not reflect increased costs per advertising message if the number of recipients increases in a corresponding manner. On this account, the price index should reflect not simply the prices charged by the various media, but also changes in circulation or average audiences as well.

Advertising-price indices were constructed on the basis of the advertising-price indices for daily newspapers, magazines, spot radio, and spot television published in *Media/Scope*.[2] The resulting price index is shown in Table 5-D.2.

2. *Media/Scope* (February 1968), p. 95. The published indices for newspapers and magazines are on a cost-per-circulation basis, whereas the radio and television indices are on the basis of cost per unit of broadcast time. The television indices were adjusted to cost per audience unit by means of a time series on the number of television households and the average number of viewing hours per day; the radio series were adjusted simply on the basis of national population.

It is a composite index of price series for four advertising media. To combine the separate series, a Paasche index was computed by using the aggregate volume of advertising expenditures on each medium as weights. This index implies that changing weights are attached to each of the individual price relatives over time. In view of the rapid growth of television advertising relative to other media, such a current weighted price index will yield less arbitrary results than a Laspeyres index, which is more likely to be sensitive to the choice of the base year chosen for weighting purposes.

One further problem was encountered before a final advertising price index was obtained. Data were available only for 1950 and succeeding years, whereas our analysis required a deflated series of advertising expenditures since 1946. What was needed, therefore, was some means of projecting backward the series on advertising costs. This backward projection was carried out by estimating a number of simple regression equations in which the advertising price index was the dependent variable and various published time series were separately the independent variable. In addition to a simple time trend, alternative independent variables were the GNP deflator, the implicit deflator for government purchases of services, the implicit deflator on brokers' commissions on the sale of residential structures, the consumer price index for newspapers, and with a series on average earnings per employee in miscellaneous business services. The equations were estimated for the years between 1950 and 1966. As expected, all of the series generally increased over time and provided a relatively high correlation coefficient. However, only one series was more closely correlated to the independent variable than the time trend, and this was the series on average earnings per employee for miscellaneous business services. The estimated regression equation was:

$$Y = \underset{(3.30)}{29.34} + \underset{(0.0006)}{0.0152}\, X, \qquad r^2 = 0.97, \qquad (1)$$

where the numbers in parentheses are the standard errors of the estimated regression coefficients. To the extent that structural conditions remain constant, the yearly change in the advertising price index should equal 0.0152 times the yearly change in average earnings per employee in this sector. Backward projections were carried out on this basis from the published figures of this variable for 1946 through 1949.

The remaining series used in the various demand analyses are aggregate series that are readily available in government publications. Personal consumer expenditures in constant dollars, the implicit price deflator for consumer expenditures, and personal disposable income are from the U.S. *National Income Accounts*. Population is obtained from the *Statistical Abstract of the*

U.S. and the index of industrial production from the *Federal Reserve Bulletin*. Table 5-D.3 lists the various series used in the regression analyses, together with their sources and units of measurement.

TABLE 5-D.3    Sources and units of measurement of basic series and definitions of derived series

| Name | Symbol | Source | Units |
|------|--------|--------|-------|
| | | *Basic Series* | |
| Industry sales | $SC(i)$ | IRS Source Book Microfilms | $10^3$ dollars |
| Industry advertising | $AC(i)$ | IRS Source Book Microfilms | $10^3$ dollars |
| Industry prices | $PRICE(i)$ | See Table D–1 | Index Numbers 1947–1949 = 100 |
| Total advertising in manufacturing | $ATOT$ | IRS, *Statistics of Income* | $10^3$ dollars |
| Population | $POP$ | *Economic Report of the President*, Feb. 1968, Table B–21. | $10^3$ persons |
| Total consumer expenditure | $TCE$ | *Economic Report of the President*, Feb. 1968, Table B–1. | $10^8$ dollars |
| Implicit deflator for total consumer expenditures | $PCE$ | *Economic Report of the President*, Feb. 1968, Table B–3 | Index Number 1958 = 1000 |
| Price index for advertising | $PAD$ | See Table 5–D.2 | Index Number 1956 = 1000 |
| | | *Derived series* | |
| Per-capita real sales | $C(i)$ | $SC(i)/(PRICE(i)\cdot POP)$ | |
| Relative advertising expenditures | $A(i)$ | $AC(i)/ATOT$ | |
| Relative prices | $P(i)$ | $PRICE(i)/PCE$ | |
| Total per-capita real expenditures | $Y$ | $TCE/(PCE\cdot POP)$ | |
| Product price relative to price of advertising | $RPA(i)$ | $PRICE(i)/PAD$ | |

CHAPTER 6 **Advertising and Profit Rates**

In this chapter, we examine the impact of advertising on profit rates. As indicated in Chapter 4, we expect this impact to be positive, and our purpose here is to subject this hypothesis to empirical testing. Before proceeding, however, we discuss the variables used in the empirical analysis.

## THE VARIABLES AND SAMPLE OF INDUSTRIES

The profit-rate variable is profits after taxes as a percentage of stockholders' equity,[1] averaged within each industry for firms with assets exceeding $500,000. This procedure avoids the difficulty, noted by Stigler, of profit withdrawals in the form of executive salaries in small and closely held corporations.[2] Profit rates are also averaged for the period 1954 through 1957, which covers a complete business cycle.

Although we view the profit rate on stockholders' equity as a more appropriate variable for this analysis than the rate of return (including interest) on total assets,[3] we examined whether the empirical results are sensitive to this

1. This profit rate variable was used originally in Joe S. Bain, "Relation of Profit Rates to Industry Concentration: American Manufacturing, 1936–1940," *Quarterly Journal of Economics* (August 1951), pp. 296–297, and Joe S. Bain, *Barriers to New Competition* (Cambridge, Mass., Harvard University Press, 1956), p. 192.
2. George J. Stigler, *Capital and Rates of Return in Manufacturing Industries* (Princeton, N.J., Princeton University Press, 1963) pp. 125–127.
3. Since the market rate of interest paid by the firm will not be increased when the firm's market power increases (and indeed may be lowered), the rate of return on stockholders' equity will be a more sensitive indicator of firms' freedom from competitive constraints. Offsetting this advantage is the disadvantage that rates of return on equity will be more sensitive to the leverage of the firm than will rates of return (including interest) on total assets.

judgment. The simple correlation coefficient between the profit rate on stock-holders' equity and the rate of return on total assets is 0.93. In addition, the correlation coefficients between each of these variables and the 1954 four-firm concentration ratio[4] are 0.36 and 0.33, respectively. These results suggest that our empirical findings are not likely to be sensitive to the choice of a specific profit-rate variable.[5]

In the light of the discussion in preceding chapters, it is useful to examine the absolute volume of advertising expenditures by existing firms as well as the advertising:sales ratio. The latter variable probably provides a good indication of the absolute cost disadvantage of the new entrant at small scales of entry but is likely to be a less accurate index of the effects of advertising on economies of scale and absolute capital requirements.

For these reasons, we calculate two measures of advertising intensity: advertising outlays per dollar of sales for firms with assets exceeding $500,000, and average advertising expenditures per firm among the largest firms that account for half of industry output.[6] Both advertising variables are averages for the years 1954 through 1957.

Although advertising per firm is positively correlated with advertising per dollar of sales, the positions of two important industries change radically depending on which variable is used to measure advertising intensity. Tires and tubes and motor vehicles have quite low advertising:sales ratios, but both are among the small group of industries with high or very high average advertising outlays per firm among the leading firms.

Concentration is measured by the average four-firm concentration ratios published by Stigler.[7] Since these ratios are based on national markets, a dummy variable is introduced where the relevant market boundaries are local rather than national.

Economies of scale in production presumably exist primarily at the plant

4. In 2 cases out of 41, our industry classifications differed from those presented by Stigler, from whose book the statistics on rates of return on total assets and four-firm concentration ratios were gathered. In both of these cases, screens and venetian blinds, and radio, TV, and phonograph, it appeared that Stigler had combined these industries with smaller, miscellaneous industries. In these calculations, therefore, we used data for the more aggregated industry to stand for its major component.

5. See also the equations predicting profit margins on sales reported in Chapter 8 below.

6. The procedure used was to select successive asset size classes of firms until 50 percent or more of industry sales was covered. The proportion of sales in the boundary class required to reach this degree of coverage was used to determine the amount of advertising and the number of firms from the size class included in both numerator and denominator of the measure of advertising per firm. For some industries, the largest size class accounted for more than 50 percent of sales. In such cases, the measure is simply average advertising per firm in the largest size class.

7. Stigler, *Capital and Rates of Return in Manufacturing Industries*, pp. 214–215.

level rather than at the firm level. In the absence of better estimates for most of the industries in the sample, a measure is derived from the size distribution of plants within each industry. Since cost minimization is an element of profit maximization, large multiplant firms should operate plants that are sufficiently large to realize available scale economies. Where demand is not a limiting factor, moreover, competition among firms should lead directly to plants that equal or exceed minimum efficient scale.[8]

At the same time, small plants may exist. These may have been built in an earlier period, before demand had expanded or a technology that required large scale had been developed, or they may be due to the entry of small firms. They may also exist in pockets of the market that are geographically segmented or may specialize in narrow product lines that are not representative of the industry generally. It is important, therefore, to select a measure that is not sensitive to the entry of single-plant firms of suboptimal scale.

The measure used is average plant size among the largest plants accounting for half of industry output. This average plant size is divided by total output in the relevant market to obtain the scale economies variable used in the regression analyses.[9]

A test of the reliability of this variable can be made by comparing minimum efficient scale as a percentage of industry output with Bain's estimates. Not only did Bain concentrate on a smaller number of industries but also he used varied forms of information. Therefore, his estimates can be viewed as a benchmark against which to appraise various methods of estimating economies of scale. We examine both the method described above and an alternative method, the Survival Technique, as used by Weiss.[10]

Of the 20 industries examined by Bain, data on the size distribution of plants are available for 19. Across these industries, the correlation coefficient between Bain's estimates and those derived from the method proposed above is 0.89.[11] Estimates based on the Survival Technique are available for 13 of the industries studied by Bain, and the correlation between these estimates and those given

8. Since the bulk of the evidence suggests that cost curves in manufacturing are L-shaped rather than U-shaped, plants which exceed minimum efficient scale will typically be efficient plants. See J. Johnston, *Statistical Cost Analysis* (New York, McGraw Hill, 1960), pp. 44–168.

9. An alternate measure based on average plant size among the largest plants accounting for 70 percent of output was also constructed. This variable was highly correlated with the variable used.

10. Leonard W. Weiss, "The Survival Technique and the Extent of Sub-Optimal Capacity," *Journal of Political Economy* (June 1964), pp. 246–261.

11. In these calculations, Bain's estimates of minimum efficient scale for the steel industry refer to steel works and rolling mills, while for the copper industry they refer to primary copper.

by Bain is 0.66. When the comparison is limited to the same 13 industries, the correlation coefficient between estimates derived from the size distribution of establishments and those published by Bain is 0.86. The method proposed above is therefore more consistent with Bain's estimates than are those computed from the Survival Technique,[12] and is used in the succeeding analysis.

The amount of capital required for entry at the scale of a single efficient plant is an additional factor that may create barriers to entry. Our definition of this variable is based upon the estimates given above of economies of scale. The average output level of plants at estimated minimum efficient scale is multiplied by the ratio of total assets to gross sales for the industry.[13]

The rate of growth of demand is measured by the ratio of industry sales in 1957 to those in 1947.[14] A period of this length was chosen to emphasize the long-run effects of the growth of demand, and the terminal years selected were both years of nearly full employment for the economy as a whole.

Industries are classified into two groups on the basis of the two variables that measure technical entry barriers: economies of scale and absolute capital requirements. A dummy variable indicating industries with high technical entry barriers is used in some regression equations.[15]

Similarly, industries are divided into two classes on the basis of the two advertising variables. A variable identifying industries with high advertising expenditures is used as an alternative measure of advertising intensity.[16]

Three of the industries—soft drinks, bakery products, and dairy products— sell in local markets, and a dummy variable is introduced to identify these industries in some equations. This variable is needed when the national concentration ratios are used, but it is not required in conjunction with the

12. In addition, the Survival Technique has a great disadvantage of frequency yielding indeterminate results. See Weiss, "The Survival Technique," pp. 258–259.

13. This measure is likely, on the average, to understate capital requirements. The book value of total assets will normally be less than their replacement cost, as a result of inflation in preceding years. In addition, a new firm is likely to have higher input costs while it is learning the production and distribution techniques required in the market.

14. The ideal measure, of course, would be the rate at which the demand curve shifted over time. The rate of growth of sales is an exact measure only if the price elasticity of demand is unity or if prices did not change over the period.

15. High technical entry barriers are assumed to exist if either the scale of an efficient plant exceeded 10 percent of the market or the capital required for efficient entry equaled at least $50 million. In addition, high barriers are assumed where scale economies fell between 6 and 9.9 percent *and* if capital requirements amounted to more than $25 million.

16. High entry barriers due to advertising are assumed either when the advertising:sales ratio exceeded 8 percent or when advertising expenditures among leading firms averaged more than $20 million per firm. The same classification is given to industries where the average ratio fell between 4 percent and 8 percent *and* average annual expenditures were between $5 million and $20 million.

economies-of-scale variable, which is estimated relative to the relevant market, whether national or local.

Under conditions of imperfect competition, the price elasticity of industry demand may have an independent effect upon profit rates, although the strength of this effect may depend on the height of entry barriers and the degree of coordination in pricing among firms in the market. In Chapter 5, satisfactory demand equations were obtained for a sufficient number of industries to warrant the inclusion of estimates of price elasticities of demand in the analysis. As explained below, a somewhat more restricted sample of industries is used to estimate those equations that include either short-run or long-run price elasticity of demand as an independent variable.

Since advertising is an important factor only in the consumer-goods sector of the economy, the empirical analysis is confined to industries in this sector.[17] Of the 41 industries included in the analysis, 29 produce nondurable consumer goods, and the remaining 12 produce consumer durables. In size, the industries range from motor vehicles, with average sales of over $20 billion per year, to hats, with average sales of only $122 million per year. Spurious size effects are absent, however, since the dependent variable is expressed in ratio form.

In Chapter 5, representative demand equations were selected for 38 industries, of which 5 are based on composite industries including two other industries. If we assume that the price elasticities of demand estimated for the composite industries are appropriate for its components, we can use the same figure for each.[18] Estimates of both long-run and short-run price elasticities are derived from these equations for each of the 38 industries,[19] and regression analyses that included the price elasticity of demand as an independent variable were confined to this sample of industries. Because of the differences in sample size, we first present the results of estimating those models that do not include either price elasticity.

## MAJOR EMPIRICAL RESULTS

The simple correlation coefficients between profit rates and each explanatory variable are presented in Table 6.1. All of the coefficients have the expected sign and all are statistically significant in at least one functional form. Moreover, the logarithmic relation appears appropriate in the case of the growth-of-demand variable, whereas the opposite is the case with regard to the

17. The petroleum industry is excluded because of the difficulty of obtaining profit data comparable to other industries in view of the special tax treatment of that industry.

18. The demand equation for tobacco was used for both cigarettes and cigars; that for grain and cereals was used for both grain mill products and cereals. The demand equation for furniture and fixtures was used for furniture.

19. The excluded industries are sugar, women's clothing, and paints. The reasons for their exclusion are discussed in Chapter 5.

TABLE 6.1.   Simple correlation coefficients: profit rates and market structure[a]

| Variable | Natural units | Logarithms |
|---|---|---|
| Growth of demand | 0.44[c] | 0.54[c] |
| Capital requirements | .43[c] | .57[c] |
| Economies of scale | .26 | .37[c] |
| Advertising:sales ratio | .42[c] | .27[b] |
| Advertising per firm | .43[c] | .50[c] |
| Concentration ratio (4 firms) | .36[c] | .35[b] |

[a]Tests of significance are made on the basis of one-tail $t$ tests.
[b]Statistically significant at the 5-percent level.
[c]Statistically significant at the 1-percent level.

advertising:sales ratio. Since the latter variable is already expressed as a percentage, it is measured in units comparable to those for the dependent variable.

The core of the empirical work in this chapter is the multiple-regression equations that relate profit rates to various combinations of the explanatory variables. A set of preliminary coefficients for these equations is presented in Table 6.2. As may be observed, the two advertising variables are never statistically significant when both are introduced into the same equations, although each variable is significant when the other is omitted. This finding is not unexpected since the two advertising variables are obviously related.[20] Note further that in these equations the advertising:sales ratio is a slightly stronger variable than the absolute volume of advertising per firm.

Although absolute capital requirements and the rate of growth of demand are both highly significant variables in a number of equations, the effect of economies of scale is quite weak. The estimated regression coefficients for the latter variable are never statistically significant, and indeed are negative in three equations. These results suggest therefore that both absolute capital requirements and the growth rate of demand may have significant effects on profit rates. Another interesting feature of these equations is that the estimated regression coefficients for concentration are never statistically significant and indeed are negative in four cases out of six.

A further set of coefficients for regression equations is presented in Table 6.3. In these equations, the effect of advertising is measured by the advertising:sales ratio. The advertising coefficients in these equations are always statistically significant regardless of which other variables are also included. Moreover, they are quite stable and vary only between 0.318 and 0.337.

The effects of absolute capital requirements and the growth rate of demand are again evident. These coefficients are statistically significant in all cases. Similarly, the concentration ratio and the economies-of-scale variable are

20. The simple correlation coefficient between these two variables is 0.37.

TABLE 6.2. Coefficients for regression equations explaining profit rates: 41 industries[a]

| Equation number | Intercept | Advertising: sales ratio | Advertising per firm | Economies of scale (log) | Absolute capital requirements (log) | Growth of demand (log) | Concentration ratio | Local industry dummy variable | $R^2$ |
|---|---|---|---|---|---|---|---|---|---|
| (1) | 0.0232 (0.51) | 0.272 (1.55) | 0.00000056 (0.90) | −0.00409 (0.52) | 0.0134[b] (2.03) | 0.0234 (1.52) | −0.000236 (0.43) | 0.0339 (1.37) | 0.55[c] |
| (2) | 0.0454[b] (1.87) | 0.268 (1.68) | 0.00000057 (1.18) | 0.00118 (0.23) | 0.00617 (1.50) | 0.0338[c] (2.54) | — | — | .52[c] |
| (3) | 0.0264 (0.57) | 0.283 (1.58) | 0.00000064 (1.00) | −0.00535 (0.67) | 0.0198[c] (3.82) | — | −0.000558 (1.08) | 0.0429[b] (1.75) | .52[c] |
| (4) | 0.0362 (0.77) | 0.297 (1.62) | 0.00000050 (0.77) | 0.000621 (0.08) | — | 0.0433[c] (3.50) | 0.000370 (0.77) | 0.0127 (0.54) | .49[c] |
| (5) | 0.0458[c] (3.39) | 0.235 (1.48) | 0.00000071 (1.27) | — | 0.0124[b] (1.98) | 0.0243 (1.60) | −0.000375 (0.79) | 0.0250 (1.40) | .55[c] |
| (6) | 0.00075 (0.02) | 0.354[b] (2.36) | — | −0.00718 (1.02) | 0.0131[b] (1.99) | 0.0245 (1.60) | 0.000069 (1.60) | 0.0410[b] (1.75) | .54[c] |
| (7) | 0.059 (1.49) | — | 0.00000106[b] (1.94) | 0.000849 (0.12) | 0.0140[b] (2.09) | 0.0244 (1.56) | −0.000591 (1.16) | 0.0251 (1.02) | .52[c] |

[a]Values of $t$ in parentheses.
[b]Statistically significant at the 5-percent level.
[c]Statistically significant at the 1-percent level.

TABLE 6.3. Coefficients for regression equations explaining profit rates: 41 industries[a]

| Equation number | Intercept | Advertising: sales ratio | Capital requirements (log) | Economies of scale (log) | Growth of demand (log) | Concentration ratio | Local-industry dummy variable | $R^2$ |
|---|---|---|---|---|---|---|---|---|
| (1) | 0.0390[c] (4.85) | 0.337[b] (2.32) | 0.00842[c] (2.81) | — | 0.0311[b] (2.42) | — | — | 0.50[c] |
| (2) | 0.0425[b] (1.75) | 0.332[b] (2.21) | 0.00807[b] (2.12) | 0.000780 (0.15) | 0.0315[b] (2.38) | — | — | .50[c] |
| (3) | 0.0375[c] (3.14) | 0.318[b] (2.17) | 0.0107[b] (1.73) | — | 0.0269[b] (1.78) | −0.000065 (0.16) | 0.0258 (1.43) | .52[c] |
| (4) | 0.0779[c] (3.86) | 0.325[b] (2.04) | — | 0.00745 (1.64) | 0.0433[c] (3.41) | — | −0.00168 (0.09) | .43[b] |
| (5) | 0.0361[c] (4.41) | 0.320[b] (2.26) | 0.00984[c] (3.16) | — | 0.0281[b] (2.19) | — | 0.252 (1.44) | .52[c] |

[a]Values of $t$ in parentheses.
[b]Statistically significant at 5-percent level.
[c]Statistically significant at 1-percent level.

also statistically insignificant. Furthermore, the multiple-correlation coefficient for these equations is always significant. The included variables typically account for more than half of the total variation in industry profit rates.

In Table 6.4, another set of coefficients is presented in which the impact of advertising is represented by a dummy variable identifying those industries in which high advertising barriers appear to exist. As suggested above, the presence of high advertising barriers should depend on both high advertising: sales ratios and a high absolute volume of advertising expenditures, so that this variable reflects both dimensions of heavy advertising.[21] As can be seen, this variable is somewhat stronger statistically than the advertising:sales ratio, which may reflect the fact that it incorporates the added explanatory power associated with a high absolute volume of advertising. The estimated coefficients are always significant at a 1-percent confidence level.

An interesting feature of Table 6.4 is that the regression coefficients for capital requirements are generally lower than those in Table 6.3. This difference is probably due to the collinearity between absolute capital requirements and absolute advertising per firm, so that including the latter in determining high advertising barriers leads to a smaller coefficient for capital requirements. The coefficients for the other structural variables, however, appear relatively insensitive to the particular advertising variable used in the equation.

The local-industry dummy variable was also introduced into the equations in both tables. In all cases, its estimated parameters are significant at the 10-percent level, and reach the 5-percent level in Table 6.4. Although this variable was used originally to correct for the use of concentration ratios calculated on a national basis, it appears to have an independent effect that does not depend on the presence of the other variable. It is useful, therefore, to compare the structural features of the three local-market industries included in our sample with the others. Relevant data are presented in Table 6.5. The economy-of-scale variable is the most sensitive to this industry characteristic. As would be expected, these industries on average have much higher values of the ratio of minimum efficient scale to market than do the national industries. It appears, therefore, that the local-market dummy variable represents the increased importance of economies of scale as well as the higher concentration levels often found in local markets.

As noted above, a number of the explanatory variables included in Tables 6.3 and 6.4 are collinear to some extent. However, the correlation between the advertising:sales ratio and the other independent variables is typically low.[22]

21. For a definition of this variable see note 16 above.
22. Simple correlation coefficients between the advertising:sales ratio and the other structural variables are: the log of economics of scale, 0.27; the log of capital requirements, 0.21; the log of growth of demand, 0.21; and the four-firm concentration ratio, 0.10.

TABLE 6.4. Coefficients for regression equations explaining profit rates: 41 industries[a]

| Equation number | Intercept | High advertising barrier | Capital requirements (log) | Economies of scale (log) | Growth of demand (log) | Concentration ratio | Local-industry dummy variable | $R^2$ |
|---|---|---|---|---|---|---|---|---|
| (1) | 0.0487[c] (6.83) | 0.0371[c] (2.87) | 0.00523 (1.63) | — | 0.0346[c] (2.81) | — | — | 0.53[c] |
| (2) | 0.0673[c] (3.05) | 0.0380[c] (2.93) | 0.00313 (0.78) | 0.00429 (0.89) | 0.0361[c] (2.90) | — | — | .54[c] |
| (3) | 0.0485[c] (4.47) | 0.0373[c] (2.93) | 0.00895 (1.50) | — | 0.02778[b] (1.93) | −0.000172 (0.44) | 0.0299[b] (1.74) | .57[c] |
| (4) | 0.0752[c] (4.30) | 0.0438[c] (3.59) | — | 0.00566 (1.36) | 0.0398[c] (3.45) | — | 0.0106 (0.60) | .54[c] |
| (5) | 0.0450[c] (6.17) | 0.0371[c] (2.95) | 0.00677[b] (2.08) | — | 0.0311[c] (2.55) | — | 0.0285[b] (1.71) | .56[c] |

[a]Values of $t$ in parentheses.
[b]Statistically significant at the 5-percent level.
[c]Statistically significant at the 1-percent level.

TABLE 6.5. Local-industry characteristics

| Industry | Advertising:sales ratio (percent) | Advertising per firm ($ million) | Capital requirements ($ million) | Economies of scale (percent) | Growth of demand (ratio) | Profit rate (percent) |
|---|---|---|---|---|---|---|
| Soft drinks | 6.2 | 0.26 | 0.75 | 8.2 | 1.98 | 10.0 |
| Dairy products | 8.5 | 15.12 | 2.09 | 14.2 | 1.16 | 7.9 |
| Bakery products | 2.9 | 1.97 | 2.57 | 8.3 | 1.69 | 9.2 |
| Average of three industries | 5.9 | 5.78 | 1.80 | 10.2 | 1.62 | 9.0 |
| All industries | 3.3 | 6.03 | 24.32 | 4.7 | 1.62 | 7.9 |

TABLE 6.6. Coefficients for multiple regression analysis: concentration and technical entry barriers[a]

| No. | Concentration[b] | Intercept | Capital requirements (log) | Economies of scale (log) | Local-industry dummy variable | $R^2$ |
|-----|------------------|-----------|----------------------------|--------------------------|-------------------------------|-------|
| 1 | Natural units | 49.9 | 7.08[c] (3.9) | 6.9[c] (2.6) | −11.2 (1.2) | 0.71[c] |
| 2 | Logarithms | 3.85 | 0.244[c] (5.1) | 0.238[c] (3.4) | − 0.294 (1.2) | .81[c] |

[a]Values of $t$ in parentheses.
[b]Four-firms concentration ratios.
[c]Statistically significant at the 99-percent level.

The estimated regression coefficients for both the advertising:sales ratio and the high advertising barrier are therefore relatively insensitive to changes in the specification of the other independent variables included in the equation.[23]

Significant collinearity exists, however, between capital requirements, economies of scale, and concentration. This is not surprising, for we should expect the first two variables to have some effect on the last. At the same time, concentration is affected by other factors, such as the past record of merger activity in the industry. To examine the extent to which concentration is explained by scale economies and capital requirements, two multiple regression equations are fitted. The results, which are striking, appear in Table 6.6.

Absolute capital requirements, scale economies, and the local-market dummy variable[24] together account for a substantial share of the variation in national concentration ratios. In logarithmic form, over 80 per cent of the variation is explained by these variables. What is surprising is the small share of variation left to be accounted for by other factors. With this high a degree of intercorrelation, it is understandable that the estimated coefficients for concentration are not statistically significant.[25]

23. This result, however, does not apply to average advertising expenditures per firm, which is more strongly correlated with the other explanatory variables. As a result, its statistical significance in regression analyses appear to depend upon which of the other variables are included in the estimating equation.

24. The local industry dummy variable was included because the concentration ratios are constructed on a national basis. The negative sign on the coefficient represents simply the downward bias of the national ratios in those industries.

25. One should be wary of drawing any policy conclusion on the basis of this equation. Merger activity may be correlated with entry barriers. Furthermore, there is some element of spurious correlation between the scale economies measure and concentration. The scale economies measure used here is 0.5 times the reciprocal of the number of the largest plants required to account for one-half of industry output. It is therefore related to plant concentration. Since plant concentration and firm concentration may be expected to be correlated even in the absence of variations in relative scale economies, some spurious correlation exists between concentration and relative scale economies. (The authors are indebted to Joe S. Bain for the elaboration of this point.)

The absence of a significant effect of concentration on profit rates may reflect the presence of multicollinearity, but it may also result from an improper specification of the concentration variable. In the equations reported in Tables 6.2–6.4, we specify that the effect of concentration is independent of other factors, such as barriers to entry. However, if the impact of concentration depends on the presence or absence of entry barriers, these results may be spurious, and an interaction variable should be defined and included as an independent variable in the analysis.

To the extent that firms set prices to exclude prospective entrants, high concentration should lead to high profits only in the presence of high entry barriers. Where overall entry barriers are low or moderate, this view of price behavior suggests that firms set prices to limit entry, and prices thereby are not affected by the number of firms in the industry. Even where this number is sufficiently small that effective price coordination is achieved, the firms do not raise prices for fear of attracting new entrants. In these circumstances, therefore, concentration has little effect on average prices.[26] On the other hand, when entry barriers are high, so that firms can ignore the prospective effect of new entrants, the number of competitors in the market may be crucially important.[27] An implication of this model of price behavior is that high concentration leads to high profits only where entry barriers are relatively high, whereas concentration has little effect where entry barriers are low or moderate.

To test this hypothesis, an interaction variable is defined which is the product of the continuous four-firm concentration ratio and the high overall entry-barrier dummy variable. The latter is defined on the basis of both advertising and technical barriers to entry. When overall barriers are low or moderate, this variable is zero regardless of the concentration ratio, whereas it takes the value of the concentration ratio where overall barriers are high. For most industries in the sample, this interaction variable is zero.

Although this variable has the advantage of providing an additional specification of the prospective effect of concentration on profitability, it also has a major disadvantage. Since overall entry barriers depend on the volume of advertising, the interaction variable must be correlated with the advertising variables even if the concentration ratio and the advertising variables are uncorrelated. Adding this interaction variable to equation (5) in both Tables

26. In this regard, note Bain's comment that "High concentration may be a relatively innocuous phenomenon if entry barriers can be reduced to a moderate level." Bain, *Barriers to New Competition*, p. 218.

27. This case corresponds to Bain's category of blockaded entry. Here the profit maximizing price, determined without regard to entry conditions is less than the entry-preventing price.

6.3 and 6.4 gives the results presented in Table 6.7. In the first equation, the interaction variable is statistically significant, but the presence of collinearity is evidenced by the low value of the coefficient of the advertising:sales ratio. It falls slightly below the estimates for this coefficient given in Table 6.4. The coefficient remains statistically significant at the conventional 5-percent level.

In the second equation, the high advertising dummy variable is used, and again the coefficient drops below values given for this coefficient in Table 6.4. The *t* value declines from about 2.9 to 1.7. Moreover, the estimated coefficient of the interaction variable is not statistically significant. Although these equations provide some suggestive results, it is hazardous to draw strong conclusions because of the considerable collinearity that is present. To some extent, the interaction variable measures the effect of advertising on profit rates, although it also reflects the role played by market concentration.

We also examine the impact on profits of the price elasticity of demand.[28] This analysis, however, suffers from the fact that it can be carried out for only 38 rather than the entire set of 41 industries, and the results may be influenced somewhat by the exclusion of three industries. Regression estimates are given in Table 6.8. In the first equation, the demand elasticity is not included, in order to determine the effect of reducing the sample from 41 to 38 industries. By comparing these results with those given above, we can see that the regression coefficients are not greatly altered. It appears, therefore, that our findings are not sensitive to the exclusion of the 3 industries, and we can interpret the results based on 38 industries in much the same way as those based on 41 industries.

When the estimated demand elasticities are introduced into the regression equations, either in conjunction with the concentration-interaction variable or not, the results are striking. The estimated regression coefficients on both the short-run and the long-run price elasticities are statistically significant; the coefficients for the long-run elasticities are highly significant. Moreover, the equation that includes both the concentration-interaction variable and the long-run price elasticity accounts for nearly 70 percent of the variation in industry profit rates. As expected, industries with more inelastic consumer demands have generally higher profit rates after the influence of other factors is taken into account.[29] Moreover, there appears to be some degree of col-

28. Some discussion of the effect of price elasticities is given in A. C. Johnson and Peter Helmberger, "Price Elasticity of Demand as an Element of Market Structure," *American Economic Review*, 57 (December 1967), 1218–1221.

29. When the high advertising dummy variable was used in place of the advertising: sales ratio in equations (2) and (3), very similar results were obtained. Equations comparable to numbers (5) and (6) were not estimated because of the high degree of collinearity between the high advertising dummy variable and the concentration interaction variable.

TABLE 6.7. Coefficients for regression equations explaining profit rate[a]

| Equation number | Intercept | Advertising[b] | Capital requirements (log) | Growth of demand (log) | Local industry dummy variable | Concentration ratio times high-overall-barrier dummy variable | $R^2$ |
|---|---|---|---|---|---|---|---|
| (1) | 0.0398[c] | 0.254[d] | 0.00577 | 0.0339[c] | 0.0184 | 0.000395[d] | 0.57[c] |
|  | (4.94) | (1.79) | (1.60) | (2.68) | (1.07) | (2.03) |  |
| (2) | 0.0457[c] | 0.0285[d] | 0.00552 | 0.0338[c] | 0.0246 | 0.000204 | .57[c] |
|  | (6.20) | (1.74) | (1.53) | (2.66) | (1.41) | (0.83) |  |

[a]Values of $t$ in parentheses.
[b]The advertising variable is the advertising:sales ratio in equation (1) and the high-advertising-barrier dummy variable in equation (2).
[c]Statistically significant at the 1-percent level.
[d]Statistically significant at the 5-percent level.

TABLE 6.8. Coefficients for regression equations explaining profit rates: 38 industries[a]

| Equation number | Intercept | Advertising: sales ratio | Capital requirements (log) | Growth of demand (log) | Local industry dummy variable | Demand elasticity[b] | Concentration ratio times high-ove-all-barrier dummy variable | $R^2$ |
|---|---|---|---|---|---|---|---|---|
| (1) | 0.0337[c] (3.82) | 0.319[d] (2.14) | 0.0110[c] (3.26) | 0.0257[d] (1.94) | 0.0282 (1.57) | — | — | 0.54[c] |
| (2) | 0.0418[c] (4.28) | 0.324[d] (2.23) | 0.0108[c] (3.27) | 0.0253[d] (1.96) | 0.0245 (1.40) | 0.00743[d] (1.71) | — | .58[c] |
| (3) | 0.0411[c] (5.04) | 0.396[c] (2.94) | 0.0112[c] (3.71) | 0.0217[d] (1.83) | 0.0242 (1.51) | 0.00733[c] (3.15) | — | .65[c] |
| (4) | 0.0374[c] (4.30) | 0.265[d] (1.81) | 0.00658 (1.63) | 0.0323[d] (2.43) | 0.0208 (1.17) | — | 0.000383[d] (1.87) | .58[c] |
| (5) | 0.0461[c] (4.82) | 0.268[d] (1.90) | 0.00611 (1.57) | 0.0321[c] (2.51) | 0.0166 (0.97) | 0.00782[d] (1.88) | 0.000400[d] (2.03) | .63[c] |
| (6) | 0.0440[c] (5.48) | 0.346[c] (2.60) | 0.00727[d] (2.02) | 0.0276[d] (2.32) | 0.0179 (1.13) | 0.00698[c] (3.09) | 0.000334[d] (1.83) | .68[c] |

[a] Values of $t$ in parentheses.

[b] The demand elasticity is the short-run coefficient in equations (2) and (5), and the long-run coefficient in equations (3) and (6). Since this variable is generally negative, a positive coefficient indicates that an increase in the absolute value of the elasticity will reduce profit rates.

[c] Statistically significant at the 1-percent level.

[d] Statistically significant at the 5-percent level.

linearity between the demand elasticity and the advertising:sales ratio, since the regression coefficient on the latter variable increases somewhat with the inclusion of the former.

In the light of the great importance of the price elasticity of demand in these equations, we should consider whether there may be a problem of spurious association. These price elasticities are defined as follows:

$$\text{short-run elasticity} = a_3 \, \frac{\bar{P}}{\bar{S}},$$

$$\text{long-run elasticity} = \frac{\lambda a_3}{1 - a_4} \, \frac{\bar{P}}{\bar{S}},$$

where $a_3$, $\lambda$, and $a_4$ are coefficients of the estimated demand functions, $\bar{P}$ is the average relative price of the product for the period 1954 through 1957, and $\bar{S}$ is average real per-capita sales for the same period. In both cases, the estimated coefficients are scaled by the average relative price index for the industry. A positive association between changes in relative prices and profit rates could, as a result, give rise to a possible spurious association between the elasticity as defined above and the profit rate. However, since the interindustry variation in the other elements of the price-elasticity formula ($a_3$, $a_4$, $\lambda$, and $\bar{S}$) is greater than the interindustry variation in relative prices, any biases attributable to this source are probably small.

Since it might be argued that the elasticity of demand, like concentration, should affect prices and profits only where entry is restricted, it is also appropriate to consider an interaction with the high overall entry-barrier dummy. However, a simple product of the two factors would not be appropriate, since the demand elasticities are generally negative numbers, with the highest values equal to zero.[30] In this case, a simple product of the elasticity and the high entry-barrier dummy would equal zero either where entry conditions are low or moderate or where demand is completely *inelastic*. Since an appropriate interaction variable would be zero either where entry conditions are low or moderate or where demand is highly *elastic*, we considered a variable of the form

$$E_H \left[ \frac{1}{1 - e} \right],$$

where $E_H$ is the high overall entry-barrier dummy and $e$ is the demand elasticity, which is constrained to be nonpositive. Only where $E_H$ equals one and demand is highly inelastic, so that $e$ equals or approaches zero, will this variable reach its maximum value of unity.

30. As indicated above, the estimated elasticities in three industries are positive values.

When this interaction variable was used in place of the demand-elasticity variable in the equations given in Table 6.8, however, disappointing results were obtained. When introduced into equations without the concentration-interaction variable, the second interaction variables were both negative, although positive signs were expected, but neither coefficient approached statistical significance. When introduced without the concentration-interaction variable, the estimated coefficients were positive, although again neither were statistically significant. When a three-way interaction was investigated, in which the new variable was multiplied by the four-firm concentration ratio for the industry, the coefficients were positive but never statistically significant, and they did not fit the data as well as the concentration-interaction variable alone. These results therefore suggest that the estimated impact of the elasticity of demand on profit rates, unlike that of concentration, does not depend on the condition of entry.

## HETEROSCEDASTICITY AND WEIGHTED REGRESSIONS

An examination of the residuals from a leading equation (number 5 in Table 6.3) revealed that heteroscedasticity is present, since small industries typically have large residuals. There are two possible reasons for this phenomenon: smaller industries may tend to have fewer firms, so that the variance of average profit rates is larger, and they may also have smaller firms. Previous studies have indicated that the variance of profit rates among small firms is greater than among larger firms,[31] and this would also account for a larger variance for smaller industries.

To determine an appropriate weighting scheme, an empirical approach was adopted. The variance of the residuals was calculated for successive quartiles in the distribution of industry sales. From this analysis, it appears that the use of industry sales is inappropriate as a weighting variable, since it would give too much emphasis to the largest industries. The square root of sales, however, is nearly proportional to the variance of the residuals, and was therefore chosen as a weighting variable.

The weighted regressions were fitted both for all industries and for all industries except motor vehicles, since this industry is an outlying observation with respect to some of the variables, including the weighting variable. The results appear in Tables 6.9 and 6.10. In these equations, $R^2$ for each of the weighted regressions is considerably higher than $R^2$ for its unweighted counter-

31. Sydney S. Alexander, "The Effect of Size of Manufacturing Corporation on the Distribution of the Rate of Return," *Review of Economics and Statistics* (August 1949), pp. 229–235; H. J. Sherman, *Profits in the United States* (Ithaca, N.Y., Cornell University Press, 1968), pp. 116–120.

TABLE 6.9. Coefficients for weighted regressions with advertising:sales ratio[a]

| Equation number | Industry | Intercept | Advertising: sales ratio | Capital requirements (log) | Economies of scale (log) | Growth of demand (log) | Concentration ratio | Local-industry dummy variable | Concentration ratio times high-overall-barrier dummy variable | $R^2$ |
|---|---|---|---|---|---|---|---|---|---|---|
| (1)a | All industries | 0.0367[b] (4.29) | 0.278[c] (1.97) | 0.0118[b] (4.26) | — | 0.0246[c] (2.01) | — | 0.0258[c] (1.76) | — | 0.78[b] |
| b | Motor vehicles excluded | 0.0425[b] (5.30) | 0.417[b] (3.05) | 0.00630[c] (2.00) | — | 0.0245[c] (2.21) | — | 0.0187 (1.38) | — | .70[b] |
| (2)a | All industries | 0.0612[b] (2.63) | 0.259[c] (1.73) | 0.00867[b] (2.76) | 0.00424 (0.91) | 0.0265[c] (2.12) | — | — | — | .76[b] |
| b | Motor vehicles excluded | 0.0690[b] (3.32) | 0.404[b] (2.88) | 0.00289 (0.87) | 0.00484 (1.17) | 0.0258[c] (2.31) | — | — | — | .69[b] |
| (3)a | All industries | 0.0337[b] (3.11) | 0.288[b] (2.00) | 0.00934 (1.55) | — | 0.0273[c] (1.99) | 0.000179 (0.46) | 0.0237 (1.53) | — | .78[b] |
| b | Motor vehicles excluded | 0.0411[b] (4.02) | 0.421[b] (3.02) | 0.00522 (0.92) | — | 0.0258[c] (2.06) | 0.000081 (0.23) | 0.0178 (1.24) | — | .70[b] |
| (4)a | All industries | 0.0444 (5.35) | 0.222[c] (1.70) | 0.00415 (1.11) | — | 0.0347[b] (2.95) | — | 0.0132 (0.93) | 0.000471[b] (2.81) | .82[b] |
| b | Motor vehicles excluded | 0.0458 (5.68) | 0.339[b] (2.40) | 0.00292 (0.80) | — | 0.0312[b] (2.71) | — | 0.0126 (0.92) | 0.00030 (1.68) | .72[b] |

[a]Values of $t$ in parentheses.
[b]Statistically significant at the 1-percent level.
[c]Statistically significant at the 5-percent level.

TABLE 6.10. Coefficients for weighted regressions with high advertising barrier[a]

| Equation number | Industry | Intercept | High advertising barrier | Capital requirements (log) | Economies of scale (log) | Growth of demand (log) | Concentration ratio | Local-industry dummy variable | Concentration ratio times high-overall-barrier dummy variable | $R^2$ |
|---|---|---|---|---|---|---|---|---|---|---|
| (1)a | All industries | 0.0481[b] (6.44) | 0.0359[b] (3.21) | 0.00603[c] (1.91) | — | 0.0300[b] (2.64) | — | 0.0249[c] (1.83) | — | 0.81[b] |
| b | Motor vehicles excluded | 0.0510[b] (6.45) | 0.0323[b] (2.78) | 0.00460 (1.35) | — | 0.0300[b] (2.65) | — | 0.0229 (1.67) | — | .68[b] |
| (2)a | All industries | 0.0832[b] (4.24) | 0.0378[b] (3.35) | 0.00180 (0.53) | 0.00670 (1.64) | 0.0316[b] (2.77) | — | — | — | .80[b] |
| b | Motor vehicles excluded | 0.0900[b] (4.56) | 0.0327[b] (2.83) | −0.00029 (0.08) | 0.00746[c] (1.84) | 0.0312[b] (2.80) | — | — | — | .69[b] |
| (3)a | All industries | 0.0462[b] (4.95) | 0.0361[b] (3.18) | 0.00432 (0.73) | — | 0.0320[b] (2.50) | 0.000122 (0.34) | 0.0235 (1.63) | — | .81[b] |
| b | Motor vehicles excluded | 0.0450[b] (4.99) | 0.0325[b] (2.75) | 0.00377 (0.53) | — | 0.0310[c] (2.42) | 0.000062 (0.17) | 0.0222 (1.54) | — | .68[b] |
| (4)a | All industries | 0.0505[b] (6.69) | 0.0240[c] (1.75) | 0.00310 (0.84) | — | 0.0351[b] (2.99) | — | 0.0176 (1.23) | 0.000299 (1.45) | .82[b] |
| b | Motor vehicles excluded | 0.0521[b] (6.56) | 0.0233[c] (1.69) | 0.00255 (0.67) | — | 0.0344[b] (2.90) | — | 0.0173 (1.20) | 0.000255 (1.18) | .70[b] |

[a]Values of $t$ in parentheses.
[b]Statistically significant at the 1-percent level.
[c]Statistically significant at the 5-percent level.

part. However, this is not surprising, since the weighting procedure deliberately emphasizes industries with smaller residuals and $R^2$ measures the proportion of the weighted variance of the dependent variable explained by the regression equation. Another way of looking at this is that weighting essentially involves multiplying the equation by the root of the weights (in this case by the fourth root of sales) and proceeding by ordinary least squares. The value of $R^2$ indicates the success at predicting profit rates multiplied by the fourth root of sales.[32]

The results are impressive. Nearly 80 percent of the weighted variance across all industries is accounted for by these equations and about 70 percent is explained when the outlying motor vehicle industry is excluded.

The advertising:sales ratio and the high advertising-barrier dummy variable are introduced alternatively; the latter is significant at the 1-percent level in all equations except those that include the concentration-interaction variable, in which the coefficient is significant at the 5-percent level. Where the impact of advertising is measured by the advertising:sales ratio, the estimated regression coefficients are significant at the 5-percent level when the motor vehicle industry is included, and at the 1-percent level otherwise. The collinearity between capital requirements, economies of scale, and concentration is again evident, but, in contrast to the unweighted regressions, the economies-of-scale variable is sometimes significant when introduced alongside capital requirements (and the latter variable is sometimes insignificant).

These results provide additional evidence of the stability of the coefficients for the two advertising variables. They also point to the fact that the impact of concentration is particularly important where entry restrictions are present.

## AN INTERPRETATION

Our primary finding is that heavy advertising leads to increased profits,[33] and here we suggest an interpretation of this result. Advertising in this analysis acts as a proxy for product differentiation, or, more specifically, for the product and market characteristics that permit heavy advertising expenditures to differentiate effectively the products of a firm from those of its rivals.

32. It is important to note that the increase in $R^2$ is no indication that the weighting used is the correct one. Indeed, a very high $R^2$ can be obtained by weighting with industry sales, which is clearly inappropriate. A subsequent test, however, was made on the extent of heteroscedasticity in the weighted regressions themselves. The residuals from Equation (1a) in Table 6.10 were calculated and the successive variances of these residuals were compared with the mean root sales in the relevant quartile. The fact that the two variables were nearly proportional provides some confirmation of the use of the square root of sales as the weighting variable.

33. The results are also consistent with the view that high profits lead to high advertising. This alternate view is examined in some detail in the next chapter.

Although these product and market characteristics are not easily measured, they are typically characterized by heavy advertising expenditures. The measured impact of advertising results then from the impact of product differentiation of profitability and from the effectiveness of heavy advertising expenditures in exploiting the gains from product differentiation.[34]

In the next chapter, we consider the various economic factors that are likely to influence the volume of advertising and present an empirical analysis of the determinants of advertising. Whatever factors are important in this analysis, however, it does appear that the volume of industry advertising expenditures depends on considerations other than the whims of individual managers. Product and market characteristics make advertising a more profitable activity in some industries than in others, and there are no reasons to believe that managers in some industries are more skilled in taking advantage of their opportunities than those in others. In fact, if we assume that managers make their decisions on advertising budgets so as to maximize profits, then the differences among industries that we observe reflect not the discretionary behavior of individuals but rather the particular product and market character- istics of member firms in the industry. They indicate the extent to which heavy advertising permits the achievement of effective product differentiation.

The last consideration is particularly important for interpreting these statisti- cal results. Since the analysis focuses on interindustry differences in advertising outlays, and since these differences are more likely to reflect industry character- istics than the peculiarity of individual managers, the empirical results have few behavioral connotations. They do not imply that an industry can earn higher profit rates simply by spending more on advertising. They do not suggest that firms which currently spend little on advertising should expand their advertising budgets if their objective is to achieve higher returns. Rather they reflect the fact that firms and industries with higher optimal advertising expenditures earn higher rates of return than firms in less advantageous market positions.

In Chapter 4, we suggested that, in some market circumstances, heavy advertising may serve as a barrier to the entry of new firms. In such circum- stances, leading firms will spend large sums on advertising so that high profits may be earned without fear of attracting new firms into the industry. If new

34. Using a framework similar to that presented above, a recent paper found that these empirical results were present also in producers' goods industries. Since advertising is frequently only a secondary source of product differentiation in these industries, the authors concluded that their finding was probably due to the including of many consumer good product lines in these industries. See Louis Esposito and Frances F. Esposito, "Foreign Competition and Domestic Industry Profitability," *Review of Economics and Statistics*, 53 (November 1971), pp. 346–348.

entrants could simply imitate the advertising efforts of established firms and gain comparable levels of consumer acceptance at the same level of expenditures, then high profits would lead to new entry and a subsequent decline in profits. If, on the other hand, new entrants cannot achieve similar market results from the same aggregate volume of expenditures, high profits may represent an equilibrium position for the industry.

A finding, therefore, that high industry outlays on advertising lead directly to high long-run profits indicates that high advertising levels serve to restrict entry. Indeed, the empirical analysis presented in this chapter may be viewed as a test of the entry-preventing effect of heavy advertising. Without this effect, profits in industries characterized by heavy advertising would be no greater on the average than in industries where advertising levels are lower. These results therefore provide empirical confirmation of the hypothesized relation between advertising and entry conditions.

Others have suggested that the effect of advertising on entry barriers has been primarily a subject of speculation. We have presented empirical findings that bear directly on this issue. The presence of restricted entry conditions can be inferred when high profits are maintained through time. To the extent that high profits follow from heavy advertising, there is empirical support for the conclusion that advertising serves as a barrier to entry.

# APPENDIX 6-A  DATA SOURCES AND TECHNICAL ADJUSTMENTS

The industry data used are reported at or aggregated to the level of IRS "minor industries," which are roughly comparable to SIC 3-digit industry groups. The source for each variable is listed in Table 6-A.1.

TABLE 6–A.1.  Sources of data

| Variable | Source |
|---|---|
| Profit rate | IRS *Source Book of Statistics of Income*; average values for 1954–1957 |
| Advertising | IRS *Source Book of Statistics of Income*; average values for 1954–1957 |
| Concentration | George J. Stigler, *Capital and Rates of Return in Manufacturing Industries*, pp. 206–215. |
| Economies of scale relative to market | 1954 *Census of Manufactures* |
| Absolute capital requirements | 1954 *Census of Manufactures* and IRS *Source Book of Statistics of Income* |
| Rate of growth of demand | IRS *Source Book of Statistics of Income* |
| Local-market dummy variables | Carl Kaysen and Donald F. Turner, *Antitrust Policy*, statistical appendix |

The sample was chosen originally to gain complete coverage of all consumer-goods industries. All "miscellaneous" industries were eliminated, however, because of the obvious conceptual problems. In addition, three other industries were dropped from the sample: newspapers, though technically a manufacturing industry, was considered to have sufficient "service" elements to make its inclusion inappropriate; petroleum refining was omitted because of the unusual statistical problems that result from the tax treatment of mineral depletion; and motor vehicle parts was dropped because of the lack of comparable Census data. Average profit rates and advertising:sales ratios for the remaining 41 industries are presented in Table 6-A.2.

TABLE 6–A.2.   Average profit rates and advertising:sales ratios in 41 consumer-goods industries, 1954–1957

| Industry | Profit rate (percent) | Advertising:sales ratio (percent) |
|---|---|---|
| Soft drinks | 10.0 | 6.2 |
| Malt liquors | 7.2 | 6.8 |
| Wines | 7.3 | 5.2 |
| Distilled liquors | 5.0 | 2.1 |
| Meat | 4.6 | 0.6 |
| Dairy products | 7.9 | 2.2 |
| Canning | 6.4 | 2.9 |
| Grain mill products | 7.0 | 1.9 |
| Cereals | 14.8 | 10.3 |
| Bakery products | 9.3 | 2.9 |
| Sugar | 5.8 | 0.2 |
| Confectionery | 10.6 | 3.5 |
| Cigars | 5.3 | 2.6 |
| Cigarettes | 11.5 | 4.8 |
| Knit goods | 3.8 | 1.3 |
| Carpets | 4.5 | 2.0 |
| Hats | 1.6 | 2.2 |
| Men's clothing | 5.9 | 1.2 |
| Women's clothing | 6.1 | 1.8 |
| Millinery | −1.3 | 0.8 |
| Furs | 5.7 | 1.0 |
| Furniture | 9.7 | 1.5 |
| Screens and blinds | 9.3 | 1.6 |
| Periodicals | 11.7 | 0.2 |
| Books | 10.1 | 2.4 |
| Drugs | 14.0 | 9.9 |
| Soaps | 11.7 | 9.2 |

TABLE 6–A.2.   (continued)

| Industry | Profit rate (percent) | Advertising:sales ratio (percent) |
|---|---|---|
| Paints | 9.9 | 1.5 |
| Perfumes | 13.5 | 15.3 |
| Tires and tubes | 10.2 | 1.4 |
| Footwear | 7.6 | 1.5 |
| Hand tools | 11.4 | 4.2 |
| Household and service machinery (nonelectrical) | 7.3 | 1.9 |
| Electrical appliances | 10.3 | 3.5 |
| Radio, TV, and phonograph | 8.8 | 2.2 |
| Motorcycles and bicycles | 5.2 | 1.1 |
| Motor vehicles | 15.5 | 0.6 |
| Instruments | 12.0 | 2.0 |
| Clocks and watches | 1.9 | 5.6 |
| Jewelry (precious metal) | 5.3 | 3.2 |
| Costume jewelry | 1.4 | 4.0 |

The variables are defined and explained in the text. The calculation of the technical entry-barrier variables and the rate of growth of demand involved using both Census and IRS data. The various specific adjustments made to reconcile data drawn from these two sources and reported at different levels of aggregation are described in the next two sections.

## TECHNICAL BARRIERS TO ENTRY

These variables are based on data from the 1954 *Census of Manufactures*. To carry out these computations, it is necessary to relate industries as defined by the Census Bureau to those of the Internal Revenue Service. This is done on the basis suggested by the Census Link Project.[1]

Within SIC 4-digit industries, average plant size among the largest plants that account for 50 percent of industry output is used as the estimate of minimum efficient plant scale (*MES*). Data on shipments are used in all cases where available; in the few remaining cases, the calculations are based on value added. When the ratios of *MES* to industry output are obtained, the average percentage among component 4-digit industries within the relevant

1. U.S. Bureau of the Census, *Enterprise Statistics: 1958, Part 3*, (Washington, D.C., U.S. Government Printing Office, 1964).

IRS industry is calculated, using shipments as weights where available and value added as weights elsewhere.

In determining the capital-requirements variable, the scale of an efficient plant is measured in most instances by the value of shipments but in a few by value added. In the latter cases, these figures are multiplied by the ratio of shipments to value added for the same 4-digit industry but in a later year.

When estimates of *MES* measured in shipments for all 4-digit industries are obtained, these are averaged, using value added as weights, to derive the value in the larger IRS industry. These averages are then multiplied by the appropriate assets:sales ratio for the IRS industry, and the resulting figures are used to represent the level of capital required for efficient entry.

In the case of the motor vehicle industry, Census data are unavailable. Bain's estimates for this industry are therefore used for both the extent of scale economies and the level of capital requirements.

For the three local industries—soft drinks, dairy products, and bakery products—it is assumed that the appropriate market is the typical large metropolitan area. Output data are not available for 4-digit industries by standard metropolitan area. Consequently, value-added data for larger 3-digit groupings are used. Average value added in large metropolitan areas for the 3-digit industry[2] is multiplied by the ratio of total national shipments in the relevant 4-digit industry to total value added in the associated 3-digit industry to obtain the estimate of 4-digit industry shipments within the typical local market. This figure is then used as the denominator in the estimate of *MES* to market for the 4-digit industry.[3] Where necessary, the resulting estimates are aggregated to the IRS minor-industry level as described above.

## RATE OF GROWTH OF DEMAND

This variable is the ratio of IRS gross sales in 1957 to that in 1947. In a few cases, however, IRS data are not available for both years and alternative procedures are used.

In 1947, IRS industries cigars and cigarettes are aggregated as tobacco manufacturers. Census data on the value of shipments in 1947 and 1957 are therefore used to compute this variable for both industries. In 1947, IRS data for screens and venetian blinds are included in miscellaneous furniture. As a result, Census value-added data for both 1947 and 1957 are utilized. Similar

2. Output data were available for 56 Standard Metropolitan Areas for the beverage industry (SIC 208); 59 such areas for bakery products (SIC 205); and 61 such areas for dairy products (SIC 202).

3. These corrections were made for the following subindustries: SIC 2081—bottled soft drinks; SIC 2021—creamery butter; SIC 2027—fluid milk and other products; SIC 2051—bread and related products.

data problems exist in the cases of drugs, perfumes, radio, TV, and phono-
graphs, instruments, and costume jewelry. In all of these instances, Census
data in 1947 and 1957 are used. With regard to perfumes and costume jewelry,
information on value of shipments is available in both years and is therefore
utilized, whereas value-added data are used in the other cases.

# CHAPTER 7 The Determinants of Advertising Expenditures

While the previous chapter examined the impact of advertising on profit rates, the present chapter concerns the determinants of advertising. Why do firms in some industries spend large sums for this purpose while others spend relatively little? As in the previous analysis, our focus is on alternate equilibrium levels of advertising, which depend on the specific product and market characteristics of the industry as well as on the position of individual firms within the industry.

The specification and estimation of cross-section regression equations explaining advertising:sales ratios is therefore the principal objective of this chapter. In the final section, however, this analysis is integrated with the profit-rate analysis of the previous chapter, and simultaneous estimates of equations predicting profit rates and advertising:sales ratios are presented.

Consider the schematic diagram given in Fig. 7.1. As stressed at the conclusion of the previous chapter, our analysis there dealt with the effect of product differentiation, together with other exogenous variables, on profit rates. These relations are indicated by the arrows directed at profits. We emphasized that the coefficient of the advertising variable in the regression equations should be interpreted as indicating the effect on profit rates of the product and market characteristics associated with a given optimal level of advertising rather than with the discretionary volume of advertising set by the firm. Advertising was therefore viewed as a structural rather than a behavioral variable. The advertising variables could therefore be viewed as proxies for the factors associated with product differentiability that cannot be measured.

In this framework, profits may affect advertising in two ways. First, there

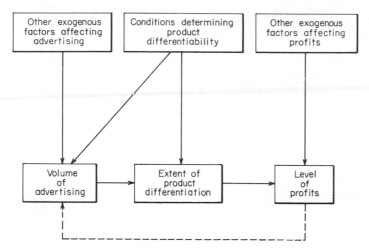

Fig. 7.1.   Schematic diagram on relations between advertising, profits, and
product differentiation

may be a possible direct link from profits to advertising, as represented by the broken line in the diagram. This would be the situation, for example, where firms' spending on advertising is determined in part by guidelines related to available cash flow or to profits. Second, and perhaps more important, because the factors determining product differentiability cannot be measured, the level of profits may represent the influence of these factors on advertising. In either instance, the estimated coefficients for the profit-rate equations in Chapter 6 are biased, and therefore simultaneous-equation estimates of the parameters of these equations are needed.

Ideally, we should specify equations relating advertising directly to the exogenous factors determining the differentiability of the product. Unfortunately, measures of product differentiability, by its nature an *ex ante* concept, are impossible to obtain. Even measures of the *ex post* concept, the degree of product differentiation in the market, are not readily obtainable. We therefore fall back on a more indirect approach, and examine those variables that may be related to the marginal effectiveness of advertising and hence may influence the volume of advertising outlays.

It is convenient to divide the possible variables that we shall consider into those that relate to the characteristics of demand in the market and those that relate to the interaction of producers within the market. Three variables related to the characteristics of product demand are used: the rate of growth of demand, a dummy variable distinguishing durable from nondurable products, and the price elasticity of demand. We now examine the rationale for including each of these variables.

## DETERMINANTS OF ADVERTISING: DEMAND VARIABLES

As noted in Chapter 2, the demand for advertising by consumers must be distinguished from the demand for advertising by firms. While the latter demand is operative in the market, consumer behavior affects the volume of advertising through two channels. First, the extent of consumer disutility with the receipt of advertising messages may have a significant impact on the effective supply schedule for these messages. Second, the effectiveness of advertising in influencing consumer decisions has a major effect on advertising budgets. Since advertising effectiveness is likely to differ among the products produced in different industries, we examine this matter in some detail.

In large part, the factors that determine consumer demand for advertising also influence the effectiveness of advertising. As mentioned above,[1] these factors reflect largely the cost of and returns from alternative sources of information. Where the cost of gaining more objective information is low, or prospective returns are high, consumers rely less on advertising and the effectiveness of advertising messages is correspondingly low. In the opposite circumstances, the level of advertising effectiveness is relatively high.

Various hypotheses regarding the effectiveness of advertising are suggested by this approach. The first is that for equal costs of search and equal distribution of relative prices, more objective information will be sought where consumer budgets for a particular commodity class are generally high than where they are low. A given percentage decline in price represents a larger saving in the first case than the second and, therefore, more effort will be spent in obtaining information from more objective sources. Where consumer budgets are high, therefore, advertising effectiveness is likely to be low, and advertising budgets are likely to be smaller.

Advertising effectiveness will depend also on the cost of gaining better information. Where relevant product information can be readily obtained by inspection, for example, there will be less need for more costly alternative sources of information. There will also be less need for strong reliance on advertising. On the other hand, where significant features of the product are not revealed by inspection, alternative sources of information become more important. The costs of search may therefore be heavily dependent on whether essential product characteristics are revealed through inspection or whether other sources of information are required to determine the quality of the product. Advertising messages should have a smaller impact on consumer decisions in the former case than in the latter.

This hypothesis follows from our discussion of the effects of alternative

1. See Chapter 2, pp. 12–14.

sources of consumer information but is also consistent with the observations of others. In his classic study of the impact of advertising, Borden argued that these messages are likely to be particularly effective when "hidden qualities of the product" are important to the consumer:

> When these hidden qualities are present, consumers tend to rely upon the brand, and advertising can be used to associate the presence of the qualities with the brand. Conversely, when the characteristics of a product which are significant to a consumer can be judged at time of purchase, brand tends to lose some of its significance and advertising is not needful in building mental associations regarding these characteristics.

The important issue is whether a "buyer can inspect the articles and judge their worth at the time of purchase."[2]

Consumer information is gained from experience with the product as well as from inspection. To the extent that consumers gain information from accumulated experience with a product, the impact of advertising on consumer decisions should be relatively low.[3] What should be important here is the frequency with which a product is purchased in a time period within which product characteristics are relatively stable.[4]

Two variables are included in the empirical analysis in an attempt to allow for the effects of these factors. The first is the rate of growth of demand in the industry. Since consumer experience with a product is likely to be inversely related to advertising effectiveness, we expect to find newer products associated with a high volume of advertising. Moreover, if newer products are characterized by relatively high rates of growth demand, rapid demand growth should also be associated with higher advertising.

Another variable related to the characteristic discussed above is the simple distinction between durable and nondurable products. However, the net effect of this factor on advertising cannot be determined a priori. Consumer budgets per unit of time on many consumer nondurables are quite low, which suggests relatively extensive advertising. However, these products are generally purchased quite frequently, which suggests the opposite. Note, however, that frequency of purchase is important because it leads to in-

2. Neil H. Borden, *The Economic Effects of Advertising* (Chicago, R. D. Irwin, 1944), pp. 425–426.

3. A similar hypothesis is put forward in Peter Doyle, "Advertising Expenditure and Consumer Demand," *Oxford Economic Papers*, 20 (November 1968), 405.

4. Even if a consumer had purchased a new automobile every year so that at age 50 he had purchased 25, he might still have accumulated little information regarding, say, the distribution of repair costs in view of changing product qualities over time.

creased consumer experience with the product. Where this effect of purchase frequency is absent, either because product characteristics are effectively hidden from the consumer, as in the case of various drugs, or because new product varieties are continually introduced, consumer experience with the product will fail to develop, and advertising effectiveness may remain high. Since the two effects of durability on the effectiveness of advertising are not necessarily equal, this product attribute is introduced into the empirical analysis to indicate the net effect of these two factors.

An additional demand variable that may influence the volume of advertising is the price elasticity of demand. Since the original work of Dorfman and Steiner, the importance of this factor has been recognized.[5] Their analysis implied that for a given functional relation between advertising and its marginal effect on sales, the more elastic is demand and the smaller is the (signed) price elasticity of demand for the firm, the smaller is the optimal level of advertising.

The Dorfman-Steiner result applies to the elasticity of the firm's demand curve, which of course must be distinguished from the elasticity of the market demand curve. However, any difference between the two elasticities is specifically foreclosed in their model, which refers to monopolistic markets. Although the firm's elasticity may be influenced by the market parameter, it is affected by other factors as well, and indeed in the case of pure competition is infinite, regardless of the market elasticity.[6] Given possible divergences between the two elasticities, the relationship between advertising and the market elasticity of demand requires further consideration.

Although, when other factors are held constant, higher market elasticities may be expected to result in higher firm elasticities, this does not establish that more elastic market demand curves lead to less advertising. Since advertising is frequently designed specifically to reduce firm demand elasticities, we cannot look to the cet. par. relationship for this purpose. Rather, we need to consider the effect of the market elasticity on the incentive to spend funds on advertising and on the interaction that exists between advertising and the market elasticity. When the market demand curve is relatively elastic, firm demand curves may be similarly elastic unless substantial advertising is carried out to achieve effective product differentiation. In these circumstances, the

5. Robert Dorfman and Peter O. Steiner, "Optimal Advertising and Optimal Quality," *American Economic Review*, 44 (1954), pp. 828–836.
6. The relationship between market and firm demand elasticities forms the basis of the Rothschild index of monopoly. See K. W. Rothschild, "The Degree of Monopoly," *Economica*, n.s., 9 (February 1942), 24–40; and John Perry Miller, "Measures of Monopoly Power and Concentration: Their Economic Significance," NBER, *Business Concentration and Price Policy* (1955), pp. 125–126.

firm's demand elasticity, and the price it can set, depend on the volume of advertising. The marginal return from advertising is therefore relatively high. In the opposite case, however, when the market demand curve is already inelastic, the gains from heavy advertising, and hence the marginal return on these expenditures, may be lower. Thus the market elasticity is likely to affect the marginal return from advertising as well as the firm's elasticity. As a result, the net effect of the market elasticity of demand on the volume of advertising cannot be determined analytically.

This conclusion can be seen with the help of a diagram used originally by Dorfman and Steiner.[7] In Fig. 7.2, both the marginal gross return from ad-

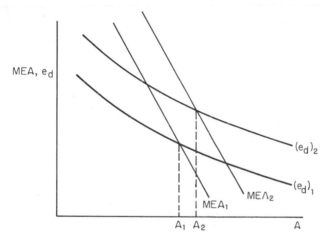

Fig. 7.2.　Advertising and the price elasticity of firm demand

vertising $MEA$ and the firm's elasticity of demand $e_d$ are measured on the vertical axis, and the volume of advertising $A$ is indicated on the horizontal axis. If the two variables decline with advertising, the functions are as drawn, and the equilibrium value is given by their intersection.[8] Since both functions shift upward as the market elasticity increases, two pairs of functions are drawn, the pair with subscript 2 being reached at a higher level of the market elasticity. As drawn, a higher market elasticity is associated with a larger volume of advertising, but this is arbitrary and depends on the relative effect of the market elasticity on the firm elasticity and the marginal returns from advertising.

7. See Dorfman and Steiner, "Optimal Advertising and Optimal Quality," Figure 1C, p. 829.

8. Dorfman and Steiner note that the second order conditions require that the MEA function cut the $e_d$ function from above and argue that this is typically the case. *Ibid.*, pp. 829–830.

This discussion suggests that the direction of the impact of the market elasticity of demand cannot be determined a priori, but rather depends on the relative strength of conflicting effects. However, the direction of the effect of a change in the market elasticity at *given* profit margins can be unambiguously determined. Under conditions of profit maximization, the elasticity of firm demand is given by the profit margin (because $(P - MC)/P = 1/-e$), and therefore the net impact of market elasticities on advertising expenditures must depend on other considerations. Hence, following the arguments suggested above, the more elastic is the market demand curve and the lower is the (signed) price elasticity of demand, the higher is likely to be the volume of advertising.

## DETERMINANTS OF ADVERTISING: MARKET STRUCTURE VARIABLES

The effectiveness of advertising on the sales and profits of an individual firm depends not only on the characteristics of the demand for its products, but also on the extent to which the firm benefits from its advertising activities with respect to other firms in the industry and to potential entrants. Advertising has some characteristics of a public good, and there may be positive or negative effects of a firm's advertising upon the sales of other firms in the industry. These external effects raise two issues. The first is the extent to which the benefits to the firm diverge from the benefits to the industry and the direction of this divergence. The second is the extent to which firms may anticipate a reaction by their competitors to any increase in their advertising. Both factors affect the marginal gain to the firm from additional investments in advertising.

Where the product is homogeneous, the advertising of any one producer leads to increased sales for all. Since the individual firm does not benefit from these positive externalities, we should expect advertising to be very low in markets in which a large number of small firms produce a relatively homogeneous product. As concentration increases in such an industry, previously external benefits become internalized; under conditions of monopoly, they are fully internalized. Hence, for relatively homogeneous products, we should expect a positive relation between concentration and the level of advertising.

Where the product is heterogeneous—as a result either of other factors or of advertising activities, or both—the situation is more complex. In markets with a large number of firms, there is now the strong likelihood that advertising will primarily benefit the individual firm at the expense of its competitors. In contrast to the homogeneous products case, there are now *negative* externalities, which the firm will ignore in determining its own advertising outlays.

An increase in concentration in such a market gives rise to conflicting effects. The negative externalities become internalized and hence act to deter advertising. If concentration increases to the point where an oligopolistic market structure is reached, firms may anticipate that their rivals will react to an increase in their advertising, which provides an additional deterrent to increases in advertising. Both of these factors would suggest a *negative* relation between concentration and the level of advertising in such markets. On the other hand, to the extent that increases in concentration result in higher price-cost margins, the benefits from additional advertising are increased. Furthermore, given the difficulties of competing through price in an oligopolistic situation, advertising may become the main channel of rivalry between competing producers, suggesting that an increase in concentration up to a certain point might lead to increased advertising activities as rivals respond competitively to each other's advertising. In this case, of course, when concentration increases to the point where either monopoly or fully collusive oligopoly is reached, we would expect advertising to decline. The total effect of concentration on advertising would therefore appear to be ambiguous in the case of heterogeneous products, but the partial effect—at given price-cost margins— will be negative unless the impact of advertising on entry barriers is strong.

Where entry-limit pricing exists, the effects of the firm's own advertising upon entry barriers will become more important as the size of the representative firm increases in relation to the market. Furthermore, to the extent that rivals' advertising also raises entry barriers, the recognition of mutual interdependence, which occurs under tight oligopoly conditions, could possibly provide a further stimulus to advertising where the entry-barrier effects of the group's advertising are strong.

In the case of relatively homogeneous products, these entry-barrier effects may be weak, but to the extent that they occur, they reinforce the positive relation between concentration and advertising that would otherwise exist. In the case of heterogeneous products, the effects of advertising upon entry barriers are likely to be stronger, and, more important, they will give rise to a positive partial association between advertising and concentration opposite to the negative partial association resulting from the sales externalities discussed above.

The expected qualitative partial effects of changes in concentration upon the volume of advertising under alternative market situations are depicted in Table 7.1. Given the possible ambiguity of the effect of concentration on advertising, the correct specification would involve the interaction of concentration with some measure of product differentiability. In the absence of such a measure, we simply include concentration in the equation determining advertising:sales ratios with no a priori restriction on its sign.

TABLE 7.1. Qualitative effects of concentration on advertising under different market conditions[a]

|  | Type of product | |
|---|---|---|
| Entry condition | Heterogeneous | Homogeneous |
| Blockaded | − | + |
| Limit pricing: | | |
| Weak effects of advertising on entry barriers | − | + |
| Strong effects of advertising on entry barriers | + | + |

[a]This table shows the direction of the *partial* effects on relative advertising levels of increases in concentration, all other variables, in particular price-cost margins, being held constant.

As suggested above, heavy advertising outlays tend to raise barriers to the entry of new firms, which should also influence advertising decisions. To understand the nature of this effect, we consider how the decisions of the firm are affected by the condition of entry. The discussion presented here is based on the analysis of a formal model of the firm's advertising and pricing decisions presented in the appendix to this chapter.[9] To simplify the discussion, we first assess the case where the firm is either a monopolist or a monopolistic competitor. Subsequently, we determine the extent to which the recognition of oligopolistic rivalry may affect our conclusions.

The general conditions determining the optimal volume of advertising by the firm are: under blockaded entry ($PL \geq PM$),

$$(PM - MC)(Q_A + A_{A'} \frac{dA'}{dA}) = 1; \tag{1}$$

under limit pricing ($PL < PM$),

$$(PL - MC)(Q_A + Q_{A'} \frac{dA'}{dA}) - Q_P(MC - MR)$$

$$(PL_A + PL_{A'} \frac{dA'}{dA}) = 1, \tag{2}$$

where $PM$ is the unconstrained profit maximizing price, $PL$ is the entry limit price, $Q$ is output, $MC$ is marginal production cost, $A$ is advertising by the firm, $A'$ is advertising by the firm's rivals, $MR$ is marginal revenue, and subscripts indicate partial derivatives.

Under unconstrained maximization, $MR = MC$, and the second term in

9. A similar model has been employed by Williamson. See Oliver E. Williamson, "Selling Expense as a Barrier to Entry," *Quarterly Journal of Economics*, 77 (February 1963), 112–128.

equation (2) vanishes. Under limit pricing, $MC > MR$, and the second term is necessarily positive.[10]

From these two conditions, the special cases where oligopolistic rivalry does not exist may be determined by setting $dA'/dA = 0$. Under blockaded entry,

$$(PM - MC)Q_A = 1. \tag{3}$$

Note that, since $(PM - MC)/PM = 1/-e_d$, this condition is equivalent to the Dorfman-Steiner result. Under limit pricing,

$$(PL - MC)Q_A - Q_P (MC - MR) PL_A = 1. \tag{4}$$

We can make use of these conditions to determine the probable impact of the different variables in the model on the volume of advertising under various conditions. In this analysis, we require the additional assumption that the marginal effect of advertising on output sold $Q_A$ diminishes as the volume of advertising increases over the relevant range.[11] Given this assumption, we can observe the partial effect of any variable through its effect on the foregoing conditions. Where a variable has a positive effect on the left-hand side of an equation, this indicates that advertising must increase in order to reduce $Q_A$ sufficiently to satisfy the relevant maximization condition.

Table 7.2 presents a tabulation of the direction of the partial effects of changes in specified variables under a variety of market conditions. Note that for many of the variables, the direction of this effect can be determined unambiguously.

Several interesting implications of these conditions can be noted. First, comparing the limit-pricing and the blockaded-entry conditions, we note that the second term is necessarily positive when the limit-pricing constraint is binding, since marginal costs exceed marginal revenue under such conditions. Hence, comparing two industries with the same realized profit margin, $P - MC$, we expect, other things being equal, that advertising will be *lower* where entry is blockaded, that is, where entry barriers are relatively high.

Since the height of the entry barrier is determined partly by the volume of advertising and partly by technical and financial factors, there would appear to be an element of simultaneity here. We obviate this difficulty be allowing only high technical entry barriers to influence advertising in the regression analysis presented below.

From Table 7.2 it is clear also that the only variables that apparently have an ambiguous partial effect on the volume of advertising are the limit price and

10. Since $Q_P < 0$, and $[PL_A + PL_{A'} \dfrac{dA'}{dA}] \geq 0$.

11. We also assume that $PL_A$ is not decreasing over the relevant range.

TABLE 7.2.  Direction of the partial effects[a] of changes in variables upon the volume of advertising

| Variable | Symbol | Entry condition | |
|---|---|---|---|
| | | Blockaded (unconstrained maximization) | Limit pricing |
| A. *Ignoring oligopolistic interdependence*[b] | | | |
| Price-cost margin[c] | $P - MC$ | $+$ | $+$ |
| Limit price[d] | $PL$ | $0$ | $+$ if $Q_A > -2Q_P PL_A$<br>$-$ if $Q_A < -2Q_P PL_A$ |
| Effect of advertising | $PL_A$ | $0$ | $+$ |
| Effect of advertising on output | $Q_A$ | $+$ | $+$ |
| B. *Oligopolistic interdependence recognized*[e] | | | |
| Strength of rivals' response | $\dfrac{dA'}{dA}$ | $+$ for homogeneous products<br>$-$ for heterogeneous products | $+$ for homogeneous products |
| | | | heterogeneous products:<br>$+$ if $(-Q_P)$<br>$(MC - MR)PL_{A'} >$<br>$(PL - MC)(-Q_{A'})$<br>$-$ if $(PL - MC)(-Q_{A'}) >$<br>$(MC - MR)PL_{A'}(-Q_P)$ |
| Limit price | | $0$ | $+$ if $(Q_A + Q_{A'} \dfrac{dA'}{dA}) >$<br><br>$(PL_A + PL_{A'} \dfrac{dA'}{dA})$<br>$(-2Q_P)$<br>$-$ if $(-2Q_P)$<br>$(PL_A + PL_{A'} \dfrac{dA'}{dA}) >$<br><br>$(Q_A + Q_{A'} \dfrac{dA'}{dA})$ |
| Other variables | | Same as in Part A | |

C. *Notation*

$P$ = Price

$MC$ = Marginal production costs

$PL$ = Limit price: price above which entry will occur

$PM$ = Unconstrained profit-maximizing price; under limit pricing, $PM > PL$

Table 7.2.    (continued)

$PL_A$ = Partial effect of change in firm's advertising on limit price

$Q_A$ = Partial effect of change in firm's advertising on output

$Q_P$ = Partial effect on output of change in price

$\dfrac{dA'}{dA}$ = Total effect of change in firm's advertising on advertising of rivals

$PL_{A'}$ = Partial effect of change in rivals' advertising on limit price

$Q_{A'}$ = Partial effect of change in rivals' advertising on output sold by firm: for homogeneous product, $Q_{A'} > 0$; for heterogeneous product, $Q_{A'} < 0$

$e_d$ = Price elasticity of demand

---

[a]These partial effects are determined from the maximization conditions derived in Appendix 7–A.

[b]Part A of this table would apply to monopolistic or monopolistically competitive markets, and to oligopolistic markets where the firm ignores rivals' reactions.

[c]Under blockaded entry, $P = PM$; under limit pricing, $P = PL$. The partial effect shown in the latter case is determined at given values of $MC - MR$.

[d]Under blockaded entry, this partial effect takes into account the dependence of output sold on the limit price.

[e]Part B of this table would apply where the firm takes into account its rivals' advertising responses. Note that we assume throughout that oligopolistic uncertainty does not affect the pricing decision.

the strength of rivals' advertising response. When the limit-price constraint is binding, an increase in the limit price gives rise to the effects of opposite sign. First, the rise in the limit price increases profit margins, which stimulates advertising. Second, this rise will reduce the gap between marginal cost and marginal revenue, which tends to reduce advertising. The precise condition determining the direction of the net effect is derived in Appendix 7-A and shown in Table 7.2. However, since variations in the limit price must, by definition, be accompanied by variations in entry barriers, the ambiguity discussed here has to do with the joint impact of an increase in entry barriers and in net profit margins. Although this joint impact may be either positive or negative, depending on the relative importance of limit pricing and of unconstrained pricing, the *partial* effects of the profit margin and the technical entry-barrier variables remain unambiguously positive and negative respectively.

Unlike the situation under blockaded entry, the price elasticity of the firm's demand curve under limit pricing may have an independent influence. As demand becomes less elastic, marginal revenues would fall, thereby increasing the second term in equation (2). Hence, other things being equal, advertising would tend to increase, suggesting that this (signed) elasticity should have a positive effect. For the reason presented above, however, changes in the market elasticity of demand may influence not only the price elasticity of the firm's demand curve, but also the marginal effectiveness of the firm's advertising. Hence, under limit pricing, the effect of the market elasticity of demand remains undetermined for it depends on the relative strengths of conflicting factors.

In the light of our earlier discussion of the role of concentration, it is interesting to note that the effects of an increase in rivals' response (or in the firm's recognition of their response) have an ambiguous effect. For the cases of homogeneous products and for heterogeneous products where the effect of advertising on the limit price is sufficiently strong (and the firm is constrained by the limit price), the recognition of rivals' reactions has a *positive* effect on the volume of advertising. In the case of heterogeneous products under unconstrained profit maximization or under limit pricing with relatively weak effects of advertising on the entry-limit price, the recognition of rivals' reactions will have a *negative* effect on the volume of advertising. These results are consistent with the arguments presented above regarding the effects of an increase in concentration, since both rivals' responses and the firm's recognition of them are likely to be larger in more concentrated markets.

Finally, we should note that the recognition of mutual interdependence affects the relative strengths of the impact of the other variables. For example, where a strong response by rivals is recognized, the effects of changes in the profit margin on the volume of advertising will be strengthened in the case of homogeneous products and weakened in the case of heterogeneous products. However, since both interactions would unduly complicate the analysis, no attempt was made to incorporate them into the regression equations presented in the following section.

## REGRESSION ANALYSIS OF ADVERTISING:SALES RATIOS

This analysis has pointed to the importance of several variables for inclusion in cross-section regression equations explaining advertising. One of these variables is the profit margin on sales. However, our earlier results indicate that this variable cannot be treated as exogenous, since it is itself influenced by advertising and by some of the exogenous variables discussed above. This indicates that both the advertising and the profit equations need to be estimated by means of simultaneous estimation techniques.

Although we have derived a list of variables for inclusion in the structural equation determining advertising, we can assign a priori restrictions on the signs of these coefficients in only three cases. Profit margins and the rate of growth of demand should have a positive effect on advertising, and entry barriers resulting from technical conditions should have a negative effect. For the remaining variables—the price elasticity of demand, the dummy variable identifying product durability, and the concentration ratio—the direction of the effects on advertising cannot be specified a priori for the reasons given above.

As in the case of the profit-rate equations, the dependent variable must be scaled by an appropriate measure of industry size in order to avoid associations that reflect variations in industry size alone. The advertising:sales ratio was therefore selected as the dependent variable in the equation explaining advertising, and the profit margin on sales (net of advertising) was specified as a possible determinant of advertising:sales ratios. The remaining independent variables in the equation—the rate of growth of demand, the price elasticity of demand, industrial concentration, and the two dummy variables identifying durable goods and industries with high technical entry barriers—do not require further scaling.

Before we examine the estimated regression equations, it is interesting to consider the distribution of advertising:sales ratios across the 41 industries in the sample. The distribution is highly skewed. Twenty-seven industries have advertising:sales ratios below 3 percent, eight have ratios between 3 and 6 percent, and only six have ratios that exceed 6 percent. In the latter group perfumes have an advertising:sales ratio of 15 percent; cereals and drugs, 10 percent each; soap, 9 percent; malt liquor, 7 percent; and soft drinks, slightly more than 6 percent. At lower levels, cigarettes and wines have ratios of about 5 percent each. These figures suggest that the major effects of advertising are not likely to be felt generally throughout this sector of the economy, but rather are concentrated in a smaller subset of industries. In most industries, even in the consumer-goods sector of the economy, advertising probably plays a relatively minor role, although it appears to play a substantial role in a few others.

An additional feature of this distribution is that the set of industries with advertising:sales ratios above 6 percent is composed entirely of the producers of nondurables. Industries that produce consumer durables appear to spend less on advertising as a proportion of sales. Despite the greater frequency of purchase typical of nondurables, the blandishments of advertising messages are likely to have greater impact on consumer decisions in these industries.

The effect on advertising:sales ratios of product durability as well as other factors are reflected in the regression-equations presented in Table 7.3. Only the first equation applies to all 41 industries in the sample. As can be seen, the association between the consumer-nondurables sector and heavy advertising is again indicated by a significant negative coefficient on the durable-industry dummy variable. In addition, the presence of high entry barriers, which are

**TABLE 7.3.** Coefficients of regression equations explaining advertising:sales ratios[a]

| Equation number | Intercept | Durable-industry dummy variable | High-technical-barrier dummy variable | Growth of demand (log) | Concentration ratio (log) | Demand elasticity[b] | No. of industries | $R^2$ |
|---|---|---|---|---|---|---|---|---|
| (1) | -0.00565 (0.20) | -0.0178[c] (1.69) | -0.0154 (1.16) | 0.0204 (1.55) | 0.0118 (1.38) | — | 41 | 0.17 |
| (2) | -0.00567 (0.19) | -0.0212[c] (1.94) | -0.0135 (0.98) | 0.0199 (1.49) | 0.0127 (1.40) | — | 38 | .19 |
| (3) | -0.00888 (0.29) | -0.0224[c] (1.99) | -0.0137 (0.98) | 0.0206 (1.52) | 0.0129 (1.41) | -0.00264 (0.53) | 38 | .20 |
| (4) | -0.00727 (0.25) | -0.0234[c] (2.14) | -0.0110 (0.80) | 0.0222 (1.67) | 0.0117 (1.30) | -0.00369 (1.31) | 38 | .23 |

[a]Values of $t$ in parentheses.
[b]The estimated short-run coefficients are used in equation (3), and the long-run coefficients in equation (4).
[c]Statistically significant at the 5-percent level.

due to scale economies or high capital requirements, have the expected depressing effect on advertising, whereas concentration has a positive influence. However, neither coefficient is statistically significant at conventional levels. The rate of growth of demand also has the expected positive effect, but its coefficient is also not statistically significant.

What is disappointing about this equation, of course, is the lack of statistical significance of the variables and the low value of the coefficient of multiple determination. The four independent variables explain only about 17 percent of the total variation in advertising:sales ratios, and the multiple-determination coefficient is not statistically significant. What this suggests is that we have not measured the primary factors that determine the effectiveness of advertising expenditures, and this failure has severely restricted the explanatory power of the equation. These omitted variables are related to the extent to which the product can be readily differentiated by advertising.

As indicated previously, estimates of the price elasticity of demand are available for 38 of the 41 industries in the sample. The equation is reestimated for these 38 industries, and the short-run and long-run demand elasticities are added to the equation. As can be seen, the estimated coefficients for this variable are both negative, although neither is statistically significant. Although a negative coefficient runs counter to the sign predicted by the Dorfman-Steiner model, under the assumption that typical firm demand elasticities resemble their market counterparts, a negative relation can be explained by the analysis indicated in Fig. 7.2. To the extent that relatively elastic market demands provide an incentive to increase advertising, precisely to create more inelastic demands for the firm, the relation between market and typical firm demand elasticities may be weak. In such a case, there is no contradiction between these results and the implications of the Dorfman-Steiner model.

## A TWO-EQUATION MODEL EXPLAINING ADVERTISING AND PROFITS

To this point, we have not examined empirically the effect of profit margins on the volume of advertising. For this purpose, a two-equation model is needed in which both profits and advertising are endogenous variables. A second but equally important objective of this analysis is to examine the apparent effect of simultaneous-equation bias in the advertising coefficients in the profit rate equations given in the previous chapter.

Just above, a model of optimal advertising expenditures was discussed in which advertising was influenced by the profit margins realized in the industry. There are, however, other explanations of a possible effect of profits on advertising. Profits constitute a major share of residual funds after obligatory expenses, and advertising is sometimes viewed as a deduction from this residual. Thus, in a review of firm budgetary procedures, it was reported that "treating advertising expenditures as a discretionary deduction from profits rather than an unavoidable cost of marketing" was a common practice.[12] In many instances, the degree of ignorance of the prospective impact of advertising is high and these outlays are a form of "playing it safe." And the extent to which this policy is pursued depends on the volume of discretionary funds. In this approach, advertising budgets are based on the level of cash flow before deduction of advertising expenditures.[13]

A simultaneous-equation model is appropriate not only because of the possible presence of reverse causality in the profit rate equation, but also because the error terms in the two structural equations are likely to be negatively correlated. Profits and advertising are linked by the identity that profits net of all deductions are derived from gross cash flow by deducting depreciation, income taxes, and advertising. Because of this linkage, transitory variations in advertising will probably be *negatively* associated with profits net of advertising. There may be other factors—omitted variables that have a common influence on both advertising and profits—which could, of course, give rise to a positive association of the error terms. However, because of the above-mentioned identity, the possibility exists of a fairly strong negative association that could affect the direction of the simultaneous equation bias in the ordinary least squares estimates of the profit and advertising equations.

Each simultaneous equation model includes two equations and an identity. The two equations explain the variability in profit rates and in advertising: sales ratios; the identity denotes the relation between some of the variables in the right-hand sides of the two equations. Two alternative specifications are made of each equation, so that four separate models are estimated. Following the results of Chapter 6, the structural variables in the profit rate equation are: the advertising:sales ratio, the volume of absolute capital requirements (in logarithmic form), the rate of growth of demand (in logarithmic form), and a local industry dummy variable. In addition, the product of the concentration ratio and the high-overall-entry-barrier dummy variable is included in specifications of the profit-rate equation for Models I and II. As indicated above, however, there is necessarily some collinearity between this interaction variable and the advertising:sales ratio, and therefore the profit rate equation is also estimated without this variable in Models III and IV.

12. Walter Taplin, *Advertising: A New Approach* (Boston, Little, Brown, 1963), p. 232.
13. In the empirical analysis, both the profit rate on sales and the ratio of cash flow to sales are used as explanatory variables, although both are calculated net of advertising because of the statistical problem which would be encountered by including advertising on both sides of a regression equation.

In the advertising equation, the structural variables are: the rate of growth of demand (in logarithmic form), a durable industry dummy variable, the concentration ratio (in logarithmic form), and the high-technical-entry-barrier dummy variable. These variables are the ones included in Table 7.3 above.[14] In addition, the ratio of after-tax profits to sales (Models I and III) and of cash flow after taxes to sales (Models II and IV) are included in alternative specifications of this equation.

When the first specification of this equation is used, the appropriate identity in the model is

$$\frac{\text{Profits}}{\text{Sales}} = \frac{\text{Profits}}{\text{Equity}} \cdot \frac{\text{Equity}}{\text{Sales}},$$

and the Equity:Sales ratio is treated as an exogenous variable. The identity appropriate for the second specification is

$$\frac{\text{Cash flow}}{\text{Sales}} = \frac{\text{Profits}}{\text{Equity}} \cdot \frac{\text{Equity}}{\text{Sales}} + \frac{\text{Depreciation}}{\text{Sales}}.$$

In this model, both the Equity:Sales ratio and the Depreciation:Sales ratio are considered exogenous.[15]

The precise specifications of the equations are shown in Tables 7.4 and 7.5. The models used may be summarized as follows:

Model I includes the concentration–high-entry-barrier interaction term in the profit rate equation, and net profits on sales in the advertising equation;

Model II includes the interaction term in the profit rate equation and the cash-flow:sales ratio in the advertising equation;

Model III excludes the interaction term and includes net profits on sales;

Model IV excludes the interaction term and includes the cash flow:sales ratio.

The estimated coefficients for the four simultaneous-equation models are given in Tables 7.4 and 7.5. Each equation is estimated both by ordinary least squares and by two-stage least squares.[16]

14. Estimated demand elasticities are not included in the first set of equations because the analysis was carried out for the complete set of industries in the sample.

15. A related two-equation model in which advertising and concentration are the two endogenous variables is presented in Douglas F. Greer, "Advertising and Market Concentration," *Southern Economic Journal*, 38 (July 1971), 19–32.

16. In the first stage of the two-stage least squares estimation, each dependent variable was regressed on all of the exogenous variables, including the equity: sales ratio (and, in the case of the cash flow model, the depreciation: sales ratio). The predicted values of the advertising:sales ratio were then used in the second stage estimation of the profit rate equations. Predicted values of the profit:sales (or cash flow:sales) ratios were generated from the predicted values of the profit rate on equity using the relevant identity. These values were then used in the second stage estimates of the equations explaining advertising:sales ratios.

TABLE 7.4. Coefficients for simultaneous regression equations: models I and II[a]

| Model | Dependent variable | Estimation method | Intercept | Advertising: sales ratio | Profit rate on sales | Cash flow rate on sales | Capital requirements (log) | Growth of demand (log) | Local industry dummy variable | Durable-industry dummy variable | Concentration ratio times high-overall-barrier dummy variable | Concentration ratio (log) | High-technical-barrier dummy variable |
|---|---|---|---|---|---|---|---|---|---|---|---|---|---|
| I 1 | Profit rate | OLSQ | 0.0398[c] (4.94) | 0.254[b] (1.78) | — | — | 0.00577 (1.60) | 0.0339[c] (2.68) | 0.0184 (1.07) | — | 0.000345[b] (2.03) | — | — |
| 2 | Profit rate | 2SLSQ | 0.0341[c] (3.49) | 0.501[b] (1.92) | — | — | 0.00580 (1.55) | 0.0303[b] (2.24) | 0.0174 (0.97) | — | 0.000317 (1.48) | — | — |
| 3 | Advertising: sales ratio | OLSQ | 0.00116 (0.05) | — | 0.875[c] (3.09) | — | — | -0.00174 (0.13) | — | -0.0140 (1.47) | — | 0.00459 (0.57) | -0.0169 (1.42) |
| 4 | Advertising: sales ratio | 2SLSQ | 0.00451 (0.18) | — | 0.980[c] (3.07) | — | — | -0.00329 (0.23) | — | -0.0136 (1.41) | — | 0.00283 (0.34) | -0.0168 (1.41) |
| II 2 | Profit rate | 2SLSQ | 0.0339[c] (3.47) | 0.507[b] (1.95) | — | — | 0.00580 (1.54) | 0.0302[b] (2.23) | 0.0174 (0.97) | — | 0.000315 (1.47) | — | — |
| 3 | Advertising: sales ratio | OLSQ | -0.00772 (0.30) | — | — | 0.696[c] (2.95) | — | -0.00220 (0.15) | — | -0.0163[b] (1.69) | — | 0.00611 (0.76) | -0.0192 (1.60) |
| 4 | Advertising: sales ratio | 2SLSQ | -0.00563 (0.22) | — | — | 0.716[c] (2.84) | — | -0.00204 (0.14) | — | -0.0162[b] (1.69) | — | 0.00521 (0.64) | -0.0190 (1.57) |

[a]Values of $t$ in parentheses.
[b]Statistically significant at the 5-percent level.
[c]Statistically significant at the 1-percent level.

TABLE 7.5. Coefficients for simultaneous regression equations: models III and IV[a]

| Model | Dependent variable | Estimation method | Intercept | Advertising: sales ratio | Profit rate on sales | Cash flow rate on sales | Capital requirements (log) | Growth of demand (log) | Local industry dummy variable | Durable-industry dummy variable | Concentration ratio (log) | High-technical-barrier dummy variable |
|---|---|---|---|---|---|---|---|---|---|---|---|---|
| III 1 | Profit rate | OLSQ | 0.0361[c] (4.41) | 0.320[b] (2.23) | — | — | 0.00984[c] (3.16) | 0.0281[b] (2.19) | 0.0252 (1.44) | — | — | — |
| 2 | Profit rate | 2SLSQ | 0.0309[c] (2.94) | 0.477 (1.51) | — | — | 0.00973[c] (2.95) | 0.0273[b] (2.04) | 0.0249 (1.39) | — | — | — |
| 4 | Advertising: sales ratio | 2SLSQ | 0.00163 (0.06) | — | 0.868[c] (2.46) | — | — | 0.000011 (0.001) | — | -0.0146 (1.52) | 0.00442 (0.54) | -0.0176 (1.48) |
| IV 2 | Profit rate | 2SLSQ | 0.0309[c] (2.96) | 0.477 (1.52) | — | — | 0.00973[c] (2.95) | 0.0273[b] (2.04) | 0.0249 (1.39) | — | — | — |
| 4 | Advertising: sales ratio | 2SLSQ | -0.00688 (0.27) | — | — | 0.620[b] (2.31) | — | 0.00140 (0.01) | — | -0.0168[b] (1.75) | 0.00650 (0.80) | -0.0192 (1.59) |

[a]Values of $t$ in parentheses.
[b]Statistically significant at the 5-percent level.
[c]Statistically significant at the 1-percent level.

In the profit rate equations, the primary effect of introducing simultaneity into the estimating procedures is on the coefficient and standard errors of the advertising:sales ratio, which is the single endogenous variable on the right-hand sides of the equations. In each model, the estimates follow the same pattern. The regression coefficients, estimated by two-stage least squares, are always larger than their counterparts, and in Table 7.4 they are nearly twice as large. At the same time, the standard errors of these coefficients are also substantially larger in the two-stage least-squares estimates, and the $t$ values decline. Although the decline is relatively slight in the equations presented in Table 7.4, and the coefficients remain statistically significant, the $t$ values fall sufficiently in Table 7.5 that the coefficients are no longer statistically significant at conventional confidence levels.[17]

Before we interpret these results, it is useful to note one characteristic of two-stage least-squares estimation. Although this procedure provides consistent estimates, it generally leads to larger standard errors of the regression coefficients than in the case of ordinary least squares.[18] A side effect of removing simultaneous-equation bias from the regression estimates is to reduce the efficiency of the estimates, and it is therefore not surprising that the $t$ values decline even though the coefficients increase.

Simultaneous-equation techniques were introduced to examine whether the ordinary least-squares estimates are biased upward. What is apparent, however, is that any bias in the original estimates is more likely to be negative, since the two-stage estimates are always greater than before.

In the equations predicting advertising:sales ratios, the most striking result is the strong influence on advertising of either the profit rate on sales or the cash flow rate on sales. The estimated coefficients do not appear to depend on which estimating procedure is used, although the standard errors are again slightly higher with two-stage least squares. Thus, an increase in net profits of $1 is associated with an increase in advertising of between 85 cents and $1. Since profits are measured *net* of advertising, this coefficient however does *not* indicate that 85 or 98 cents out of each dollar of gross profits (including advertising) is allocated to advertising. A similar interpretation is appropriate

17. The coefficients remain significant at the 10 percent confidence level.
18. After discussing the properties of various estimation methods for structural equations, Christ concludes that "Least Squares is in general inconsistent, and (if its expectations exist) biased for every sample size and in the limit, but it has the minimum variance (or approximate variance) among the methods discussed here," which include two-stage least squares. Carl F. Christ, *Econometric Models and Methods* (New York, Wiley, 1967), pp. 464–465. In addition, Christ summarizes the results of various Monte Carlo studies and finds that the variances of the regression estimates in least squares are generally lower than obtained from other estimators. *Ibid.*, pp. 477–481.

for Models II and IV, which include the cash flow variable, since it is also measured net of advertising. Note also that the growth of demand variable in these equations is effectively zero, which contrasts with the results given in Table 7.3 above, where no discretionary-funds variable was included. Thus, some doubt is cast on the view that advertising is greater where product demand is expanding rapidly.

To estimate the parameters of simultaneous-equation models that include the impact of the price elasticity of demand on both profits and advertising, the sample was limited as before to 38 industries. Only Models I and III are reestimated, and the results are presented in Table 7.6. As can be seen, the estimated coefficients are not widely different from those presented above.The impact of the long-run demand elasticity on profit rates is again indicated, as the relevant coefficients are all highly significant. Unlike the equations presented in Table 7.3 above, however, the advertising equations considered here include the profit rate on sales as an additional explanatory variable. With this specification, the estimated coefficients for the long-run demand elasticity are always statistically significant, regardless of whether the equation is estimated by ordinary least squares or by two-stage least squares. These results suggest that there is an inverse relation between the price elasticity of market demand and advertising.[19]

As indicated in Chapter 6, the error terms in the profit-rate equations are heteroscedastic, so that an appropriate weighting procedure will increase the efficiency of the estimates. However, there was no indication of heteroscedasticity in the residuals of the advertising-sales equations. Weighted regression estimates, using two-stage least squares as well as ordinary least squares, were therefore computed only for the profit rate equations.[20] The results are presented in Tables 7.7 and 7.8, where the model numbers and equation numbers correspond to those used in Tables 7.4 and 7.5.

The difference between the two tables is that the first is based on all 41 observations, whereas the second is based on 40 observations, with motor vehicles excluded. As noted in the previous chapter, motor vehicles is an outlying case in terms of the weighting variable, and the advertising:sales ratio is an inadequate measure of product differentiation in this industry. Although the ratio is low, the absolute volume of advertising expenditures per firm is very large. Since the absolute volume of expenditures as well as the volume relative to sales should affect competitive conditions, the advertising: sales ratio in this industry is a particularly inappropriate variable with which to measure the impact of advertising on profit rates.

19. See the discussion concerning Figure 7.2 above.
20. The weighting variable used is the same as that used in Chapter 6.

TABLE 7.6. Coefficients for simultaneous regression equations with price elasticity of demand included: 38 industries[a]

| Model | Dependent variable | Estimation method | Intercept | Advertising:sales ratio | Profit rate on sales | Long-run demand elasticity | Capital requirements (log) | Growth of demand (log) | Local industry dummy variable | Durable-industry dummy variable | Concentration ratio times high-overall-barrier dummy variable | Concentration ratio (log) | High-technical-barrier dummy variable |
|---|---|---|---|---|---|---|---|---|---|---|---|---|---|
| I 1 | Profit rate | OLSQ | 0.0440c (5.48) | 0.346c (2.60) | — | 0.00698c (3.09) | 0.00727b (2.02) | 0.0276b (2.32) | 0.0179 (1.13) | — | 0.000334b (1.83) | — | — |
| 2 | Profit rate | 2SLSQ | 0.0410c (4.57) | 0.495b (2.19) | — | 0.00722c (3.14) | 0.00722b (1.97) | 0.0256b (2.06) | 0.0171 (1.06) | — | 0.000292 (1.51) | — | — |
| 3 | Advertising:sales ratio | OLSQ | -0.00228 (0.09) | — | 0.951c (3.47) | -0.00442b (1.82) | — | -0.00130 (0.10) | — | -0.0198b (2.09) | — | 0.00428 (0.53) | -0.0127 (1.07) |
| 4 | Advertising:sales ratio | 2SLSQ | -0.00181 (0.07) | — | 0.904c (3.00) | -0.00461b (1.88) | — | 0.000822 (0.06) | — | -0.0201b (2.12) | — | 0.00425 (0.52) | -0.0124 (1.04) |
| III 1 | Profit rate | OLSQ | 0.0411c (5.04) | 0.396c (2.94) | — | 0.00733c (3.15) | 0.0112c (3.71) | 0.0217b (1.83) | 0.0242 (1.51) | — | — | — | — |
| 2 | Profit rate | 2SLSQ | 0.0411c (4.55) | 0.399 (1.62) | — | 0.00734c (3.03) | 0.0112c (3.59) | 0.0217b (1.81) | 0.0241 (1.50) | — | — | — | — |
| 4 | Advertising:sales ratio | 2SLSQ | -0.00381 (0.15) | — | 0.876c (2.65) | -0.00448b (1.83) | — | 0.00188 (0.14) | — | -0.0209b (2.20) | — | 0.00514 (0.63) | -0.0132 (1.11) |

[a]Values of t in parentheses.
[b]Statistically significant at the 5-percent level.
[c]Statistically significant at the 1-percent level.

TABLE 7.7.  Coefficients for weighted regression equations explaining profit rates: 41 industries[a]

| Model | Estimation method | Intercept | Advertising:sales ratio | Capital requirements (log) | Growth of demand (log) | Local industry dummy variable | Concentration ratio times high-overall-barrier dummy variable |
|---|---|---|---|---|---|---|---|
| I 1 | OLSQ | 0.0444[c] (5.35) | 0.222[b] (1.70) | 0.00415 (1.11) | 0.0347[c] (2.95) | 0.0132 (0.93) | 0.000471[c] (2.81) |
| 2 | 2SLSQ | 0.0397[c] (4.22) | 0.402[b] (1.98) | 0.00465 (1.21) | 0.0327[c] (2.68) | 0.0130 (0.89) | 0.000436[c] (2.49) |
| II 2 | 2SLSQ | 0.0396[c] (4.20) | 0.407[b] (2.01) | 0.00466 (1.21) | 0.0327[c] (2.67) | 0.0130 (0.89) | 0.000435[c] (2.49) |
| III 1 | OLSQ | 0.0367[c] (4.29) | 0.278[b] (1.97) | 0.01181[c] (4.26) | 0.0246[b] (2.01) | 0.0258[b] (1.76) | — |
| 2 | 2SLSQ | 0.373[c] (3.85) | 0.256 (1.07) | 0.01182[c] (4.26) | 0.0247[b] (2.01) | 0.0260[b] (1.76) | — |
| IV 2 | 2SLSQ | 0.0371[c] (3.84) | 0.262 (1.10) | 0.01182[c] (4.26) | 0.0247[b] (2.01) | 0.0259[b] (1.76) | — |

[a]Values of $t$ in parentheses.
[b]Statistically significant at the 1-percent level.
[c]Statistically significant at the 5-percent level.

TABLE 7.8. Coefficients for weighted regression equations explaining profit rates: 40 industries (excluding motor vehicles)[a]

| Model | Estimation method | Intercept | Advertising:sales ratio | Capital requirements (log) | Growth of demand (log) | Local industry dummy variable | Concentration ratio times high-overall-barrier dummy variable |
|---|---|---|---|---|---|---|---|
| I 1 | OLSQ | 0.0458[c] (5.68) | 0.339[b] (2.40) | 0.00292 (0.80) | 0.0312[c] (2.71) | 0.0126 (0.92) | 0.000310 (1.68) |
| 2 | 2SLSQ | 0.0417[c] (4.66) | 0.561[c] (2.47) | 0.00295 (0.78) | 0.0279[b] (2.28) | 0.0121 (0.85) | 0.000214 (1.04) |
| II 2 | 2SLSQ | 0.0417[c] (4.65) | 0.564[c] (2.48) | 0.00295 (0.78) | 0.0279[b] (2.28) | 0.0121 (0.85) | 0.000213 (1.04) |
| III 1 | OLSQ | 0.0425[c] (5.30) | 0.417[c] (3.05) | 0.00630[b] (2.00) | 0.0245[b] (2.21) | 0.0187 (1.40) | — |
| 2 | 2SLSQ | 0.0411[c] (4.71) | 0.508[b] (1.99) | 0.00583[b] (1.74) | 0.0240[b] (2.13) | 0.0176 (1.27) | — |
| IV 2 | 2SLSQ | 0.0410[c] (4.69) | 0.515[b] (2.02) | 0.00579[b] (1.72) | 0.0239[b] (2.12) | 0.0176 (1.26) | — |

[a]Values of $t$ in parentheses.
[b]Statistically significant at the 5-percent level.
[c]Statistically significant at the 1-percent level.

In Models I and II, the weighted equations estimated by the two techniques show the same pattern as the unweighted equations; this is less clear in Models III and IV. Where weighted equations are estimated without motor vehicles, the regression coefficients of the advertising:sales ratio are substantially larger when simultaneous-equation techniques are used. Moreover, the co-efficients remain statistically significant in all cases. When weighted equations are estimated that include the motor-vehicle industry, the two-stage least-squares estimates of the advertising coefficient are substantially larger than those estimated by ordinary least squares and remain statistically significant in Models I and II. These coefficients, however, are slightly lower and no longer significant in Models III and IV.

Taken as a whole, these econometric results provide some limited support for the analysis of the determinants of advertising developed earlier in this chapter. The main determinants of the volume of advertising in relation to sales are the profit margin, the price elasticity of industry demand, and the two dummy variables identifying durable goods and high technical entry barriers. Neither concentration nor the rate of growth of demand appears to have much effect on advertising:sales ratios.

The simultaneous-equation estimates of the effects of advertising on profits are larger than the corresponding ordinary least-squares estimates presented in Chapter 6. These results, therefore, provide additional support for the hypothesis that advertising has an important impact on profits. In the next chapter, we examine how these empirical findings are influenced when advertising is treated as a capital outlay rather than as a current expense.

# APPENDIX 7-A

In this appendix, we analyze a model of the firm under different market circumstances and derive the conditions for the optimal volume of advertising by the firm as presented in the body of this chapter.

We assume that the firm maximizes profits, given a demand function $Q = Q(A, A', P)$, a cost function $C = C(Q)$, and an entry limit pricing constraint $P \leq PL$, where $Q$ is output, $P$ is price, $A$ is the firm's advertising, $A'$ is the advertising of its rivals, $C$ is the total cost of production, and $PL$ is the limit price, that is, the price above which new entrants would penetrate the market.

For simplicity, we assume that production is under conditions of constant marginal cost:

$$C_Q = MC.$$

where subscripts indicate partial differentiation.

The signs of the partial derivatives of the demand function with respect to the firm's decision variables are specified as follows:

$$Q_P < 0, \ Q_A > 0.$$

The response of the firm's output to the advertising of its rivals depends on the characteristics of the products: for homogeneous products, $Q_{A'} > 0$; for heterogeneous products, $Q_{A'} < 0$. Under oligopolistic market conditions, the firm may assume that its rivals will react to an increase in its advertising. This reaction is described by the total derivative $dA'/dA$.

As demonstrated below, where the entry-limit pricing constraint is binding, the firm's decisions are influenced by the effect of its advertising on the limit price. We describe this effect by the total derivative

$$\frac{dPL}{dA} = PL_A + PL_{A'} \cdot \frac{dA'}{dA},$$

where $PL_A$ and $PL_{A'}$ are the partial derivatives of the limit price with respect to the advertising by the firm and by its rivals. We assume that $PL_A$ and $PL_{A'} \geq 0$.

Consider the first-order conditions for profit maximization under different entry conditions. Where entry is blockaded ($P < PL$), advertising and price are two decision variables[1] and the first-order conditions for profit maximization are derived by partially differentiating the profit function

$$\pi = PQ(P,A,A') - C(Q) - A \tag{1}$$

with respect to $P$ and $A$. The result is

$$\frac{\partial \pi}{\partial P} = Q + PQ_P - C_Q Q_P = 0,$$

or

$$\frac{P - MC}{P} = \frac{1}{-e}, \tag{2}$$

where $e$ is the price elasticity demand, and

$$\frac{\partial \pi}{\partial A} = P\left(Q_A + Q_{A'} \cdot \frac{dA'}{dA}\right) - C_Q\left(Q_A + Q_{A'} \cdot \frac{dA'}{dA}\right) - 1 = 0,$$

or

$$(P - MC)\left(Q_A + Q_{A'} \cdot \frac{dA'}{dA}\right) = 1. \tag{3}$$

If $dA'/dA = 0$, as in the case of monopoly or monopolistic competition, this simplifies to

$$(P - MC)\, Q_A = 1,$$

which, given (2), is equivalent to the Dorfman-Steiner result:

$$PQ_A = -e.$$

We now turn to the more complex case where the entry-limit pricing constraint is binding ($P = PL$). Now the firm maximizes profits by using a single

1. Note that we ignore the problem of oligopolistic interdependence in pricing. Hence the analysis applies to oligopolistic markets where the firm is a price leader, or to monopolistic markets.

decision variable—advertising—but takes into account any effects of advertising on the entry-limit price. Then

$$\pi = PL \cdot Q(A,A',P) - C(Q) - A,$$

$$\frac{d\pi}{dA} = PL\left(Q_A + Q_{A'}\frac{dA'}{dA} + Q_P\frac{dPL}{dA}\right) + Q\frac{dPL}{dA}$$

$$- C_Q\left(Q_A + Q_{A'}\frac{dA'}{dA} + Q_P\frac{dPL}{dA}\right) - 1 = 0, \tag{4}$$

or

$$(PL - MC)\left(Q_A + Q_{A'}\frac{dA'}{dA}\right) + [(PL - MC)Q_P + Q]\frac{dPL}{dA} = 1.$$

It may be readily demonstrated that if the entry-limit price $PL$ equals the unconstrained profit-maximization price $PM$, the second term on the left-hand side vanishes. Equation (4) may be manipulated to obtain a more readily interpreted expression. We represent the conventional (unconstrained) marginal revenue function by $MR = \partial(PQ)/\partial Q$.

Since $MR = P + Q/Q_P$, or $P - MR = Q/-Q_P$

the second term in equation (4) may be rewritten as

$$-Q_P\left[\frac{Q}{-Q_P} - (PL - MC)\right]\left(PL_A + PL_{A'}\frac{dA'}{dA}\right)$$

or

$$-Q_P(MC - MR)\left(PL_A + PL_{A'}\frac{dA'}{dA}\right).$$

Hence, the equation

$$(PL - MC)\left(Q_A + Q_{A'}\frac{dA'}{dA}\right) - Q_P(MC - MR)$$

$$\left(PL_A + PL_{A'}\frac{dA'}{dA}\right) = 1 \tag{5}$$

is equivalent to equation (4).

It is now obvious that if the entry-limit price equals the unconstrained price, the second term vanishes, and we arrive at the blockaded-entry result. Where the entry-limit price constraint is binding ($PL < PM$), $MC > MR$, and the second term in equation (4) or (5) is necessarily positive. Hence, we conclude that the effect of an operative limit price constraint is to increase the volume of advertising (at a given profit margin).

These expressions may be used to consider the impact on advertising of changes in any of the variables in these maximization conditions. By partially differentiating the relevant expression with respect to each variable of interest, we can determine its effect upon industry parameters. When the partial derivative is positive, it indicates that the variable has a positive impact, since advertising must increase sufficiently to reduce $Q_A$ in order to satisfy the maximization condition. We consider each variable in turn:

1. Price-cost margin $(P - MC)$. Under blockaded entry, this variable necessarily has a positive impact. Under limit pricing, changes in price-cost margins have a positive impact if $MC - MR$ remains unchanged; otherwise its effect is ambiguous, and is that described for the next variable $(PL)$.

2. The entry limit price $(PL)$. Under blockaded entry, this variable necessarily has no effect. Under limit pricing, the direction of effect is ambiguous. Partially differentiating[2] the left-hand side of equation (4) with respect to $PL$, we obtain

$$\left( Q_A + Q_{A'} \frac{dA'}{dA} \right) + 2Q_P \left( PL_A + PL_{A'} \frac{dA'}{dA} \right).$$

Since $Q_p < 0$, this expression is positive if

$$\left( Q_A + Q_{A'} \frac{dA'}{dA} \right) > - 2Q_P \left( PL_A + PL_{A'} \frac{dA'}{dA} \right).$$

If this inequality holds, an increase in $PL$ due to factors other than advertising will lead to an increase in advertising. If the inequality is reversed, an increase in $PL$ will reduce the volume of advertising.

Note that the effect of the recognition of oligopolistic interdependence will normally make it less likely that increases in $PL$ will have a positive effect on the volume of advertising, since $Q_{A'} < 0$ in the usual case of heterogeneous products, and $PL_{A'} > 0$.

3. The marginal impact of advertising on output $(Q_A)$ has a positive effect on the volume of advertising. The marginal impact of advertising upon the entry limit price $(PL_A)$ has a positive effect where the limit-pricing constraint is binding (and zero otherwise). Shifts in these two variables reflect changes in product differentiability.

As discussed in the body of this chapter, three variables that may influence product differentiability are the durability of the product, the rate of growth of demand, and the price elasticity of market demand.

4. The strength of rivals' reactions as recognized by the firm $(dA'/dA)$ has

---

2. Note that, since $Q$ depends directly on $PL$, it is not held constant in the partial differentiation.

an ambiguous effect. For the use of homogeneous products, where $Q_{A'} > 0$, the recognition of mutual dependence necessarily stimulates advertising. Under limit pricing where advertising affects entry barriers, this effect is strengthened.

With heterogeneous products ($Q_{A'} < 0$) and blockaded entry, the recognition of mutual interdependence will reduce the volume of advertising (at given profit margins). Under limit pricing of heterogeneous products, however, the recognition of mutual interdependence gives rise to conflicting effects. Partially differentiating the left-hand side of equation (5) with respect to $dA'/dA$, we obtain:

$$(PL - MC)\, Q_{A'} - Q_P\, (MC - MR)\, PL_{A'}.$$

This expression is positive if

$$-Q_P\, (MC - MR)\, PL_{A'} > -Q_{A'}\, (PL - MC),$$

and negative if the inequality is reversed. Hence, the recognition of mutual dependence could have a positive effect on advertising (at given profit margins) where the effect of advertising on entry barriers is strong.

# CHAPTER 8 Advertising as a Capital Investment

An important criticism that has been raised regarding empirical results such as those presented in the previous two chapters is that the investment aspects of advertising are ignored.[1] It is argued that the high partial impact of advertising upon the measured rate of return might be attributable to the fact that advertising represents an investment that should be amortized, whereas under conventional accounting procedures, advertising is expensed.

Although this argument has a good deal of superficial appeal, the problem of the deviation between "true" or internal rates of return and measured or "book" rates of return is far more complex than has generally been recognized. In general, the mere capitalization of advertising expenditures will not suffice to correct the book rate of return, even if all other expenditures of a capital nature are properly treated in the accounts of the firm. As demonstrated below, any bias in the measured rate of return attributable to expensing advertising depends upon: the rate of growth of the firm, deviations from the growth path during the period of observation, firms' policies with respect to the distribution or reinvestment of any monopoly rents, the time pattern of net revenues from investments in fixed capital, and the reactions of competitors (including those in other industries) to changes in advertising intensity.

As a result, under some circumstances, the conventional book rate of return may well be closer to the true rate of return than an alternative calculated on the basis of a naïve capitalization formula. Furthermore, the internal rate of return itself has some limitations as an indicator of monopoly power, at least

1. See L. G. Telser's discussion of "Advertising and the Advantages of Size," *American Economic Review* (May 1969), pp. 121–123.

as usually calculated. The plowing back of monopoly profits into financial assets, or via diversification into other industries (with lower average rates of return), will bias rates of return toward competitive levels.[2]

One approach to the problem of treating advertising as a capital investment is illustrated by the work of Weiss.[3] This involves constructing estimates of the "goodwill stock" generated by advertising on the basis of constant exponential decay rates (based in part on fragmentary empirical estimates of market-share models) and observed past advertising expenditures.

Let $GW$ be goodwill stock, $A$ be the volume of advertising investment, and $\delta$ be the rate of decay of advertising; then

$$GW_t = A_t + (1 - \delta)GW_{t-1}.$$

From this measure, corrected measures of net income and equity were developed:

$$E_t^* = E_t + GW_t,$$

$$\pi_t^* = \pi_t + A_t - \delta GW_{t-1}.$$

The ratio of these two corrected measures was used by Weiss as a corrected rate of return. As Weiss points out, the rate of return so corrected may exceed or fall short of the "book" rate of return, depending basically on whether or not the book rate of return exceeds the rate of growth of the goodwill stock.

Weiss's work represents an important step forward in the analysis of advertising, and we note with interest and satisfaction that our own hypotheses survive the test of both an application to new data (Weiss used 1963–64 instead of 1954–1957) and the use of these "corrected" rates of return.

However, this approach is generally inadequate for the following reasons:

1. The demand functions presented in Chapter 5 indicate that a simple model of exponential decay is an inadequate representation of the time pattern of the effects of advertising upon industry sales. The Generalized Koyck model used implies that some portion of advertising expenditures should be written off during the year they are made, and the residual then depreciated at constant rates.

2. Stock-adjustment demand models imply, and the results reported in Chapter 5 confirm, that the typical time pattern of effects upon sales of advertising for durable goods is very different from that for nondurable goods.

2. It is interesting to note that the favorable treatment of capital gains under the income tax laws provides an incentive for firms to reinvest rather than to distribute funds in excess of their requirements within their own industry.

3. L. W. Weiss, "Advertising, Profits, and Corporate Taxes," *Review of Economics and Statistics* (November 1969), pp. 421–429.

Hence the use of a common depreciation rate for all industries may give invalid results.

3. This approach ignores the negative goodwill created by the advertising of competitors within the industry as well as the effects of advertising in other industries. It implicitly assumes that all the advertising by firms in the industry generates only positive asset values which are added up to obtain the net goodwill stock.

The approach we adopt is to construct alternative measures of adjusted rates of return and adjusted profit margins on sales based on the market demand equations presented in Chapter 5.[4] Since a flexible stock-adjustment model is used, the first two difficulties above are avoided.

The selection of a demand function for the industry rather than market-share functions for individual firms (assuming data for individual firms were available for enough industries, which is not the case) obviates the third difficulty. The difference between an amortization schedule based on an industry demand function and that based on market-share functions for firms within the industry reflects the rivalrous effects of advertising within the industry. Since these rivalrous effects by definition give rise to negative goodwill for competitors within the industry equal to the positive goodwill for the firm doing the advertising, the total goodwill for the industry as a whole is not affected. Hence it is preferable to base amortization schedules on time patterns derived from demand functions rather than from market-share functions.[5] The form of the demand function also permits adjustments for the negative effects of advertising in other industries.

Two adjusted rate-of-return measures are examined. The first represents an attempt to approximate better the internal rate of return. The construction of this measure involves deducting the depreciation of advertising rather than current advertising outlays from the numerator of the rate of return and adding the capital value of advertising to the denominator of the return.

Although we analyze this measure, it suffers from three weaknesses: (a) the inadequacy of the internal rate of return as a measure of monopoly power within the industry and the fact that the adjusted rate of return calculated

<hr />

4. Two industries—sugar and paints—were omitted from the analysis because satisfactory demand functions were not obtained. See Chapter 5 above.

5. It is noteworthy that the rates of decay of the interindustry effects of advertising appear to be considerably more rapid than the rate of decay of the rivalrous effects. (For references to various estimates of depreciation rates based on market share models, see Weiss, "Advertising, Profits, and Corporate Taxes.") This indicates that customers won over from rivals within an industry are more easily retained (in the absence of an increase in the competitors' advertising) than customers who are induced to switch their purchases from other industries' products.

in this approach will be affected by firms' policies with respect to the distribution of surplus, (b) the fact that the adjusted rate of return may be negatively associated with advertising intensity even though advertising earns a profit rate that exceeds the cost of capital for industries in which the rate of return in the absence of advertising exceeds the rate of return on advertising investment, and (c) the sensitivity of this measure to errors in the estimated depreciation rates.

An alternative adjustment involves the direct application of the principle of charging capital costs to the current period. Book net revenues may be adjusted by adding back advertising expenditures made during the period and subtracting that portion of advertising expenditures which should be expensed, together with the net capital costs attributable to current and past advertising. These capital costs include not only the deterioration of the effects of past advertising that occurs during the period (which is analogous to the depreciation of physical assets) but also the imputed capital costs on the net amount invested. In addition, any capital gains or losses on the intangible capital should be added or subtracted.

The resulting corrected net revenue divided by the book value of stockholders' equity then represents the rate of return adjusted to incorporate these capital costs. This measure has the advantage that it will be positively associated with advertising intensity if the rate of return on advertising investments exceeds the cost of capital, and will have a zero association with advertising if the rate of return of advertising equals the cost of capital. In addition, this adjusted rate is linearly related to an appropriately scaled measure of monopoly rents on advertising, and is less sensitive to the reinvestment of surplus infinancial assets.

There is one disadvantage in using this measure, in that it involves an asymmetric treatment of fixed capital and advertising capital. If we were to test hypotheses concerning the effects of increases in fixed capital upon the rate of return, this measure would clearly be inappropriate, since increases in fixed capital would lower the rate of return if the monopoly yield on advertising capital exceeded the monopoly yield on fixed capital.

None of the hypotheses we test pertain directly to the effects of increases in fixed capital investment. However, the absolute capital requirements variable used in our regressions is affected by the degree of capital intensity of the industry, and the estimate of its impact upon the rate of return may be distorted as a result.

An alternative measure which obviates this difficulty is the profit margin on sales net of all estimated capital costs. This measure preserves the symmetry of treatment of fixed capital and advertising capital, and has the additional advantage of being relatively insensitive to the reinvestment of monopoly rents in financial assets.[6] Its main drawback is that it is more reasonable to formulate certain hypotheses concerning entry barriers in terms of effects on rates of return than in terms of effects on price-cost margins. However, the latter problem may be allowed for by scaling the appropriate independent variables by a measure of capital intensity.

All of the adjustments to profit rates or margins presented in this chapter require the estimation of the stock of capital generated by advertising. Following the usage of others, we shall refer to this capital as "goodwill." The generation of goodwill stocks involves the use of appropriate amortization formulas linking goodwill stocks to advertising flows.

As noted previously, advertising by a firm not only generates positive goodwill for the firm, but also may generate negative goodwill elsewhere in the economy. Three effects of a firm's advertising may be usefully distinguished: (1) sales are attracted from rivals within the industry; (2) the relative position of the firm with respect to new entrants may be improved, thereby permitting the firm to set a higher price-cost margin; and (3) sales are attracted from other industries (or perhaps even from savings). We shall refer to these as the "rivalrous," "entry-barrier," and "interindustry" effects of advertising respectively.

Rivalrous advertising creates negative as well as positive asset values. Hence, when aggregating across firms in an industry, that portion of advertising which is rivalrous should in principle be deducted (and hence currently expensed) before any calculation of net goodwill-stock values for the industry is made.

Similarly, advertising by other industries creates negative goodwill that may offset the positive goodwill created by the industry's own advertising efforts. Only the entry-barrier effects of advertising create an unambiguously positive intangible asset that is not at least partly offset by the activities of rivals or firms in other industries. Hence, although advertising may have lasting effects on sales, a substantial portion of advertising expenses incurred in a year should logically be written off in that year as being required to maintain the firm's market share in the face of advertising rivals and to fight off the encroachment of competing products from other industries.

6. As is discussed below, the adjusted net margin is defined as follows:
$$b_4 = \frac{\pi + AD - DEP - rGW - rE}{S}.$$
Since the imputed cost of capital of all equity is deducted from the margin, investments of surplus in financial assets which yield the cost of capital do not affect the adjusted net margin.

Because the net effect of rivalrous advertising upon industry goodwill is zero, the amortization formulas used for the correction of industry rates of return are derived from the market demand functions rather than from functions explaining the market shares of individual firms. Two sets of measures based on market demand functions are calculated: the first set ignores the negative effects of advertising in other industries, and the second set takes these effects into account.

Hence we construct and analyze six measures of adjusted profit rate: the two adjusted rates of return and the adjusted net profit margin discussed earlier, all calculated both with and without allowance for the negative effects of advertising in other industries. Before we proceed to the specification and analysis of these measures, however, it is constructive to examine more rigorously the effects upon the ordinary book rate of return of expensing advertising.

## THE EFFECTS OF ADVERTISING ON THE BOOK RATE OF RETURN: A THEORETICAL ANALYSIS

Although advertising outlays during a period may affect future as well as current sales, there are a number of differences between advertising on the one hand and both capital expenditures and developmental expenditures (research, development, product design, exploration, and so forth) on the other that invalidate the simple capitalization approach. Indeed, as will be demonstrated below, it is quite possible for advertising to impart a *negative* bias to the book rate of return. This bias would be magnified if one applied typical amortization procedures based on the rate of decay of the sales effects of advertising.

Two essential characteristics differentiate advertising from capital expenditures. First, unlike capital expenditures, advertising expenditures do not noticeably precede the beginning of the sales and net revenue streams that they generate; that is, there is little or no gestation lag.[7] For capital expenditures, by contrast, a significant gestation lag will probably exist while plant is constructed and equipment put in place.[8]

Second, a portion of the advertising outlays in any period can be viewed as maintenance expenditures necessary to maintain the goodwill established by previous advertising expenditures. In contrast, the maintenance of plant and

7. The demand equations estimated in Chapter 5 show that advertising in a year typically has a major impact on sales during that year, and are therefore consistent with a zero or a very short gestation lag.

8. For estimates of the lags between capital appropriations and capital expenditures, see Shirley Almon, "The Distributed Lag between Capital Appropriations and Expenditures," *Econometrica* (January 1965), pp. 178–196.

equipment is identified separately from capital expenditures in the books of the firm, and is, of course, treated as a current expense.

The contrast between advertising and developmental expenditures is even more marked. Although the latter are expensed, they represent expenditures that typically precede capital expenditures related to new products or processes; hence the gestation lag is typically longest of all for these types of expenditures.[9]

Because of the gestation lag and the lumping of expenditures required to maintain advertising capital with expenditures to increase advertising capital, the effects of advertising upon the book rate of return depends upon the typical time pattern of revenues (net of all current expenses) from an investment in plant and equipment, as well as upon the difference between the growth rate of the firm and its internal rate of return. Only if we are prepared to make specific assumptions about this time pattern can we draw conclusions about the direction and magnitude of any distortions in the book rate of return introduced by advertising.

The problem of the relation between book and internal rates of return has recently been examined thoroughly by Thomas Stauffer.[10] On the basis of this work, one may draw the following conclusions for a firm under conditions of equilibrium growth:

1. The book rate of return is an unbiased measure of the internal rate of return if the growth rate is equal to the internal rate of return.[11]

2. If the growth rate is less than the internal rate of return, the sign as well as the magnitude of the bias attributable to the expensing of advertising depends on the time pattern of net revenues from fixed capital, the typical life of fixed capital, and the time pattern of sales effects of advertising. The magnitude of the bias, of course, will also depend on the difference between the growth rate and the internal rate of return.

9. In some industries where a portion of the capital stock appreciates through age—the obvious examples being wines and distilled liquors—there is a long gestation lag for inventory capital as well.

10. T. R. Stauffer, "The Measurement of Corporate Rates of Return and the Marginal Efficiency of Capital" (unpub. diss. Harvard University, June 1971). Our results, however, are not identical with those presented by Stauffer. Stauffer's conclusion that a bias due to advertising exists when the growth rate equals the internal rate of return results from a minor approximation error in his analysis. Some aspects of Stauffer's work have been published. T. R. Stauffer, "The Measurement of Corporate Rates of Return: A Generalized Formulation," *Bell Journal of Economics and Management Science* (Autumn 1971), pp. 434–469.

11. For a summary discussion of alternative rate of return concepts and an explanation of the condition that the book rate is equal to the internal rate when the latter equals the growth rate, see E. Solomon, "Alternative Rate of Return Concepts and their Implications for Utility Regulation," *Bell Journal of Economics and Management Science* (Spring 1970), pp. 65–81.

3. Since biases from other sources (the expensing of developmental expenditures and the use of inappropriate depreciation rates for fixed capital) undoubtedly exist, the effect of expensing advertising upon the accuracy of the book rate as a measure of the internal rate cannot be readily determined.

Let us consider two examples of the time pattern of net revenue streams from fixed investments. The first case is that of a constant revenue stream with no gestation lag between investments in capital goods or in advertising and the start of the flow of net revenues. In this situation the bias depends only on the time pattern of sales effects of advertising, the difference between the internal rate of return and the growth rate, and the relative importance of advertising. The formula for the bias is as follows:

$$R - r = \frac{Ad}{E} \cdot \frac{\lambda(r - g)}{(1 + g - \lambda)(1 + r)},$$

where $R$ is the book rate of return, $r$ is the internal rate of return, $(1 - \lambda)$ is the rate of decay of the sales effect of advertising, $g$ is the growth rate, and $Ad/E$ is the advertising:equity ratio. Hence for this case, provided $\lambda$ is not equal to zero, there is a positive bias due to advertising when $g < r$ and a negative bias when $g > r$.

Let us now consider the case where the net cash flow from fixed investments declines exponentially at the rate $1 - \theta$ over the life of fixed capital. For this more general case, the bias now depends on the time pattern of revenues from fixed investments and the life of fixed capital as well as on the factors mentioned in the previous case. The formula for the bias is as follows:

$$(R - r) = \frac{Ad}{E} \left\{ \frac{1 + r - \lambda}{1 + g - \lambda} \cdot \frac{1 - [1/(1 + r)]^N}{1 - [1/(1 + g)]^N} \cdot \right.$$

$$\left. \frac{1 - [\theta/(1 + g)]^N}{1 - [\theta/(1 + r)]^N} \cdot \frac{g}{r} \cdot \frac{1 + g}{1 + r} \cdot \frac{1 + r - \theta}{1 + g - \theta} - 1 \right\} \cdot$$

The complex term in braces is evaluated for alternative values of $\lambda$ and $\theta$ and typical values of $r$ and $g$ in Table 8.1. These illustrative results show that, even when the internal rate of return exceeds the growth rate, the bias due to advertising could be either positive or negative, depending on the particular value of the two rates of decay $1 - \lambda$ and $1 - \theta$, and on the life of fixed capital, $N$. For this case, the bias varies inversely with all three variables. Across a range of reasonable values of these parameters, both positive and negative biases are obtained. These results serve to emphasize the conclusion that appropriate procedures for adjusting book rates of return can be devised only on the basis of specific assumptions about the time pattern of net revenues from investments in fixed capital.

The discussion so far has focused upon the case of a firm or industry under

TABLE 8.1.  Illustrative bias factors[a]

| N | $\theta$ | $\lambda = 0.50$ | $\lambda = 0.75$ |
|---|---|---|---|
| 10 | 1.00 | 0.074 | 0.138 |
|    | 0.95 | .018 | .079 |
|    | .90  | .003 | .063 |
| 20 | 1.00 | .074 | .138 |
|    | 0.95 | −.022 | .036 |
|    | .90  | −.068 | −.013 |

*Notation*

$g$ = growth rate of the industry
$r$ = internal rate of return
$1 - \lambda$ = rate of decay of sales effect of advertising
$1 - \theta$ = rate of decay of revenues from fixed capital
$N$ = life of fixed capital

[a]These factors, multiplied by the ratio of advertising to equity, yield the bias in the book rate of return attributable to advertising (under steady-state growth conditions); $g - 0.04$ and $r = 0.08$ in all cases; no gestation lag.

conditions of equilibrium growth. Any systematic biases related to advertising that persist across industries under these conditions will naturally result in biased estimates of the impact of advertising upon measured rates of return.

However, it is worth while to examine the effects of departures from equilibrium growth. In general, in the absence of appropriate amortization formulas for all expenditures of a capital nature, fluctuations in these expenditures will give rise to fluctuations in the difference between the book and internal rates of return. The resulting errors of measurement in the dependent variable increase the noise in the data, with reduced goodness of fit and lower statistical significance of independent variables as a consequence.

More important, however, transitory fluctuations in advertising give rise to systematic biases related to this transitory component that will bias the regression coefficient of advertising downward. Because advertising is expensed, years with unusually high advertising will show book rates of return lower than normal and years with unusually low advertising will show book rates of return higher than normal (although, in each case, the "normal" book rate may of course also be biased). The resulting negative association between transitory fluctuations in advertising and book rates of return will impart a negative bias to the cross-section regression coefficient of book rates of return on advertising.[12] This negative bias may partly or fully offset any positive bias associated with a high normal level of advertising.

12. This phenomenon probably accounts for the results reported in the previous chapter, where it was found that the simultaneous estimates of the impact of advertising on profits are larger than the ordinary least squares estimates.

## ADJUSTMENTS TO BOOK RATES OF RETURN:
## A FRAMEWORK OF ANALYSIS

Given the ambiguity of the biases involved and the difficulty of devising an appropriate correction procedure in the absence of data on the time pattern of revenues from capital investments, there is some question as to how to proceed. Our primary objective is, of course, to deal with the possibility that there may be a systematic bias in the cross-section estimates, rather than to derive corrected estimates of book rates of return per se. In the absence of data on developmental expenditures and on the correct and book depreciation schedules for fixed capital, corrections applied only to advertising investments will not necessarily yield more accurate measures of the internal rate of return in any case.

To deal with the possible cross-section bias, on the other hand, corrections applied to advertising investments alone may be sufficient, since the most likely source of biases systematically related to measures of advertising intensity would thereby be eliminated. We are, of course, still faced with two difficulties discussed above, namely, the dependence of the bias on the time pattern of revenues from fixed investments and the problem whether the negative effects of advertising investments in other industries should be taken into account.[13]

To provide the most stringent test for any bias in our results, we have constructed corrected rates of return on the basis of conservative assumptions about the time pattern of revenues and the effects of advertising in other industries. Since a constant net revenue stream from new investments would always yield a positive bias when the internal rate of return is greater than the growth rate, we base our calculations upon this assumption.[14] Because the existence of negative effects of advertising in other industries would tend to reduce the possible biases in the book rates of return, we carry out one set of

13. We made no attempt to estimate the impact of advertising upon profit rates over time. Our reasons for avoiding this monumental empirical task as are follows: (1) Since book profit rates will be affected by the various measurement problems discussed in this chapter, variation in book rates over time may be inadequate indicators of the time pattern of net profits. (2) Changes in depreciation arrangements under the tax laws have occurred during the period, thereby creating noncomparabilities of rates of return over time. (3) The effects of cyclical variables, such as variations in capacity utilization, upon profits in a time series context may overwhelm the effects of advertising. (4) The effects of changes in other relevant structural or behavioral variables would have to be examined. Since annual time series data on these measures is not available and/or is difficult to construct, only inadequately specified models could be examined in any case.

14. See Appendix 8-A for a demonstration that the use of a sufficiently low depreciation rate may result in the apparent elimination of excess rates of return.

calculations that ignores these negative effects. These assumptions enable us to derive amortization and expensing formulas for advertising directly from the estimated demand functions for the industries.

Before we proceed with this analysis, it is useful to consider its relation to the basic issue that is central to this study: the effect of advertising upon competition. In this connection, two alternative and not necessarily conflicting hypotheses can be put forward:

Hypothesis I: The internal rate of return is positively related to the relative level of advertising;

Hypothesis II: Investments in advertising typically yield rates of return above the cost of capital.

The first hypothesis may be tested, on the basis of the assumptions stated above, by utilizing the corrected rates of return on investment in equity and goodwill developed below. If the corrected rate of return is significantly positively correlated with the relative intensity of advertising, this provides confirmation of the hypothesis.

The second hypothesis is tested by the partial correlation between corrected rates of return and the relative intensity of advertising only if we are prepared to make the additional assumption that advertising is the sole source of excess profits. If excess profits exist for other reasons, and advertising investments themselves yield excess returns, the relation between advertising intensity and the corrected rate of return will be positive only among those industries in which the rate of return in the absence of advertising is lower than the rate of return on advertising investments. A negative partial correlation will exist for those industries in which the rate of return in the absence of advertising exceeds the yield on advertising investments. Therefore it is possible that the partial correlation between these variables across a sample of industries could be either insignificant or negative, even though the yield on advertising investments typically exceeds the cost of capital, because of the other factors that give rise to excessive rates of return.

The second hypothesis must therefore be tested via a different approach. As is described below, estimates of profits net of all capital costs may be constructed, and may be expressed either as an adjusted rate of return on equity or as an adjusted net margin on sales. The resulting adjusted rates of return and adjusted net profit margins are then introduced as dependent variables in appropriately modified cross-section regressions, with relative advertising intensity included as one of the explanatory variables. Hypothesis II is then tested by the significance of the partial regression coefficients of the adjusted rate of return or adjusted net profit margin on the advertising:sales ratio. A significant positive coefficient would indicate that the effect of advertising intensity upon rates of return or gross margins is greater than the amount required to offset the current and capital costs associated with the advertising outlays. Insignificant or negative coefficients would lead us to reject Hypothesis II.

Finally, we should point out that since the amortization formulas used are based on the estimated time pattern of the real sales effects of advertising, no allowance is made for possible differences between that pattern and the time pattern of advertising's effects on price-cost margins. There are two reasons for this, one practical and the other conceptual. First, estimates of the time pattern of these effects are not available. Second, and more important, the increase in the price-cost margins may reflect the monopolistic effects of advertising, and the use of a formula that may capitalize or partly capitalize monopoly rents should be avoided. We feel that the approach we have adopted, which is to treat all advertising expenditures as if they were as necessary for production and sales as are other costs, and then to examine whether there is evidence of monopoly returns associated with these expenditures, is conservative in this respect. To apply arbitrarily lower depreciation rates when amortizing advertising to allow for the possible longer life of the monopolistic effects of advertising would involve at least a partial capitalization of the monopoly returns. Hence, one would be not only deducting the full costs of advertising investments (whereas, strictly speaking, only that portion not associated with monopoly rents should be deducted) but also deducting the imputed capital costs of the value of the monopoly goodwill itself. The results would, of course, understate the monopolistic effects of advertising activities.

When advertising increases the difficulties of entry into an industry, its effect is analogous to that of a government tax on entry, which creates valuable monopoly rights for those already established in the industry. An apt analogy involves the treatment of the costs of purchasing legal monopoly rights in an industry. If one included the market value of these rights in the denominator of rates of return for the New York City taxi industry, for example, one might conclude from an analysis of these rates of return that there is no problem of monopoly pricing in that industry.

## ESTIMATION OF GOODWILL STOCKS

As demonstrated above, it is possible to derive an amortization formula for advertising only if we are prepared to make specific assumptions about the time pattern of revenues from fixed investments. In this section, we develop estimates of the goodwill stock based on the assumption that the net revenues from fixed investments are constant over the life of these investments. These estimates will therefore overstate the goodwill stock generated by advertising for those industries in which the net revenues decline over the life of a capital project. The adjusted rates of return in such industries will hence be biased downward where the growth of goodwill is less than the book rate of return and upward where the growth rate exceeds the book rate of return.[15]

Goodwill stocks may be generated by means of formulas based on the demand equations presented in the previous chapter. Two sets of estimates are constructed on the basis of alternative formulations of the effects of advertising by other industries. In the first set, we ignore the negative effect of advertising in other industries; advertising is allowed to generate only positive goodwill in the industry that makes the expenditures. In the second set, we make allowance for the negative effect of a general increase in advertising upon the effectiveness of the industry's own advertising. Hence advertising in an industry generates not only positive goodwill in that industry but negative goodwill in other industries.

Let us first derive the formula appropriate under the assumption that advertising in other industries as well as population growth and future price changes may be ignored. Consider the Generalized Koyck demand model,

$$C_t = a_1 \Delta A_t + a_1 \lambda A_{t-1} + a_4 C_{t-1} + Z_t,$$

where $C_t$ is per-capita real sales at time $t$, $A_t$ is advertising in the industry, $Z_t$ represents the effects of all other variables, and $a_1$, $\lambda$, and $a_4$ are coefficients from the regression equation. This model implies that each dollar's worth of advertising made at time $t$ yields the following stream of sales:

| Period | Sales effect[16] |
|--------|------------------|
| 1 | $a_1$ |
| 2 | $a_1 (\lambda + a_4 - 1)$ |
| 3 | $a_4 a_1 (\lambda + a_4 - 1)$ |
| 4 | $a_4^2 a_1 (\lambda + a_4 - 1)$ |
| . | . |
| . | . |
| . | . |
| $t$ | $a_4^{t-2} a_1 (\lambda + a_4 - 1).$ |

Note that, after the initial period, the sales effects of advertising decay at the rate $1 - a_4$. Hence the goodwill stock (the present value of the net revenue stream generated by advertising made in a period) will also decay at the rate $1 - a_4$ starting at the end of that period.

Hence our problem simplifies to that of determining the fraction of current advertising that should be expensed; the remainder represents additions to

15. See the example of exponentially declining net revenues discussed above. See also T. R. Stauffer, "The Measurement of Corporate Rates of Return," Chapter 3.

16. The coefficients $a_1$, $\lambda$, and $a_4$ are from the Generalized Koyck Demand Model and are defined in Chapter 5 above.

goodwill. Since we want to construct a goodwill stock analogous to a fixed-capital stock at replacement cost, we divide advertising expenditures in a period into that portion chargeable to the current period and that portion chargeable to future periods (and hence added to goodwill initially) on the basis of the present values of the net incomes generated. Since we assume that the net profit per dollar of sales is constant, we simply calculate the ratio of the present value of sales generated during the period to the present value of sales generated in the current and all future periods. The resulting fraction is the proportion of current advertising chargeable to current expense.

The present value of current sales is simply $a_1$. The present value of all sales is

$$a_1 \left[ 1 + (\lambda + a_4 - 1) \sum_{i=0}^{\infty} \frac{a_4^i}{(1+r)^{i+1}} \right],$$

where $r$ is the appropriate discount rate. The latter expression simplifies to

$$a_1 \left( \frac{r+\lambda}{1+r-a_4} \right).$$

Hence current advertising may be divided into that portion charged to current expense ($CE$) and that portion added to the goodwill stock ($AGW$) according to the following formulas:

$$CE_t = \left( \frac{1+r-a_4}{r+\lambda} \right) A_t,$$

$$AGW_t = \left( \frac{\lambda-1+a_4}{r+\lambda} \right) A_t$$

The goodwill stocks at the end of each period may therefore be generated by means of the equation

$$GW_t - GW_{t-1} = AGW_t - DEP_t,$$

where $DEP_t$ is the deterioration of the previous goodwill that occurs during period $t$ and is given by

$$DEP_t = (1 - a_4)GW_{t-1}.$$

Hence

$$GW_t = \left( \frac{\lambda-1+a_4}{r+\lambda} \right) A_t + a_4 \, GW_{t-1}.$$

It is evident that, in addition to the coefficients of the demand equations, we require estimates of the discount rate and a procedure for initializing the goodwill stock. The discount rate used is based on interest rates and stock yields for the corporate sector as a whole, the same rate being used in each industry.[17] A case could be made for using a different rate (depending on the debt:equity ratio for the industry) for each industry, but such refinements do not appear worth while because the resulting estimates are not particularly sensitive to changes in the discount rate used.

We initialize the generating process in 1946, and assume that the initial goodwill at the beginning of that year is zero.[18] Since 1954 is the first year for which the adjusted rates of return are calculated, goodwill stocks and related adjusted rates of return over the period relevant for the cross-section analysis will not be sensitive to changes in initial goodwill stocks. Furthermore, in view of the effect of various wartime restrictions and shortages on consumer purchases and on advertising, the zero initialization may be appropriate.

For several durable-goods industries (and for two nondurable-goods industries) the straightforward application of this procedure yielded negative goodwill stocks throughout the relevant period. For these industries, the dynamic demand functions imply that the future effects of today's advertising are negative because current additions to stocks of goods induced by advertising have a subsequent negative effect on future spending. In these cases we decided to adopt the convention of simply expensing advertising, which means that the book rates of return are not adjusted in any way for these industries.

For the remaining industries, it is noteworthy that, with two exceptions, the resulting estimates of the goodwill stocks are smaller than the annual flows of advertising expenditures. These results reflect two characteristics of the demand equations. First, a substantial portion of advertising is expensed in the current period, and hence never contributes to the goodwill stock. Second, the depreciation rates applied to the stocks themselves are relatively high. As a result, the typical life of the interindustry effects of advertising is quite short.

As already noted, these estimates do not take into account the impact of competitive advertising in other industries. Also ignored are the effects of price changes and population growth. Since the demand equations are estimated in real per-capita terms, anticipated increases in prices and population will affect the division of advertising between charges to current expense and additions to goodwill. In addition, increases in prices and population, whether anticipated or not, will give rise to capital gains on the goodwill stock that

17. The cost of capital used is 6.35 percent. This is obtained as a weighted average of the BAA bond yield and the earnings: price ratios for equities, taking into account the deductibility of interest charges from the corporation income tax. The weights used are the relative volumes of debt and equity in all manufacturing. Experimentation with the alternative measure of the BAA bond yield itself indicated that the goodwill stock estimates are not sensitive to changes in the cost of capital.

18. For industries for which data for 1946 and/or 1947 are not available, estimates of advertising based on the pattern of advertising in manufacturing as a whole over the period 1946–1948 and industry advertising in 1947 or 1948 were used.

serve to offset a portion of the depreciation that would otherwise occur. All of these complexities are taken into account in our second estimated goodwill-stock series.

The simplest procedure is first to derive the formula for the generation of positive goodwill, which takes into account population growth and price increases, and then to develop the formula for the negative goodwill generated by advertising in other industries. Let $q$ represent the anticipated growth rate of the price· population factor. The formula for allocating advertising between current expenses and additions to goodwill now becomes

$$AGP_t = A_t \left( \frac{\lambda - 1 + a_4}{r + \lambda - qa_4} \right),$$

where $AGP$ represents additions to the positive goodwill stock, and

$$CE_t = \frac{1 + r - (1 - q)a_4}{r + \lambda - qa_4}.$$

The formula for the depreciation of the goodwill stock is the same:

$$DEP_t = GP_{t-1} (1 - a_4),$$

where $GP$ represents the positive goodwill stock.

In this situation, however, both anticipated and unanticipated capital gains will occur. The former reflect the effects of anticipated increases in prices and population; the latter reflect the effects of unanticipated changes in these variables. The anticipated capital gains are

$$ACGP_t = q \cdot GP_{t-1} \cdot a_4;$$

the unanticipated capital gains or losses are

$$UCGP_t = \left[ \frac{P_t Pop_t}{P_{t-1} Pop_{t-1}} - 1 - q \right] \cdot GP_{t-1} \cdot a_4.$$

The generation formula for the positive goodwill stock is now

$$GP_t = GP_{t-1} - DEP_t + ACGP_t + UCGP_t + AGP_t.$$

Let us now consider the negative goodwill generated by the advertising of other industries. First note that the specification of the demand equations implies that the effect of advertising in other industries is to reduce the effectiveness of the industry's own advertising. A stable level of advertising in other industries would not affect any of the foregoing formulas and hence would not generate negative goodwill stocks. We therefore calculate the value of negative goodwill as the offset to the positive goodwill that results from the increase in advertising in other industries above its level in the initial year:

$$AGN = AGP \left( \frac{ATOT_0}{ATOT_t} - 1.0 \right).$$

The formulas for depreciation, anticipated capital gains, and unanticipated capital gains are analogous to those relating to the positive goodwill stock: for depreciation,

$$DEPN_t = GN_{t-1}(1 - a_4);$$

for anticipated capital gains;

$$ACGN_t = q \cdot GN_{t-1} \cdot a_4;$$

and for unanticipated capital gains,

$$UCGN_t = \left( \frac{P_t Pop_t}{P_{t-1} Pop_{t-1}} - 1 - q \right) \cdot GN_{t-1} \cdot a_4.$$

The net goodwill-stock and related series for each industry are obtained by simply adding together the positive and negative components.

In order to derive these estimates, we require an estimate of $q$, the combined growth rate of price and population, for each industry. We simply assume that anticipated growth over this period may be approximated by the 1948–1957 trend in the price · population factor.[19]

The resulting goodwill-stock estimates we shall henceforth refer to as complex measures, in contrast to the simple measures developed previously which ignore the complications of population growth, price changes, and the growth of advertising in other industries.

## CALCULATIONS OF ADJUSTED RATES OF RETURN AND ADJUSTED PRICE-COST MARGINS; INTERINDUSTRY REGRESSION RESULTS.

The goodwill-stock estimates described above may be used[20] to calculate ajdusted rates of return and adjusted price-cost margins, as has already been

19. To be specific, the average annual rate of growth between 1948 and 1957 in the product of industry price times population is used as the estimate of $q$.

20. One minor adjustment to the goodwill stock estimates described above was required. The data used to estimate the demand functions covered all corporations in each industry, and the goodwill stock estimates discussed above are of comparable coverage. Since the profit rate analyses are based on data for firms with assets above $500,000 (for an explanation of this choice, see Chapter 6 above), the goodwill stocks had to be adjusted to make them comparable to the other data used in the profit rate analyses. The adjustment procedure is as follows:

$$GW_{53}^* = GW_{53} \cdot \frac{\overline{Ad^*}}{\overline{Ad}}$$

where $GW$ is the goodwill stock at the end of the year, $Ad$ is the average advertising over the period 1954–57, and a superscript * identifies the variable as pertaining to firms with assets above $500,000. $GW^*$ for the years 1954–1957 was then generated using the goodwill stock generation formulae and observed advertising data for firms with assets above $500,000 over those years.

discussed. Two adjusted rates of return are calculated. Denoting the unadjusted book rate by $b_1$ and the two adjusted rates of return by $b_2$ and $b_3$ respectively, we have the following formulas:

$$b_1 = \frac{\pi}{E},$$

$$b_2 = \frac{\pi + Ad - CE - DEPG}{E + GW},$$

$$b_3 = \frac{\pi + Ad - CE - DEP - rGW}{E},$$

where $\pi$ is net profits, $E$ is stockholders equity, $Ad$ is current advertising, $CE$ is that portion of advertising which is expensed, $DEPG$ is the depreciation on the goodwill stock, $r$ is the cost of capital, and $GW$ is the value of the goodwill stock.

The first adjusted rate, $b_2$, is an estimate of the rate of return on all capital. Under certain conditions, $b_2$ may be regarded as a better approximation of the true internal rate of return than $b_1$. It is therefore appropriate to use $b_2$ to test the hypothesis that the internal rate of return itself varies with the intensity of advertising.

The second adjusted rate, $b_3$, represents a rate of return corrected for current and capital costs of advertising. This measure, or the alternative measure of adjusted price-cost margin described below, is appropriate for testing the hypothesis that investment in advertising earned a rate of return above the cost of capital.

Since $b_3$ involves an asymmetric treatment of fixed investment and advertising investments, it is also instructive to examine the adjusted price-cost margin, denoted by $b_4$ and specified as follows:

$$b_4 = \frac{\pi + Ad - CE - DEPG - rE - rGW}{S},$$

where $S$ is current sales. As is obvious from this specification, $b_4$ is a measure of the profit margin on sales net of all capital costs. Hence advertising and fixed capital investments are treated symmetrically (recall that $\pi$ is already net of depreciation on fixed capital). Appropriate regression equations explaining $b_4$ therefore provide an alternative test of the hypothesis that the yield on advertising investments is greater than the cost of capital. In order to preserve comparability with our other results, regressions with all of the independent variables scaled for capital intensity as well as regressions with the original set of independent variables are estimated.[21]

21. In these alternative regressions, all variables, including the constant term, are multiplied by the ratio (Equity + Goodwill)/Sales.

In the previous chapters we have examined the effect of advertising:sales ratios on rates of return; an alternative formulation of the general hypothesis that the relative intensity of advertising is related to rates of return or price-cost margins could be considered. In addition to the ordinary advertising:sales ratio, the total user cost of advertising expressed as a percentage of sales is used as an alternative variable. This variable is defined as follows:

$$Adj \frac{Ad}{S} = \frac{CE + DEPG + \rho GW}{S} \, ,$$

where $\rho$ is the cost of capital before tax.[22]

Before we proceed to the cross-sectional regression results, it is worth discussing the relation between the alternative measures. Averages for the 1954–1957 period of book rates of return, the two adjusted rates of return and the adjusted net profit margin for the 39 industries are presented in Table 8.2. Means, standard deviations, and correlations between these measures are tabulated in Table 8.3. The results obtained are most interesting. In contrast to what many would have expected, the means of the two adjusted rates of return are slightly *higher* than the mean of the book rate of return. More important, the correlations between the three rate-of-return measures are uniformly very high.

The high intercorrelation between the three rate-of-return measures reflects not only the properties of the demand equations, but also the fact that growth rates of advertising were quite high during the postwar period. Growth rates of advertising and sales for the postwar period are presented in Table 8.4. It is noteworthy that the average growth rate of advertising exceeded that of sales, and was also about the same as average book rate of return for 1954–1957. As a result, for most industries, the estimated biases attributable to advertising in the book rate of return are small, and are about as frequently negative as positive.

The correlation between the adjusted net profit margin and the alternative rate-of-return measures is somewhat lower. This is, of course, not surprising, since interindustry variations in the equity:sales ratio will affect the relation between adjusted net margins and the various rates of return, except for those industries in which the adjusted net margin is zero.

These high correlations indicate, of course, that these data will probably not permit us to discriminate between the hypothesis that advertising affects

22. $\rho$ is a weighted average of before tax earnings price ratios and the BAA interest rate. The total user cost measure is therefore defined in before-tax terms. For industries where advertising is expensed, the simple Ad/Sales ratio is used. The adjusted Ad/Sales ratio used in regressions explaining rates of return and net margins adjusted on the basis of the complex goodwill stock estimates is defined net of capital gains.

TABLE 8.2.  Average book rates of return, adjusted rates of return, and adjusted net margins: 39 industries[a]

| Industry | Book rate of return, $b_1$ | Adjusted rates of return | | Adjusted net margin, $b_4$ |
|---|---|---|---|---|
| | | $b_2$ | $b_3$ | |
| Soft drinks | 0.09988 | 0.09997 | 0.10012 | 0.01906 |
| Malt liquor | .07162 | .07087 | .07222 | .00353 |
| Wines | .07261 | .07456 | .07515 | .00453 |
| Distilled liquor | .05007 | .04960 | .04945 | −.00482 |
| Meat[b] | .04644 | .04644 | .04644 | −.00177 |
| Dairy products | .07936 | .07909 | .07937 | .00412 |
| Canning | .06428 | .06522 | .06550 | .00074 |
| Grain mill products | .07020 | .06905 | .06933 | .00126 |
| Cereals | .14811 | .13796 | .14625 | .03341 |
| Bakery products | .09279 | .09295 | .09344 | .00877 |
| Confectionery[b] | .10650 | .10650 | .10650 | .01668 |
| Cigars | .05299 | .05210 | .05191 | −.00574 |
| Cigarettes | .11471 | .11419 | .11630 | .02278 |
| Knit goods | .03762 | .03757 | .03753 | −.01064 |
| Carpets[b] | .04533 | .04533 | .04533 | −.00980 |
| Hats[b] | .01575 | .01575 | .01575 | −.02524 |
| Men's clothing[b] | .05941 | .05941 | .05941 | −.00134 |
| Women's clothing | .06079 | .108647 | .10518 | .00839 |
| Millinery[b] | −.01335 | −.01335 | −.10335 | −.01201 |
| Furs | .05724 | .05790 | .05797 | −.00271 |
| Furniture[b] | .09661 | .09661 | .09661 | .01183 |
| Screens and blinds[b] | .09301 | .09301 | .09301 | .01128 |
| Periodicals[b] | .11660 | .11660 | .11660 | .01410 |
| Books | .10106 | .10084 | .10140 | .01815 |
| Drugs | .13981 | .13935 | .14451 | .05624 |
| Soaps | .11653 | .11554 | .11593 | .01771 |
| Perfumes | .13534 | .13414 | .14268 | .03076 |
| Tires and tubes[b] | .10236 | .10236 | .10236 | .01409 |
| Footwear[b] | .07604 | .07604 | .07604 | .00421 |
| Hand tools[b] | .11442 | .11442 | .11442 | .02869 |
| Household and service machinery (nonelectrical) | .07315 | .07293 | .07299 | .00393 |
| Electrical appliances[b] | .10253 | .10253 | .10253 | .01467 |
| Radio, TV, and phonograph | .08789 | .08409 | .08578 | .00611 |

Table 8.2. (continued)

| Industry | Book rate of return, $b_1$ | Adjusted rates of return | | Adjusted net margin, $b_4$ |
|---|---|---|---|---|
| | | $b_2$ | $b_3$ | |
| Motorcycles and bicycles[b] | .05160 | .05160 | .05160 | −.00457 |
| Motor vehicles[b] | .15461 | .15461 | .15461 | .03463 |
| Instruments | .12023 | .12026 | .12101 | .02755 |
| Clocks and watches | .01873 | .01794 | .01196 | −.02681 |
| Jewelry (precious metal) | .05273 | .05112 | .05092 | −.00610 |
| Costume jewelry | .01405 | .01591 | .01540 | −.01277 |

[a]All averages are for the period 1954–1957 and are for firms with assets above $500,000. Adjustments are based on the simple goodwill stock series in each case.
[b]Advertising is fully expensed for this industry so that book and adjusted rates of return are the same. For these industries, the adjusted net margin is simply the net-profit:sales ratio.

TABLE 8.3. Means, standard deviations, and simple correlations of book and adjusted profit rates

| Variable | | Mean | Standard deviation |
|---|---|---|---|
| A. *Adjustments based on simple goodwill stocks* | | | |
| Book rate of return, | $b_1$ | 0.0795 | 0.0382 |
| Adjusted rate of return, | $b_2$ | .0797 | .0375 |
| | $b_3$ | .0808 | .0390 |
| Adjusted net margin on sales, | $b_4$ | .0075 | .0166 |
| *Correlation matrix* | | | |

| | $b_1$ | $b_2$ | $b_3$ | $b_4$ |
|---|---|---|---|---|
| $b_1$ | 1.000 | 0.993 | 0.983 | 0.928 |
| $b_2$ | | 1.000 | .996 | .933 |
| $b_3$ | | | 1.000 | .936 |
| $b_4$ | | | | 1.000 |

B. *Adjustments based on complex goodwill stocks*

| | | Mean | Standard deviation |
|---|---|---|---|
| Book rate of return, | $b_1$ | 0.0795 | 0.0382 |
| Adjusted rates of return, | $b_2$ | .0789 | .0377 |
| | $b_3$ | .0792 | .0382 |
| Adjusted net margin on sales, | $b_4$ | .0075 | .0167 |

*Correlation matrix*

| | $b_1$ | $b_2$ | $b_3$ | $b_4$ |
|---|---|---|---|---|
| $b_1$ | 1.000 | 0.998 | 0.997 | 0.930 |
| $b_2$ | | 1.000 | .9996 | .932 |
| $b_3$ | | | 1.000 | .934 |
| $b_4$ | | | | 1.000 |

TABLE 8.4.   Growth rates of advertising and sales: 39 industries

| Industry | Growth rate[a] | |
| | Advertising | Sales |
| --- | --- | --- |
| Soft drinks | 7.59 | 5.34 |
| Malt liquor | 10.48 | 2.43 |
| Wines | 8.83 | 6.88 |
| Distilled liquor | 12.18 | 2.94 |
| Meat | 7.41 | 1.87 |
| Dairy products | 7.04 | 0.98 |
| Canning | 10.54 | 6.29 |
| Grain mill products | 7.34 | 1.48 |
| Cereals | 2.58 | 5.66 |
| Bakery products | 11.06 | 4.91 |
| Confectionery | 5.50 | 1.50 |
| Cigars | 3.33 | 1.29 |
| Cigarettes | 12.76 | 3.90 |
| Knit goods | 6.36 | 2.37 |
| Carpets | 4.42 | 2.04 |
| Hats | −5.46 | −7.03 |
| Men's clothing | 2.39 | 1.64 |
| Women's clothing | 5.75 | 0.54 |
| Millinery | 1.19 | 3.26 |
| Furs | 7.48 | −1.71 |
| Furniture | 12.55 | 6.72 |
| Screens and blinds | 11.21 | 6.22 |
| Periodicals | 5.69 | 6.23 |
| Books | 9.35 | 10.50 |
| Drugs | 8.99 | 6.68 |
| Soaps | 1.84 | 3.54 |
| Perfumes | 14.43 | 12.26 |
| Tires and tubes | 11.87 | 5.39 |
| Footwear | 4.08 | 2.02 |
| Hand tools | 12.27 | 4.12 |
| Household and service machinery (nonelectrical) | 7.67 | 4.96 |
| Electrical appliances | 11.88 | 8.17 |
| Radio, TV, and phonograph | 16.46 | 15.82 |

Table 8.4.   (continued)

| Industry | Growth rate[a] | |
|---|---|---|
| | Advertising | Sales |
| Motorcycles and bicycles | −0.87 | 1.04 |
| Motor vehicles | 14.24 | 7.43 |
| Instruments | 14.14 | 13.14 |
| Clocks and watches | 2.12 | 1.06 |
| Jewelry (precious metal) | −1.39 | 0.35 |
| Costume jewelry | 25.40 | 12.67 |
| Average of all industries | 7.97 | 4.48 |

[a]These are annual average compound growth rates for the period 1948–1957.

the internal rate of return and the hypothesis that advertising earns a rate of return higher than the cost of capital. Given the high correlation between $b_2$ and $b_3$, we should not be surprised if the statistical estimates of the effects of advertising on each are very similar.

Cross-section regressions using the alternative rates of return and adjusted net-margin measures in a preferred equation selected from an earlier chapter are presented in Table 8.5. Except for one of the equations predicting the net margin, the specification of the independent variables is unchanged from equation (5) of Table 6.3. The results indicate that advertising intensity has a statistically significant and quantitatively important impact on the rate of return regardless of how the rate of return is measured. The $R^2$'s decline slightly when adjusted rates of return are used. Given that the adjustment procedures are based on estimated rather than exact measures of demand characteristics, errors of measurement are of course introduced in the adjusted rates of return, which probably accounts for the slight worsening of fit.

Coefficients for several equations predicting adjusted profit margins are shown in Table 8.5. All are consistent with the hypothesis that advertising intensity has a significant impact on net margins. However, the equation with the independent variables scaled for capital intensity yields a slightly better fit, thereby indicating that this particular specification is somewhat superior. It is notable that the rate of growth of demand comes through as a stronger variable in equations predicting net margins than it does in equations predicting rates of return. The opposite is true for capital requirements.

There is little to choose between equations using adjusted advertising:sales ratios and those using ordinary advertising:sales ratios. Equations utilizing variables adjusted on the basis of the complex goodwill-stock measures and the simple goodwill-stock measures respectively are also very similar. In

TABLE 8.5. Coefficients for cross-section regression equations predicting book and adjusted-profit rates: 39 industries

| Dependent variable | Constant | Regression coefficients | | | | R² |
|---|---|---|---|---|---|---|
| | | Advertising: sales ratio | Absolute capital require- ments (log) | Local industry dummy variable | Growth of demand (log) | |
| Book rate of return, $b_1$ | 0.036 (4.26) | 0.316 (2.14) | 0.0103 (3.16) | 0.0263 (1.48) | 0.0263 (1.99) | 0.532 |
| A. VARIABLES ADJUSTED ON BASIS OF SIMPLE GOODWILL-STOCK ESTIMATES | | | | | | |
| *Unadjusted advertising:sales ratio*[a] | | | | | | |
| Adjusted rates of return, $b_2$ | 0.039 (4.47) | 0.295 (1.94) | 0.0092 (2.78) | 0.0244 (1.35) | 0.0272 (2.01) | .491 |
| $b_3$ | 0.039 (4.25) | 0.340 (2.11) | 0.0086 (2.44) | 0.0222 (1.16) | 0.0290 (2.02) | .470 |
| Adjusted net margin, $b_4$ | −0.010 (2.68) | 0.174 (2.58) | 0.0024 (1.63) | 0.0059 (0.73) | 0.0163 (2.71) | .487 |
| $b_4{}^a$ | −0.028 (2.78) | 0.325 (2.19) | 0.0068 (1.62) | 0.0195 (0.91) | 0.0426 (3.24) | .564 |
| *Adjusted advertising:sales ratio*[b] | | | | | | |
| Adjusted rates of return, $b_2$ | 0.039 (4.49) | 0.274 (1.81) | 0.0092 (2.76) | 0.0246 (1.35) | 0.0277 (2.03) | .484 |
| $b_3$ | 0.039 (4.27) | 0.317 (1.97) | 0.0086 (2.41) | 0.0225 (1.16) | 0.0295 (2.04) | .462 |
| Adjusted net margin, $b_4$ | −0.010 (2.60) | 0.163 (2.41) | 0.0024 (1.60) | 0.0060 (0.73) | 0.0165 (2.72) | .476 |
| $b_4{}^a$ | −0.028 (2.71) | 0.299 (2.01) | 0.0068 (1.61) | 0.0198 (0.92) | 0.0434 (3.28) | .555 |
| B. VARIABLES ADJUSTED ON BASIS OF COMPLEX GOODWILL-STOCK ESTIMATES | | | | | | |
| *Unadjusted advertising:sales ratio* | | | | | | |
| Adjusted rates of return, $b_2^*$ | 0.037 (4.34) | 0.285 (1.89) | 0.0098 (2.96) | 0.0259 (1.43) | 0.0264 (1.98) | 0.501 |
| $b_3^*$ | 0.037 (4.26) | 0.300 (1.96) | 0.0996 (2.85) | 0.0253 (1.38) | 0.0273 (1.99) | .496 |
| Adjusted net margin, $b_4^*$ | −0.0107 (2.81) | 0.166 (2.48) | 0.0026 (1.76) | 0.0071 (0.89) | 0.0169 (2.83) | .501 |
| $b_4^{*a}$ | −0.030 (3.00) | 0.323 (2.17) | 0.0077 (1.88) | 0.0237 (1.13) | 0.0434 (3.32) | .587 |
| *Adjusted advrtiseing:sales ratio*[b] | | | | | | |
| Adjusted rates of return, $b_2^*$ | 0.037 (4.35) | 0.271 (1.82) | 0.0098 (2.95) | 0.0261 (1.44) | 0.0269 (1.99) | .498 |

Table 8.5.   (continued)

| Dependent variable | | Constant | Advertising: sales ratio | Absolute Capital require- ments (log) | Local industry dummy variable | Growth of demand (log) | $R^2$ |
|---|---|---|---|---|---|---|---|
| | | | | Regression coefficients | | | |
| | $b_3^*$ | 0.037 (4.27) | 0.286 (1.88) | 0.0096 (2.84) | 0.0254 (1.38) | 0.0275 (2.00) | .493 |
| Adjusted net margin, | $b_4^*$ | −0.011 (2.77) | 0.158 (2.39) | 0.0026 (1.75) | 0.0072 (0.90) | 0.0170 (2.83) | .496 |
| | $b_4^{*a}$ | −0.030 (2.95) | 0.305 (2.07) | 0.0078 (1.88) | 0.0241 (1.14) | 0.0438 (3.34) | .582 |

[a]All the independent variables are multiplied by the ratio (equity + goodwill): sales.
[b]For most industries, the adjusted advertising:sales ratio is defined as $(DEP + \rho \cdot GW_{t-1})/S$, where $\rho$ is the before-tax cost of capital and $DEP$ is defined net of capital gains; for industries where advertising is expensed, the adjusted and unadjusted ratios are equal.

every instance, the regression coefficient of advertising intensity is significant at at least the 5-percent level (on a one-tailed test).

The conclusions reached on the basis of the empirical work of preceding chapters receive additional confirmation in these results. Taken together with the findings reported by Weiss using a different approach for a different period,[23] these results indicate that the conclusion that advertising affects profit rates does not merely reflect inappropriate accounting procedures. The available evidence is therefore consistent with the view that intensive advertising in an industry permits firms to set higher price-cost margins, thereby yielding rates of return higher than those in other industries where advertising is less important.

23. L. W. Weiss, "Advertising, Profits, and Corporate Taxes. "

## APPENDIX 8-A

It may be demonstrated that the use of a sufficiently low depreciation rate can in many instances result in the apparent elimination of excess rates of return. To the extent that the goodwill stock generated represents increased monopoly power for established firms, it should not be incorporated in the denominator of any rate-of-return calculations. This is readily demonstrated for a firm under conditions of equilibrium growth.

Let the true rate of return be $r = (N - \delta K)/K$, where $N$ is revenues net of current expense, $K$ is capital assets, and $\delta$ is the depreciation rate. Suppose a lower depreciation rate $d < \delta$ is used and an estimate of the rate of return defined as follows:

$$r^* = \frac{N - dK^*}{K^*} \; ;$$

$$K^* = \sum_{i=0}^{\infty} I_{t-i} (1 - d)^i$$

and

$$K_t = \sum_{i=0}^{\infty} I_{t-i} (1 - \delta)^i.$$

Under conditions of steady growth at rate $g$,

$$K_t^* = \frac{1 + g}{g + d} I_t \text{ and } K_t = \frac{1 + g}{g + \delta} I_t;$$

hence

$$K_t^* = K_t \frac{g + \delta}{g + d}.$$

Substituting for $K^*$ in the expression for $r^*$ we obtain

$$r^* = \left[\frac{g + d}{g + \delta}\right]\left(\frac{N}{K}\right) - d.$$

Subtracting this result from $r$ gives

$$r - r^* = \frac{N}{K}\left(1 - \frac{g + d}{g + \delta}\right) - (\delta - d)$$

$$= \frac{N}{K}\left(\frac{\delta - d}{g + \delta}\right) - (\delta - d)$$

$$= (\delta - d)\left(\frac{N/K}{g + \delta} - 1\right)$$

$$= \frac{\delta - d}{g + \delta}\left(\frac{r + \delta}{g + \delta} - 1\right)$$

$$= \frac{(\delta - d)(r - g)}{g + \delta}.$$

Note that $r - r^* > 0$ if $\delta > d$ and $r > g$, and

$$\lim_{d \to 0} (r - r^*) = \frac{\delta(r - g)}{g + \delta}.$$

# CHAPTER 9 Advertising and Firm Size

In Chapter 4, we suggested that there may be important scale economies associated with advertising, in that larger firms need not spend as much proportionately as their smaller rivals to achieve the gains from effective product differentiation. While spending more than smaller firms in absolute amount, they may also be spending less in relation to sales.

One facet of this issue concerns the relation between advertising and firm size within industries. In this chapter, we consider whether large firms typically spend more or less on advertising than their smaller rivals and what factors might account for any observed differences. We also examine the relations between industry characteristics and the intraindustry distribution of advertising expenditures by size of firm.

Before looking at the empirical evidence, we need to ask how to interpret such statistical relations. Is there any direct association between relative levels of advertising expenditures among firms in an industry and the presence of scale economies? For most inputs, a negative relation between firm size and average costs per unit of output, with the quantities of other inputs held constant, would suggest the presence of economies of scale.[1] Can we draw a similar inference in regard to advertising?

There are various reasons why differences in unit advertising costs among firms of different sizes by themselves indicate little about the presence or absence of economies of scale. Where smaller firms spend relatively more on advertising than do their larger counterparts, this may be due to scale econ-

1. This inference is based on the assumption that output prices are fixed in the market and not influenced by the quantities purchased of particular inputs.

omies in advertising and a smaller firm's resulting need to spend more per unit sold to achieve the same result. Alternatively, it may be due to a smaller firm's aim to achieve a greater impact on consumer demand via advertising. In the opposite case, where smaller firms spend proportionately less on advertising, this may be due either to the presence of diseconomies of scale or to the firm's willingness to compete in a different segment of the market, where less advertising is required for consumer acceptance. Indeed, different firms in the same industry may adopt quite different strategies regarding advertising, so there may be differences in advertising:sales ratios among firms even if neither economies nor diseconomies of scale are present.

Unlike the case of production costs, widely different levels of output can be produced and sold with the same volume of advertising—even where the quantities of all other inputs remain fixed. This is because advertising is designed to affect not only the quantity of output that is sold, but also the prices at which this output is sold. Hence a lower product price may take the place of a higher volume of advertising expenditures, and there is no specific level of advertising required to sell a given volume of output.

In many markets, an important function of advertising is to permit firms to maintain price levels that equal or exceed those of their rivals. As noted before, consumers frequently consider highly advertised products as higher in "quality" than others in the market and, as a result, these products command a higher price. Where advertising outlays are low, on the other hand, firms are often unable to reach effective price parity with their rivals, for consumers view their products as substandard, and prices must be set lower to attract buyers. We have only to observe the striking price differences that exist among competing brands of aspirin, soap, or various cosmetics to recognize the significance of this effect.

In the same market, some firms may choose to engage in heavy advertising outlays and sell their products at the higher prices that such outlays permit. Others may find it more profitable to dispense with most of these expenditures, produce a more standardized product, and accept a lower price. Different unit advertising costs thereby reflect differences in firm marketing strategies as well as the effects of scale economies in advertising. As a result, we cannot interpret the findings discussed below as reflecting only economies of scale in advertising. Evidence bearing more directly on the extent of such economies is presented in the following chapter.

## RELATIVE ADVERTISING EXPENDITURE WITHIN INDUSTRIES

In this section, we examine the distribution of relative advertising expenditures within industries and seek to explain the differences that exist among industries. The measures used for this purpose are relative concentration levels. For the largest firms within an industry, concentration ratios are computed for total advertising expenditures as well as for assets and sales. Average four-firm concentration ratios for each of these variables for the period 1954–1957 are given in Table 9.1. For most industries, advertising is more highly concentrated than either assets or sales. In 28 industries out of 41, advertising is more highly concentrated than assets, and in 31 industries out of 41, it is more highly concentrated than industry sales. This indicates that the largest firms typically spend proportionately greater amounts on advertising.

However, it is instructive to examine the 10 industries in our sample where this finding is unambiguously reversed. These industries are: distilled liquors, cigarettes, periodicals, books, drugs, paints, perfumes, tires and tubes, motor vehicles, and instruments. What is striking about this group of industries is that they include many of those characterized by heavy industry advertising expenditures. The mean advertising:sales ratio of this group of 10 industries is 4.0 percent, which contrasts with an average ratio of 3.1 percent in the remaining 31 industries. Although this finding is not conclusive, there is some suggestion that industries in which the largest firms do proportionately less advertising than their smaller rivals are often those with generally higher advertising:sales ratios.

Eight-firm concentration ratios for the three variables are given in Table 9.2. When large firms in an industry are considered to include the top 8, advertising is even more highly concentrated than before. In only 7 industries out of 41 do the top 8 firms account for a smaller share of total industry advertising expenditures than they do of aggregate industry assets or sales. In three additional cases, the leading 8 firms account for proportionately more advertising than sales but proportionately less than their aggregate value of assets. In the remaining cases, the 8 largest firms account for a larger, and often a substantially larger, share than would be expected from firm size alone.

It is important to note that in the 7 industries in which advertising is less concentrated than either sales or assets, the average advertising:sales ratio is 4.6 percent, whereas in the remaining 34 industries it is 3.0 percent. Again, it appears that industries in which the largest firms do proportionately less advertising than their smaller rivals are likely to be those in which aggregate industry advertising is relatively high.

To examine this question further, concentration ratios for advertising expenditures are divided by the comparable ratios for assets and sales respectively. The mean values of these ratios are then computed for the seven industries with very high aggregate advertising as defined by both the industry

TABLE 9.1.   Four-firm concentration ratios[a]

| Industry | Concentration ratio (percent) | | |
|---|---|---|---|
| | Advertising expenditures | Assets | Sales |
| Soft drinks | 27.6 | 14.8 | 13.3 |
| Malt liquors | 24.2 | 28.3 | 22.8 |
| Wines | 39.3 | 32.7 | 31.1 |
| Distilled liquors | 48.2 | 62.0 | 56.0 |
| Meat | 58.0 | 49.1 | 48.2 |
| Dairy products | 64.7 | 61.3 | 53.4 |
| Canning | 42.5 | 31.4 | 24.9 |
| Grain mill products | 62.4 | 34.4 | 32.0 |
| Cereals[b] | 91.0 | 84.2 | 81.2 |
| Bakery products | 35.5 | 31.4 | 24.0 |
| Sugar | 41.5 | 31.1 | 39.6 |
| Confectionery | 40.0 | 34.6 | 25.4 |
| Cigars | 63.9 | 59.5 | 51.8 |
| Cigarettes | 74.6 | 79.1 | 79.8 |
| Knit goods | 15.6 | 12.3 | 7.1 |
| Carpets | 55.2 | 48.3 | 43.1 |
| Hats | 73.5 | 41.9 | 34.6 |
| Mens' clothing | 21.2 | 9.0 | 5.7 |
| Womens' clothing | 15.5 | 4.4 | 2.6 |
| Millinery | 21.8 | 12.9 | 7.5 |
| Furs | 6.7 | 6.6 | 4.7 |
| Furniture | 15.2 | 10.6 | 8.9 |
| Screens and blinds | 31.6 | 29.2 | 24.6 |
| Periodicals[b] | 2.3 | 25.4 | 33.6 |
| Books | 8.9 | 19.4 | 16.5 |
| Drugs | 14.1 | 26.5 | 23.4 |
| Soaps | 83.0 | 78.0 | 73.6 |
| Paints | 29.9 | 49.3 | 47.3 |
| Perfumes | 19.2 | 27.7 | 25.2 |
| Tires and tubes | 74.8 | 82.0 | 78.1 |
| Footwear | 37.8 | 38.4 | 26.3 |
| Hand tools | 55.1 | 21.2 | 17.2 |
| Household and service machinery (not electrical) | 40.1 | 45.9 | 37.3 |

Table 9.1. (continued)

|  | Concentration ratio (percent) | | |
| Industry | Advertising expenditures | Assets | Sales |
| --- | --- | --- | --- |
| Electrical appliances | 62.1 | 52.7 | 48.7 |
| Radio, TV and phonograph | 44.8 | 40.0 | 35.3 |
| Motorcycles and bicycles | 67.2 | 57.0 | 51.2 |
| Motor vehicles | 73.4 | 76.9 | 77.3 |
| Instruments | 33.7 | 46.4 | 39.0 |
| Clocks and watches | 60.0 | 53.2 | 47.7 |
| Jewelry (precious metal) | 38.2 | 30.7 | 25.2 |
| Costume jewelry | 56.1 | 21.9 | 16.3 |

[a]These ratios are calculated from I.R.S. statistics, which are published by asset-size class of firm. For this reason, we were forced to assume that each firm within a size class had values of advertising expenditures, assets, and sales equal to the mean value within the size class. The concentration ratios are averages for the years 1954–1957.

[b]Data on advertising expenditures for the largest firm in cereals and the largest two firms in periodicals were missing from the I.R.S. statistics. In those cases, advertising expenditures were presumably included in other expense categories on the firm's tax return. As a result, advertising levels in these two industries are understated. The concentration ratios presented above exclude those firms that were alone in their respective size classes, from the industry total as well as from the total for the largest firms. In cereals, the four-firm concentration ratios that include the omitted firm are 91.4 and 90.1 percent in terms of assets and sales respectively. The corresponding figures for periodicals are 36.0 and 36.2 percent. The adjusted figures are used to provide a more accurate basis of comparison with the advertising ratio.

TABLE 9.2.   Eight-firm concentration ratios[a]

|  | Concentration ratio (percent) | | |
| Industry | Advertising expenditures | Assets | Sales |
| --- | --- | --- | --- |
| Soft drinks | 32.6 | 20.2 | 17.9 |
| Malt liquors | 38.2 | 39.4 | 34.7 |
| Wines | 64.3 | 50.6 | 45.0 |
| Distilled liquors | 67.3 | 77.6 | 70.5 |
| Meat | 67.0 | 57.8 | 56.5 |
| Dairy products | 79.1 | 70.7 | 63.6 |
| Canning | 58.2 | 44.1 | 35.0 |
| Grain mill products | 66.5 | 46.2 | 43.3 |
| Cereals[b] | 94.3 | 93.0 | 91.0 |
| Bakery products | 51.7 | 44.3 | 37.4 |

Table 9.2.   (continued)

| Industry | Concentration ratio (percent) | | |
|---|---|---|---|
| | Advertising expenditures | Assets | Sales |
| Sugar | 56.3 | 46.4 | 52.5 |
| Confectionery | 54.5 | 44.9 | 35.8 |
| Cigars | 76.9 | 73.1 | 66.6 |
| Cigarettes | 97.5 | 96.2 | 96.3 |
| Knit goods | 28.7 | 17.4 | 11.5 |
| Carpets | 74.6 | 69.9 | 60.7 |
| Hats | 84.4 | 53.8 | 47.0 |
| Mens' clothing | 25.5 | 13.3 | 9.1 |
| Womens' clothing | 19.6 | 6.6 | 4.0 |
| Millinery | 27.2 | 18.6 | 11.3 |
| Furs | 13.2 | 10.3 | 7.8 |
| Furniture | 20.0 | 15.0 | 12.3 |
| Screens and blinds | 43.2 | 42.6 | 37.4 |
| Periodicals[b] | 5.0 | 33.3 | 43.8 |
| Books | 19.0 | 28.5 | 24.3 |
| Drugs | 27.7 | 42.8 | 37.8 |
| Soaps | 86.8 | 80.8 | 76.6 |
| Paints | 38.6 | 57.4 | 54.6 |
| Perfumes | 35.7 | 43.5 | 39.2 |
| Tires and tubes | 92.2 | 91.8 | 87.2 |
| Footwear | 45.2 | 44.0 | 30.6 |
| Hand tools | 59.6 | 29.2 | 23.7 |
| Household and service machinery (not electrical) | 50.7 | 55.5 | 48.6 |
| Electrical appliances | 72.7 | 65.3 | 62.1 |
| Radio, TV and phonograph | 66.5 | 56.6 | 52.6 |
| Motorcycles and bicycles | 89.2 | 81.6 | 77.5 |
| Motor vehicles | 92.7 | 94.6 | 94.6 |
| Instruments | 48.8 | 54.9 | 47.3 |
| Clocks and watches | 86.7 | 76.3 | 73.1 |
| Jewelry (precious metal) | 50.9 | 40.8 | 35.0 |
| Costume jewelry | 61.4 | 30.4 | 21.9 |

[a,b]See the notes to Table 9.1.

advertising:sales ratio and the absolute volume of average advertising expenditures among the leading firms.[2] The average values for the remaining industries in the sample are also computed.

The empirical findings are given in Table 9.3. As can be seen, the average ratio for industries with heavy advertising expenditures is less than unity in

TABLE 9.3.   Effect of aggregate industry advertising on intraindustry distribution of advertising

| | Concentration ratio in advertising divided by concentration ratio in assets or sales | | | |
| | Four-firm ratios | | Eight-firm ratios | |
| Variable | Assets | Sales | Assets | Sales |
|---|---|---|---|---|
| Average of 7 industries[a] with high advertising, $\bar{X}_1$ | 0.875 | 0.938 | 0.931 | 0.986 |
| Remaining 33 industries, $\bar{X}_2$ | 1.357 | 1.728 | 1.294 | 1.597 |
| Difference, $\bar{X}_2 - \bar{X}_1$ | 0.482 | 0.790 | 0.363 | 0.611 |
| $t$ Test: $\bar{X}_1 < \bar{X}_2$ | 3.61 | 3.92 | 3.77 | 4.10 |
| Degrees of freedom | 36 | 39 | 35 | 39 |
| $t$ Test: $\bar{X}_1 < 1.0$ | 1.66 | 0.85 | 1.23 | 0.27 |
| Degrees of freedom | 6 | 6 | 6 | 6 |
| $t$ Test: $\bar{X}_2 > 1.0$ | 3.24 | 3.87 | 3.75 | 4.26 |
| Degrees of freedom | 32 | 32 | 32 | 32 |

[a]Periodicals were excluded from the analysis because they gave a highly extreme observation, probably owing to the data problem described in note b to Table 9.1.

every case, whereas the average for the remaining industries exceeds unity throughout. In addition, the differences between these ratios are statistically significant at the 1-percent confidence level in each case. Thus, there is empirical support for the view that larger firms spend proportionately less on advertising where aggregate industry advertising is high as compared with what would probably be spent, again relative to the outlays of smaller firms, where industry advertising is moderate or low.

Note that the average ratio for the seven industries with heavy advertising expenditures is always less than unity, which suggests that the leading four or eight firms generally have lower advertising:sales ratios than do the re-

2. High advertising levels are indicated for industries where (a) the average advertising: sales ratio exceeded 8 percent, (b) average advertising expenditures per firm among the leading firms, which accounted for 50 percent of industry output, exceeded $20 million, or (c) the former exceeded 4 percent *and* the latter exceeded $5 million. These same classifications were used to define the high advertising barrier to entry used in Chapter 6 above.

maining firms in the industry. We are unable to accept this hypothesis, however, with much assurance. In none of the cases was the null hypothesis rejected at the conventional 5-percent level, although it could be rejected at the 10-percent level in the first instance.

The opposite hypothesis—that larger firms spend proportionately more on advertising where industry advertising does *not* reach very high levels—fared better in an empirical test. In these industries, which constitute the majority of the sample, the largest four and eight firms generally spend more than their smaller competitors, and here the null hypothesis could always be rejected at the 1-percent level. Thus, it appears that the largest firms in any industry account for a greater share of industry advertising than would be expected on the basis of size alone, where advertising is *not* a dominant feature of competitive life.

As discussed above, there are alternative explanations for a finding that advertising is more highly concentrated in large firms than would be expected on the basis of size alone. The first is the presence of *diseconomies* of scale in advertising, so that larger firms need to spend proportionately more than their smaller rivals to achieve the same impact on consumer demand. The second explanation is that smaller firms compete in different segments of the market from those dominated by the larger firms, and that in these submarkets the same high advertising levels are not required. Although the first explanation is consistent with these findings, there is little supporting evidence that diseconomies are encountered by large advertisers, and, in fact, the analysis presented in other sections of this monograph points in the opposite direction.[3] For this reason, it seems a more likely conclusion that larger firms spend relatively more on advertising in most industries than do smaller firms because they seek to sell their products in different segments of the market. Their aim is to achieve effective market segmentation, and proportionately higher advertising outlays are devoted to this end. In contrast, the bulk of the sales of smaller firms in these industries are likely to be products that are more standardized, where less advertising is required and where unit prices, and possibly unit profits, are lower.

An example of this type of market segmentation is found in the soap industry, where soap and detergents are sold both to final consumers in packaged form and to hospitals, restaurants, and other institutions in bulk form. As expected, higher advertising expenditures are required for sales to final consumers, who generally have far less purchasing expertise than do institutional buyers. Although statistics on advertising:sales ratios in the two segments of this market are not available, we can observe that smaller firms have

3. See especially Chapter 10 below.

much higher aggregate market shares in sales of bulk soap and detergent than in their packaged counterparts.[4]

Where larger firms spend proportionately *less* on advertising, conclusions are more difficult to draw. One explanation would be the presence of economies of scale in advertising and, as reported in the following chapter, there is some evidence for the presence of these economies. Where such economies may be realized, we might expect to find lower advertising:sales ratios among larger than among smaller firms. At the same time, segments of the market where less advertising is required for effective entry may also be found in these industries. For example, the soap industry as a whole is characterized by heavy aggregate industry advertising. The relative concentration of advertising in these industries probably reflects both sets of factors.

In industries where aggregate advertising is high, so that these outlays are a particularly important feature of industry behavior, there are likely to be relatively few submarkets of any significance where advertising has only a small impact on consumer demand. In this case, smaller firms would find it difficult to survive without competing with their larger rivals via advertising. The advertising:sales ratios of smaller firms would therefore be as high as those of the leading firms; they might even be higher, to overcome any scale economies that are realized by their larger rivals.

In the remaining industries, there may be many segments of the market where heavy advertising is not compelled by consumer behavior. In these circumstances, smaller firms have the option of concentrating their sales in these submarkets and spending far less on advertising as a proportion of sales. And this option is more likely to be chosen where there are scale economies in advertising. The evidence is surely not conclusive, but this set of explanations is consistent with empirical observation and does suggest various hypotheses regarding the relation between advertising and firm size within industries.

## RELATIVE ADVERTISING AMONG THE LEADING FIRMS

In this section, we examine the pattern of advertising expenditures among the leading firms in an industry, in contrast to the share of those firms together relative to the rest of the industry. Do the 4 largest firms account for more or

4. The largest four firms accounted for 80 percent of synthetic organic packaged detergents (SIC 28415) in 1958 and 92 percent in 1963. In contrast, the largest four firms accounted for 47 percent of synthetic organic bulk detergents (SIC 28416) in 1958 and 39 percent in 1963. In the case of packaged and bulk soaps, the differences are even greater. The largest four firms accounted for 79 percent of packaged soaps (SIC 28413) in 1963 but for only 28 percent of bulk soaps (SIC 28413) in the same year. "Concentration Ratios in Manufacturing Industry, 1963," *Report for the Subcommittee on Antitrust and Monopoly,* Committee on the Judiciary, U.S. Senate, 89.2, 1966, p. 182.

less advertising than would be expected from firm size alone, as compared with the second 4 firms, or with the next 16 firms in the industry? Given that the leading 4 or 8 firms generally spend proportionately more on advertising than the remaining firms in the industry, does a similar pattern apply to relative expenditures between the top 4 and the second 4, or between other groups of leading firms?

The statistics analyzed are differences between size groups of firms in the relative concentration levels of advertising and sales. These are derived by first dividing the concentration ratio of advertising by that of sales for each group of firms, and then taking the difference between these ratios for different size classes. The meaning of these statistics can be understood more clearly through the formulas by which they were calculated. The first measure, $Z_1$, describes relative advertising expenditures between the four largest and the second four firms in an industry:

$$Z_1 = \frac{A_4/A_t}{S_4/S_t} - \frac{(A_8 - A_4)/A_t}{(S_8 - S_4)/S_t} \, , \tag{1}$$

where $A_4$ and $A_8$ indicated total advertising expenditures for the four and eight largest firms and $A_t$ is total advertising expenditure in the industry; $S$ indicates sales for the same groups of firms. When $Z_1$ is positive, advertising is more highly concentrated in the four largest firms than in the second four firms as compared with that what would be expected from size alone. A negative sign, on the other hand, indicates that the concentration of advertising in the top four firms is proportionately lower than within the second four firms in the industry.

The second measure concerns relative advertising expenditures between the top 4 firms in an industry and the next 16, and is defined by

$$Z_2 = \frac{A_4/A_t}{S_4/S_t} - \frac{(A_{20} - A_4)/A_t}{(S_{20} - S_4)/S_t} \, . \tag{2}$$

Similarly, relative advertising expenditures between the top 8 firms and the succeeding 12 are measured by:

$$Z_3 = \frac{A_8/A_t}{S_8/S_t} - \frac{(A_{20} - A_8)/A_t}{(S_{20} - S_8)/S_t} \, . \tag{3}$$

These variables not only describe relative concentration levels within the largest 8 and 20 firms in an industry, but also measure relative advertising outlays. This can be seen by multiplying each of the three variables by the average advertising:sales ratio in the industry. The three additional variables obtained, denoted by $Z_1^*$, $Z_2^*$, and $Z_3^*$ respectively, reflect differences in advertising:sales ratios between particular groups of firms. Thus,

$$Z_1^* = \left[ \frac{A_4/A_t}{S_4/S_t} - \frac{(A_8 - A_4)/A_t}{(S_8 - S_4)/S_t} \right] \cdot \frac{A_t}{S_t} \qquad (4)$$

$$= \frac{A_4}{S_4} - \frac{A_8 - A_4}{S_8 - S_4} \cdot \qquad (5)$$

This variable thereby measures the unit advertising differentials between the top 4 and the second 4 firms in an industry. Comparable results hold for $Z_2^*$ and $Z_3^*$. Where any of these variables is positive, the advertising:sales ratio of the largest firms exceeds the ratio for the smaller firms, whereas the opposite results hold when the coefficient is negative.

The original $Z_i$ variables have a similar interpretation. This is seen most easily by dividing $Z_i^*$ by the industry advertising:sales ratio to obtain the original variable $Z_i$. Therefore,

$$Z_i = \frac{\Delta A/S}{A/S} = \frac{\text{Unit advertising differential}}{\text{Average unit advertising outlay}}, \qquad (6)$$

where the word "unit" indicates that advertising outlay is measured in relation to sales. Thus $Z_i$ measures the unit advertising differential expressed as a fraction of average unit advertising outlay for the industry as a whole; $Z_i$ is the *relative* differential in unit advertising outlays.

The calculated absolute and relative values of these unit advertising differentials are given in Tables 9.4 and 9.5. When comparisons are made between

TABLE 9.4.  Unit advertising differentials: relative values

| Industry | Top 4 vs. next 4, $Z_1$ | Top 4 vs. next 16, $Z_2$ | Top 8 vs. next 12, $Z_3$ |
|---|---|---|---|
| Soft drinks | +0.9946 | +0.9658 | +0.6885 |
| Malt liquors | −.1154 | −.0090 | +.0922 |
| Wines | −.5327 | −.1348 | +.3289 |
| Distilled liquors | −.4529 | −.3759 | −.2290 |
| Meat | +.1012 | +.0881 | +.0602 |
| Dairy products | −.1985 | −.0149 | +.3189 |
| Canning | +.1584 | +.3629 | +.5166 |
| Grain mill products | +1.5813 | +1.4673 | +.9284 |
| Cereals | +0.7852 | +0.6293 | +.3398 |
| Bakery products | +.2704 | +.3988 | +.5095 |
| Sugar | −.0993 | −.0579 | −.0104 |
| Confectionery | +.1725 | +.3071 | +.3381 |
| Cigars | +.3523 | +.4140 | +.3917 |

Table 9.4.  (continued)

| Industry | Top 4 vs. next 4, $Z_1$ | Top 4 vs. next 16, $Z_2$ | Top 8 vs. next 12, $Z_3$ |
|---|---|---|---|
| Cigarettes | −.4544 | −.3760 | +.1196 |
| Knit goods | −.8488 | −.5969 | −.1643 |
| Carpets | +.1748 | +.2783 | +.3453 |
| Hats | +1.2446 | +1.6150 | +1.4879 |
| Mens' clothing | +2.5040 | +2.5042 | +1.5504 |
| Womens' clothing | +3.1190 | +3.4180 | +3.1097 |
| Millinery | +1.5049 | +1.5854 | +1.5072 |
| Furs | −0.6939 | −0.7375 | −0.4838 |
| Furniture | +.3208 | +.2806 | +.1735 |
| Screens and blinds | +.3741 | +.3137 | +.1411 |
| Periodicals | −.1952 | −.3438 | −.4439 |
| Books | −.7610 | −.7444 | −.1011 |
| Drugs | −.3345 | −.4394 | −.3772 |
| Soaps | −.1614 | +.0199 | +.1398 |
| Paints | −.5694 | −.8306 | −.9952 |
| Perfumes | +.2238 | −.4893 | −.3929 |
| Tires and tubes | −.9546 | −.2945 | +.3596 |
| Footwear | −.3017 | −.1607 | −.0489 |
| Hand tools | −2.5070 | +2.3101 | +1.5256 |
| Household and service machinery (nonelectrical) | +0.1368 | +0.2177 | +0.2419 |
| Electrical appliances | +.4880 | +.4470 | +.3104 |
| Radio, TV and phonograph | +.0171 | +.1674 | +.3463 |
| Motorcycles and bicycles | +.4742 | +.6398 | +.6726 |
| Motor vehicles | −.1599 | −.2179 | −.5638 |
| Instruments | −.9562 | −.4799 | +.1140 |
| Clocks and watches | +.1906 | +.3864 | +.5748 |
| Jewelry (precious metal) | +.2087 | +.3322 | +.3493 |
| Costume jewelry | +2.4946 | +2.5113 | +1.8819 |

the top 4 and the second 4 firms, the largest firms have higher advertising: sales ratios in 24 industries but spend proportionately less on advertising in 17 industries. The same division is found in comparing the 4 largest firms with the next 16. In the previous comparison against all other firms in the industry, there are only 10 such cases. There is therefore some indication that the

TABLE 9.5.   Unit advertising differentials: absolute values

| Industry | Top 4 vs. next 4, $Z_1{}^*$ | Top 4 vs. next 16, $Z_2{}^*$ | Top 8 vs. next 12, $Z_3{}^*$ |
|---|---|---|---|
| Soft drinks | 6.1665 | 5.9880 | 4.2687 |
| Malt liquor | −3.4840 | −0.0612 | 0.6270 |
| Wines | −2.7700 | −.7010 | 1.7103 |
| Distilled liquor | −0.9511 | −.7894 | −0.4809 |
| Meat | .0607 | .0529 | .0361 |
| Dairy products | −.4367 | −.0328 | .7016 |
| Canning | .4594 | 1.0524 | 1.4981 |
| Grain mill products | 3.0045 | 2.7879 | 1.7640 |
| Cereals | 8.0876 | 6.4818 | 3.4999 |
| Bakery products | 0.7842 | 1.1565 | 1.4776 |
| Sugar | −.0199 | −0.0116 | −0.0021 |
| Confectionery | .6038 | 1.0749 | 1.1834 |
| Cigars | .9160 | 1.0764 | 1.0184 |
| Cigarettes | −2.1811 | −1.8048 | 0.5741 |
| Knit goods | −1.1034 | −0.7760 | −.2136 |
| Carpets | 0.3496 | .5566 | .6906 |
| Hats | 2.7381 | 3.5530 | 3.2734 |
| Mens' clothing | 3.0048 | 3.0050 | 1.8605 |
| Womens' clothing | 5.6142 | 6.1524 | 5.5975 |
| Millinery | 1.2039 | 1.2683 | 1.2058 |
| Furs | −0.0694 | −0.0738 | −0.0484 |
| Furniture | .4812 | .4209 | .2603 |
| Screens and blinds | .5986 | .5019 | .2258 |
| Periodicals | −.0390 | −.0688 | −.0888 |
| Books | −1.8264 | −1.7866 | −.2426 |
| Drugs | −3.3116 | −4.3501 | −3.7343 |
| Soaps | −1.4849 | 0.1831 | 1.2862 |
| Paints | 0.8541 | −1.2459 | −1.4928 |
| Perfumes | 3.4241 | −7.4863 | −6.0114 |
| Tires and tubes | −1.3364 | −0.4123 | 0.5034 |
| Footwear | −0.4526 | −.2411 | −.0734 |
| Hand tools | 10.5294 | 9.7024 | 6.4075 |
| Household and service machinery (not electrical) | 0.2599 | 0.4136 | 0.4596 |
| Electrical appliances | 1.7080 | 1.5645 | 1.0864 |
| Radio, TV and phonograph | 0.0376 | 0.3683 | 0.7619 |

Table 9.5. (continued)

| Industry | Top 4 vs. next 4, $Z_1$* | Top 4 vs. next 16, $Z_2$* | Top 8 vs. next 12, $Z_3$* |
|---|---|---|---|
| Motorcycles and bicycles | .5216 | .7038 | .7399 |
| Motor vehicles | .0959 | −.1307 | −.3383 |
| Instruments | −1.9124 | −.9598 | .2280 |
| Clocks and watches | 1.0674 | 2.1638 | 3.2189 |
| Jewelry (precious metal) | 0.6678 | 1.0630 | 1.1178 |
| Costume jewelry | 9.9784 | 10.0452 | 7.5276 |

largest firms are more likely to spend less on advertising per unit sold as compared with their immediate rivals than when compared with all others. In these industries, it appears that a second tier of firms spends relatively more on advertising than either the largest firms or those that are quite small.

When comparisons are made between the 8 largest firms and the next 12, however, the findings change. In this case, 30 industries out of 41 show higher advertising:sales ratios for the larger than for the smaller firms.

Given the wide variance in advertising outlay differentials among industries, we consider whether these differentials are related to general industry characteristics. Three types of analysis were carried out. In Table 9.6a, the 41

TABLE 9.6a. Differential advertising intensity cross-tabulated with advertising intensity

| Advertising intensity[a] | Top 4 vs. next 4, $Z_1$ | | Top 4 vs. next 16, $Z_2$ | | Top 8 vs. next 12, $Z_3$ | |
|---|---|---|---|---|---|---|
| | Positive | Negative | Positive | Negative | Positive | Negative |
| High | 2 | 5 | 2 | 5 | 4 | 3 |
| Medium or Low | 22 | 12 | 12 | 12 | 26 | 8 |

[a]Based on advertising:sales ratios and advertising per firm. For a description of this classification, see Chapter 6.

TABLE 9.6b. Binomial tests of difference between industries of high advertising intensity and all other industries

| Variable | Difference in proportion negative | Standard deviation of difference | t test |
|---|---|---|---|
| $Z_1$ | 0.361 | 0.212 | 1.70* [39df] |
| $Z_2$ | .361 | .212 | 1.70* [39df] |
| $Z_3$ | .121 | .212 | 0.57 [39df] |
| $Z_1$ and $Z_3$ pooled[a] | .277 | .150 | 1.84* [78df] |

[a]Since $Z_2$ is not independent of either $Z_1$ or $Z_3$, it cannot be included in the pooling.

industry observations are cross-classified against the overall intensity of industry advertising. As is apparent, there is the same tendency for the largest firms to spend relatively less on advertising in industries characterized by a high level of aggregate advertising expenditures. Where advertising is important, 5 values for both $Z_1$ and $Z_2$ are negative and only 2 are positive, whereas in the remaining industries, where advertising plays a smaller role, only 12 industries out of 34 show negative coefficients. As can be seen, however, the results are less clear for $Z_3$, which describes comparisons between the top 8 firms and the next 12. As indicated in Table 9.6b, the difference between the proportions of negative and positive coefficients is statistically significant at the 5-percent level for both $Z_1$ and $Z_2$, but not for $Z_3$. However, if the observations for $Z_1$ and $Z_3$ are pooled, the difference is again statistically significant.

A similar analysis was carried out to test the effect of industry concentration, with the results given in Table 9.7a,b. Although the proportion of

TABLE 9.7a.  Differential advertising intensity cross-tabulated with Kaysen-Turner concentration groupings

| Concentration type | Top 4 vs. next 4, $Z_1$ | | Top 4 vs. next 16, $Z_2$ | | Top 8 vs. next 12, $Z_3$ | |
|---|---|---|---|---|---|---|
| | Positive | Negative | Positive | Negative | Positive | Negative |
| Concentrated[a] | 14 | 13 | 14 | 13 | 20 | 7 |
| Unconcentrated | 10 | 4 | 10 | 4 | 10 | 4 |

[a]Includes industries classified as either Type I or Type II oligopolies by Kaysen and Turner. Carl Kaysen and Donald F. Turner, *Antitrust Policy* (Cambridge, Mass., Harvard University Press, 1959).

TABLE 9.7b.  Binomial tests of difference between concentrated and unconcentrated industries

| Variable | Difference in proportion negative | Standard deviation of difference | t test |
|---|---|---|---|
| $Z_1$ | 0.194 | 0.212 | 0.92 |
| $Z_2$ | .194 | .212 | .92 |
| $Z_3$ | −.028 | .212 | −.13 |
| $Z_1$ and $Z_3$ pooled[a] | .083 | .150 | .55 |

[a]Since $Z_2$ is not independent of either $Z_1$ or $Z_3$, it cannot be included in the pooling.

negative unit advertising differentials is larger among the concentrated industries than among their more unconcentrated counterparts, the difference between these proportions is not statistically significant. As a result, there is little convincing evidence that overall concentration affects the relative distribution of advertising expenditures by firm size within industries.

The second analysis is based on the distribution of the unit advertising differentials across industries. Mean values of the six variables, cross-classified by aggregate industry advertising, are given in Table 9.8. As can be seen, the overall unit advertising differential is positive, which indicates that, on the average, larger firms spend proportionately more on advertising than their smaller rivals, even within the top 8 and 20 firms. The average advertising: sales ratio among the leading 4 firms is nearly one percentage point higher than that of the second 4 firms, or, alternatively, the 4 largest have an advertising:sales ratio that is approximately 30 percent higher than that of their next smaller rivals. Moreover, the differences are slightly greater when comparisons are drawn between the 4 largest firms and the next 16, and between the 8 largest firms and the next 12.

When industries are divided into two groups in terms of the importance of industry advertising, we observe the same phenomenon. In the 7 industries with high overall advertising levels, the coefficients are generally negative, which suggests that relative advertising outlays are lower for the largest firms. In the remaining industries, where advertising plays a far smaller role, the 4 largest firms typically spend proportionately more than either the next 4 or the next 16; and the 8 firms spend, on the average, proportionately more than the next 12. These differences, moreover, approach 50 percent of the average advertising:sales ratio for the industry. Thus, we conclude that larger firms typically have *higher* advertising:sales ratios than their smaller rivals *except* where advertising is a particularly important feature of industry behavior. In these industries, available evidence suggests that the leading firms spend proportionately *less* than their rivals.

The second part of Table 9.8 provides statistical tests of the significance of these differences. When advertising outlay differentials are measured on a relative basis, the observed differences between the two sets of industries are statistically significant at the 5-percent level in all three comparisons. In absolute values, however, the observed differences are not statistically significant on comparisons between the top 4 and second 4 firms, but are significant at the 10-percent level in the 2 remaining cases. In addition, the average advertising outlay differentials are not significantly negative among industries with high aggregate advertising intensity, although in the remaining 34 industries these differentials are always significantly positive.[5]

_____

5. These results are corroborated by a correlation analysis between the various measures of advertising outlay differentials and both the advertising:sales ratio in the industry and the average volume of expenditures among leading firms. The generally negative coefficients suggested again that larger firms tend to spend proportionately more where advertising is a less important feature of industry structure and conduct.

TABLE 9.8. Effect of aggregate industry advertising on intraindustry distribution of advertising within largest 8 and 20 firms

| Unit advertising cost differentials | Relative advertising differentials | | | Absolute advertising differentials | | |
|---|---|---|---|---|---|---|
| | Top 4 – next 4, $Z_1$ | Top 4 – next 16, $Z_2$ | Top 8 – next 12, $Z_3$ | Top 4 – next 4, $Z_1^*$ | Top 4 – next 16, $Z_2^*$ | Top 8 – next 12, $Z_3^*$ |
| Average of 7 industries with high advertising, $\overline{X}_1$ | −0.0309 | −0.1261 | −0.0918 | +0.1363 | −1.0240 | −0.5853 |
| Average of remaining industries, $\overline{X}_2$ | +.3772 | +.4776 | +.4793 | +1.1466 | +1.3992 | +1.3582 |
| Average of all 41 industries | +.3075 | +.3746 | +.3818 | +0.9741 | +0.9855 | +1.0264 |
| *t* Test | | | | | | |
| $\overline{X}_1 < \overline{X}_2$ | 1.70 | 2.64 | 3.06 | 0.60 | 1.42 | 1.53 |
| Degrees of freedom | 29 | 30 | 25 | 8 | 7 | 7 |
| $\overline{X}_1 < 0$ | 0.20 | 0.86 | 0.70 | −0.09 | 0.62 | 0.48 |
| Degrees of freedom | 6 | 6 | 6 | 6 | 6 | 6 |
| $\overline{X}_2 > 0$ | 2.09 | 2.72 | 3.59 | 2.26 | 2.93 | 3.97 |
| Degrees of freedom | 33 | 33 | 33 | 33 | 33 | 33 |

## RELATIVE ADVERTISING EXPENDITURES AND FIRM SIZE

The analysis above has focused on two-way comparisons between differently defined groups of large and small firms; in this section we examine relative expenditures for four groups of firms within each industry. Average unit advertising outlays[6] are calculated for the 4 largest firms in each industry, the second 4 firms, the next 12 firms (ranks 9 through 20), and all remaining firms with assets exceeding $500,000. Summary statistics are shown in Table 9.9.

TABLE 9.9.   Average unit advertising outlays (percent)[a]

| Industry | Top 4 firms | Second 4 firms | Next 12 firms | All remaining firms with assets above $500,000 |
|---|---|---|---|---|
| All industries | 4.62 | 3.83 | 3.47 | 2.25[b] |
| Seven industries with high aggregate industry advertising | 7.40 | 8.26 | 8.47 | 5.99 |
| Remaining 34 industries[b] | 4.04 | 2.92 | 2.44 | 1.45[b] |

[a]See text footnote 6.

[b]Since all firms with assets exceeding $500,000 in the motorcycles and bicycles industry are included in the top 20, these average values are based on 40 and 33 industries respectively.

When average values are computed for all industries in the sample, the results conform to our earlier findings. Highest outlays, relative to sales as well as in absolute volume, are typically made by the largest firms, and decline with diminishing firm size. However, for the 7 industries with high aggregate advertising, defined as before, the findings are quite different. The largest firms in these industries appear generally to spend more than firms *below* the top 20, but they appear to spend less, on the average, than the remaining firms *within* the top 20. At the same time, recall from the preceding section that the observed differences in advertising:sales ratios within the top 20 are not statistically significant.

These results suggest that there may be a number of industries in which the largest firms have lower unit advertising outlays than somewhat smaller firms, although they have higher outlays than the smallest firms in the industry. What seems likely is that this second tier of firms generally aims to compete

6. These measures may differ slightly from average advertising:sales ratios in that they are the ratio of aggregate advertising among, say, the four largest advertisers to aggregate sales among the four largest sellers.

directly with the leading firms, and is forced thereby to spend proportionately greater amounts on advertising. The smallest firms, on the other hand, probably produce a more standardized product and, as a result, have lower advertising: sales ratios. With this interpretation, these findings are again consistent with the view that economies of scale exist in advertising, but they can hardly be regarded as strong evidence in this direction.

If this pattern of relative advertising outlays reflects the presence of scale economies, we should expect to find it more frequently where overall advertising is high than where it is low. To determine this point, industries were divided into 4 classes, depending on which group of firms had the highest advertising:sales ratio within the industry. The 4 groups were again the leading 4 firms, the second 4, the next 12, and all remaining firms with assets above $500,000. As indicated in Table 9.10, in 23 of the 41 industries, the highest average ratio lies in the 4 largest firms. Of the 18 remaining industries, there are 12 in which the second 4 firms spent larger relative amounts than either the largest firms or the other two groups of smaller firms.

What is interesting about the groups of industries in which smaller firms spend relatively more on advertising is that aggregate advertising levels in these industries are typically higher. As can be seen, there is an inverse relation throughout between the industry advertising:sales ratio and the average size of firm with highest relative advertising outlays. It is generally where industry advertising:sales ratios are low that advertising is relatively higher for the largest firms. The differences, however, in advertising:sales ratios between the

TABLE 9.10. Industry advertising levels and relative distribution of advertising within industries

| Firms with highest advertising:sales ratio in industry | Number of industries | Average of industry advertising:sales ratio (percent) | Average absolute advertising outlay among leading firms[a] (10³ dollars) |
|---|---|---|---|
| Top 4 firms | 23 | 2.94 | $ 3,111 |
| Second 4 firms | 12 | 3.26 | 11,540 |
| Next 12 firms | 4 | 4.60 | 7,505 |
| All remaining firms with assets above $500,000 | 2 | 5.05 | 3,568 |
| All firms except top 4 | 18 | 3.76 | 9,757 |

[a]This is the average volume of expenditures per firm for the largest firms that account for at least half of industry sales. This same measure was used in the regression analysis of Chapter 6.

4 largest firms and either the second 4 or all other firms are *not* statistically significant.

Presumably, economies of scale in advertising are likely to be most important for industries in which the absolute volume of advertising by the largest firms is high. As shown in Table 9.10, average absolute advertising outlays among the leading firms are much higher for those industries in which the 4 leading firms' average advertising expenditures in relation to sales are *lower* than those of their smaller rivals. Among the 18 industries in which the smaller firms have higher advertising:sales ratios than do the top 4 firms, average absolute outlays per firm average $9.8 million. Among the 23 industries in which the 4 largest firms had the higher advertising:sales ratios, on the other hand, average absolute outlays per firm averaged only $3.1 million. The difference between these two statistics *is* significant at the 5-percent level. In these industries, firms outside the circle of market leaders apparently are compelled to compete via advertising, and they experience higher unit advertising outlays. Where absolute advertising outlay is less important, on the other hand, we generally observe higher unit outlays among the largest firms.

## CONCLUSIONS

In this chapter, we have examined various dimensions of the intraindustry distribution of advertising expenditures by firm size. The results suggest that, in most industries, larger firms spend proportionately more on advertising than their smaller rivals, for various definitions of large and small firms. However, there are a number of industries in which smaller firms spend proportionately as much as or more than the leading firms. What is noteworthy about the latter group is that it includes most of those industries with high aggregate levels of industry advertising. In both groups, however, the very smallest firms (those ranked below the top 20) spend little on advertising, both absolutely and in relation to sales.

In markets where advertising has a major impact on consumer behavior, firms that advertise little are likely to be placed at a substantial disadvantage in terms of the prices that they can realize as well as the quantities that they can sell. In these industries, smaller firms are therefore compelled to spend large sums on advertising. Where scale economies in advertising exist, moreover, smaller firms may achieve effective price parity with their larger rivals only at the cost of higher unit advertising outlays. In contrast, in most industries in which advertising plays a lesser role, smaller firms that do not engage in heavy advertising are apt to produce more standardized products without suffering price disadvantages that are as great. In these circumstances, therefore, they are more likely to advertise less and sell their output at a lower price, which would indeed lead advertising:sales ratios to be lower for smaller firms. In both cases, moreover, much smaller firms are probably forced to follow this course. The observed pattern of advertising expenditures is thereby consistent with the presence of scale economies in advertising.

A further inference that may be drawn concerns the relative effects of the two dimensions of aggregate industry advertising. Industry advertising may be considered high either because of high advertising expenditures relative to sales or because of a high absolute volume of advertising expenditures among the leading firms. Thus, advertising levels are considered high in the motor-vehicle industry despite an average advertising:sales ratio that falls below 1 percent. Through much of the empirical analysis, industry classes are defined in terms of both dimensions. When these dimensions are considered separately, however, important differences emerge. The absolute volume of expenditures appears to have a far greater impact on the intraindustry distribution of expenditures than the volume of advertising outlays relative to sales. Smaller firms are more likely to spend relatively more on advertising in industries where the dollar volume of these outlays is generally high than where advertising:sales ratios are high but at low dollar volumes. Where absolute outlays per firm are generally high, smaller firms typically spend proportionately as much as, and frequently more than, their larger rivals in an apparent effort to maintain their market positions. Therefore, it is the high dollar volume of advertising by the leading firms, rather than high outlays relative to sales, that appears particularly important.

As we indicated at the start of this chapter, these empirical results by themselves do not provide a measure of the importance of economies of scale in advertising. Since advertising typically affects the prices that are set, the full scale effects of advertising depend on relative prices as well as on relative advertising costs. Clearly, if the effective price levels are the same between two groups of firms, then to the extent that smaller firms are forced to spend more per unit on advertising, the presence of scale economies seems apparent. Since generally we may assume that the prices set by larger firms are not *lower* than those of their smaller rivals, industries in which smaller firms have higher unit advertising costs may well suggest advanges of scale. On the other hand, where smaller firms spend proportionately less on advertising, we cannot draw the opposite conclusion since there may be many circumstances in which the smaller firms set lower prices. An analysis of the advantages of scale due to heavy advertising must consider relative prices as well as relative costs. Such an analysis is presented in the next chapter.

# CHAPTER 10 Advertising and the Advantages of Size

In this chapter we examine the effects of advertising upon the relative profit positions of large and small firms and upon the minimum size of firm required to realize any economies of scale in advertising.

Although advertising may be a strategic factor in the rivalry between large firms in imperfectly competitive markets, it may also confer advantages upon large firms as a group over their smaller rivals. Advertising and the resulting product differentiation may influence the relation between large firms and small by affecting both relative costs and relative prices. These are in fact closely tied effects, for smaller firms may have to spend considerably more per unit of output than their larger rivals to achieve effective price parity. This depends, of course, on the existence and relative importance of economies of scale in advertising. Where such economies are substantial, they should influence the relative profitability of large and small firms. Both the size at which such advantages of scale are exhausted and the profit-rate disadvantages associated with lower volumes of sales are significant measures of the quantitative importance of such economies.

To determine the extent of economies of scale in advertising, ideally one should examine the relation between advertising inputs and outputs. Such an analysis would indicate whether or not an increase in inputs led to a proportionately greater increase in outputs. This approach suffers, however, from the difficulties inherent in measuring the output of advertising expenditures. Since price differences among competing products may describe the extent of product differentiation that is due directly to advertising, an important component of the "output" of large-scale advertising may be a higher price for the product. For this reason, one cannot analyze this question directly by examining unit advertising outlays in relation to firm size. On the other hand, a straight-forward analysis of the simple relation between advertising and profit rates within an industry may also be misleading, since no account would be taken of the realization of possible economies of scale in production.

Alternative approaches involve the examination of the net effect of advertising on profit rates for firms of different sizes. We deal with this problem in three ways. First, we examine the influence of industry advertising levels on the general relation between firm size and profit rates. Second, we consider the impact of these outlays on estimates of minimum efficient firm size in relation to the market. And finally, we estimate the interindustry effects of advertising intensity upon profit-rate differences between large and small firms.

Before proceeding with this analysis, we must ask whether firms are likely to stop short of realizing all available advertising economies, so that firms may be observed with suboptimal advertising budgets. That interfirm differences in advertising are likely to exist is due to a number of factors. In the first place, the high profit rates earned by larger firms in some industries will significantly exceed the opportunity cost of capital, so that smaller firms, even where they earn substantially lower profit rates, will still maintain their operations. Though growth may be desired, it may not be possible to expand sales even with expanded advertising. In markets where product differentiation is important, there may be many instances where disadvantaged firms can maintain their shares of the market with a select group of customers even though there is little hope that these shares can be increased. Finally, smaller firms with low advertising budgets may be unable to realize available scale economies because their actions call forth a sufficient reaction from larger rivals who hold stronger market positions. For any of these reasons, we should expect large and small firms to coexist in imperfectly competitive markets, with different relative advertising levels and different profit rates.

## THE OVERALL RELATION BETWEEN FIRM SIZE
## AND PROFITABILITY

The most direct way to approach the problem at hand is to posit a single relation between size and profitability for all firms in the consumer goods sector of the economy that are larger than the size required to attain minimum efficient scale in production ($MES$), while recognizing that expected profit rates at specific firm sizes will be different for different industries.[1] Given such an overall relation, we can then consider whether it is affected by industry levels of advertising. In this analysis we assume that advertising intensity has the same impact on the relation between profitability and firm size in one industry as in another. To test the proposition that there are net advantages of scale—beyond those attributable to scale economies in production—that result from heavy industry advertising, a regression model is specified:

$$\pi_{ij} = \alpha_i + \beta_1 S_{ij} + \beta_2 S_{ij} A_i + u_{ij}, \tag{1}$$

where $\pi_{ij}$ is the average profit rate in size class $j$ in industry $i$, $S_{ij}$ is the corresponding value for average firm size measured by the value of assets, $A_i$ refers to the advertising:sales ratio for the industry as a whole, and $u_{ij}$ is a random error term. Note that different intercepts are specified for each industry to account for industry differences in average profit rates.

Since scale economies in production as well as in advertising will influence the relation between firm size and profitability, we need to correct for the former. This is done simply by removing all observations from the sample for which the average firm in the size class did not exceed minimum efficient scale in production, as determined in Chapter 6. As a result, the equation is estimated only for the larger firms in each industry, although the average size of these larger firms varies considerably among industries.

This particular functional form is chosen because it permits a test of the hypothesis that $\partial \pi_{ij} / \partial S_{ij}$ is higher, after correction for scale economies in production, where average industry advertising is larger than where it is smaller. Another way of stating this hypothesis is to say that $\partial^2 \pi_{ij} / \partial S_{ij} \partial A_i$ exceeds zero. Note that, since $\beta_2$ is a direct estimate of this second cross partial derivative, the hypothesis is supported when this coefficient is positive and significant. In addition, we would expect $\beta_1$ to approach zero since average firm size should have little impact on profitability (after correction for scale economies in production) where industry advertising levels are low.

Equation (1) is not estimated directly because of the likelihood that the error terms are heteroscedastic. A previous study indicated that these error variances are approximately proportional to the reciprocal of firm size.[2] If the observations referred to individual firms, the appropriate correction would be to multiply each observation by the square root of firm size. Since the observations refer to mean values for groups of firms within asset size classes, and

1. For an extensive analysis of the relationships between firm size and profit rates see H. J. Sherman, *Profits in the United States* (Ithaca, N.Y., Cornell University Press, 1968).
2. Marshall Hall and Leonard Weiss, "Firm Size and Profitability," *Review of Economics and Statistics* (August 1967), pp. 319–331.

the number of firms in each class is not constant, the appropriate correction factor is the square root of the total value of assets in the particular size class.[3]

TABLE 10.1. Coefficients for weighted regression equations explaining profit rates by industry and firm size: 149 observations[a]

| Average value of assets per firm, $\beta_1$ | Assets per firm times industry advertising:sales ratio, $\beta_2$ | $R^2$ |
|:---:|:---:|:---:|
| $-0.705 \times 10^{-8}$ | $0.316 \times 10^{-5}$ | 0.95 |
| (0.21) | (2.77) | |
| — | $.297 \times 10^{-5}$ | .95 |
| | (4.38) | |

[a]Observations are limited to those where average firm size exceeds minimum efficient scale of plant, and refer to average values for the asset-size class of firms. Industry dummy variables are also included in the regression equations. Values of $t$ in parentheses.

The empirical results are given in Table 10.1, which refers again to the years from 1954 to 1957. As can be seen, the hypothesis that advertising promotes advantages to large size is strongly supported. The two estimates of $\beta_2$ are both highly significant and the estimate of $\beta_1$ is effectively zero. Note that the absolute size of the coefficients is unimportant because it primarily reflects the units in which assets per firm are measured—in this case, thousands of dollars. In addition to the coefficients presented, different intercepts are estimated for each industry. Note that although 41 industries are included in the sample, and 14 size classes are given for each industry, so that there are 574 possible observations, only 149 remain after those that fall below minimum efficient scale in production are removed.

Although this analysis has the advantage of providing large numbers of degrees of freedom, it suffers from the fact that the same scale and advertising effects are implied for all industries. Not only may different industries have

3. If $e$ denotes the error term in an equation analogous to (1) but which refers to the individual firms then

$$\sigma_e^2 = \frac{\sigma^2}{S}, \text{ and } \sigma_u^2 = \frac{\sigma_e^2}{N},$$

where $N$ is the number of firms in the size class. Therefore

$$\sigma_u^2 = \frac{\sigma^2}{S \cdot N}.$$

Since, however, no information is available on individual firms, we assume that the size of each firm in a size class equals the class mean, and therefore,

$$\sigma_u^2 = \frac{\sigma^2}{\overline{S} \cdot N} = \frac{\sigma^2}{\Sigma S},$$

where $\Sigma S$ is total assets of all firms in the class.

different average profit levels, which lead to different intercepts, but also they may have different slope parameters. The second analysis of the effect of scale economies in advertising specifically allows for different slope coefficients. This gain, however, is obtained at the cost of severely reducing the number of degrees of freedom available for estimating the relevant coefficients.

## ESTIMATES OF MINIMUM EFFICIENT FIRM SIZE

If scale economies in advertising are substantial, we would expect that the optimal size of firms in an industry will generally be larger than in the absence of these economies, and that the extent of the increase will depend on the volume of advertising. Since other factors influence efficient firm size, this approach measures only advertising economies that are available at firm sizes larger than those required to exhaust alternative sources of economies of scale. To the extent that such economies exist, efficient firm size should be larger, other things being equal, in industries where advertising outlays are high than where they are low. Our first task, therefore, is to obtain estimates of minimum efficient firm size for each industry in our sample.

To examine the relation between firm size and profit rates within industries, we assume, following earlier studies,[4] a functional relation between rate of return and firm size that allows profit rates to increase with size, but at a decreasing rate such that profit rates approach an asymptote. Using this functional form, we can determine that level of firm size at which the asymptote is effectively reached. This provides an estimate of that firm size at which virtually all of the advantages of scale in terms of higher profit rates are exhausted. Note that we examine here the gross rather than the net effect of firm size. This is done because we are not concerned with the effect on profits of size per se as much as with the entire set of advantages that may be associated with firm size. This level of firm size serves as an estimate of minimum efficient firm size[5] in each industry.

The empirical analysis consists of estimating for each industry in our sample a regression equation across size classes of the form

$$\pi = a + b\,\frac{1}{S} + c\,\frac{1}{S^2} + u, \tag{2}$$

4. See S. S. Alexander, "The Effect of Size of Manufacturing Corporations on the distribution of Rate of Return," *Review of Economics and Statistics* (August 1959), pp. 229–235; H. O. Stekler, *Profitability and Size of Firm* (Berkeley, Institute of Business and Economic Research, University of California, 1963); and Hall and Weiss, "Firm Size and Profitability."
5. While we use the term "minimum efficient firm size," we do not mean that such a size is necessary to obtain efficiency in any normative sense, but rather that it is the minimum size at which all of the private advantages of scale are attained.

where $\pi$ denotes the average profit rate on stockholders' equity in the particular size class, $S$ denotes average firm size, and $u$ is an error term. Although 14 asset size classes are included in the published IRS statistics, the bottom 3 classes are not used in the analysis since the profit-rate statistics were considered especially unreliable. These classes include firms with total assets of less than \$100,000, for which profit withdrawals in the form of executive salaries are likely to be important.[6] Although data for 11 size classes are available for most industries, a smaller number of observations was used in some cases because there are no firms in one or more size categories.

Because of the problem of heteroscedasticity, the same weighting scheme was applied in estimating equation (2) as was used in estimating equation (1). As indicated above, the estimated regression equation is used to estimate the value of the function as it approaches the asymptotic value $\hat{a}$. Since the function never actually reaches this value, we evaluate it at a point that is arbitrarily close to the value of the asymptote; in the analysis below, we evaluate the function at 99 percent of $\hat{a}$. This value is obtained by solving the following equation for $S$:

$$0.99\hat{a} = \hat{a} + \hat{b}\,\frac{1}{S} + \hat{c}\,\frac{1}{S^2}, \tag{3}$$

where $\hat{a}$, $\hat{b}$, and $\hat{c}$ are the estimated regression coefficients.[7]

The resulting estimates of minimum efficient firm size are given in Table 10.2. Note that estimates are given for only 29 industries out of the 41 included in the sample. In the remaining cases, the coefficient $\hat{b}$ had a positive sign so that the function approached the asymptote from above rather than from below, and therefore estimates of $MEF$ could not be obtained. In these cases, it appeared that the larger firms did not generally have higher profit rates. A comparative analysis of the characteristics of these industries in relation to the other 29 is presented in the next section (see Table 10.4).

In addition to the estimates of $MEF$, Table 10.2 provides estimates of the

6. See George J. Stigler, *Capital and Rates of Return in Manufacturing Industry* (Princeton, N.J., Princeton University Press, 1970), pp. 125–127. In earlier parts of this study, and in the analysis of profit rate differences below, we excluded two additional size classes, confining the analysis to firms with assets above \$500,000. To exclude these additional observations in the estimation of the equations relating profit rates to firm size would have cost two scarce degrees of freedom. Visual inspection of the profit rate data revealed that profit rates for the first three size groups were highly volatile, with a number of large positive and large negative observations. However, the profit rates of firms in the next two size classes did not show such volatility. In order to avoid reducing a small number of degrees of freedom even further, we decided to include these two size classes, at the possible cost of introducing some systematic error into the estimated coefficients.

7. The largest positive root of the quadratic equation is taken to represent the appropriate economic magnitude.

TABLE 10.2. Estimates of minimum efficient firm and plant size (value of assets, in millions of dollars)

| Industry | Minimum efficient firm size | Standard error of estimate[a] | Minimum efficient plant size | Average size of firms | |
|---|---|---|---|---|---|
| | | | | Top 4 | Second 4 |
| Soft drinks | 14.2 | 19.5 | 0.8 | 38.4 | 11.9 |
| Malt liquors | 123.5 | 32.6 | 20.3 | 129.4 | 46.7 |
| Distilled liquors | 340.8 | 199.5 | 14.7 | 301.4 | 77.2 |
| Dairy products | 18.9 | 14.7 | 2.1 | 342.4 | 52.7 |
| Canning | 64.6 | 23.1 | 6.7 | 190.6 | 79.2 |
| Grain mill products | 26.5 | 23.7 | 4.2 | 150.5 | 51.4 |
| Cereals | 43.6 | 41.4 | 36.5 | 100.9 | 4.6 |
| Bakery products | 7.7 | 10.3 | 2.6 | 154.0 | 46.6 |
| Sugar | 78.1 | 47.6 | 31.0 | 110.3 | 42.4 |
| Confectionery | 61.6 | 23.4 | 10.3 | 69.2 | 21.1 |
| Cigars | 41.8 | 30.9 | 5.4 | 38.2 | 8.5 |
| Cigarettes | 39.3 | 23.5 | 99.6 | 558.5 | 174.8 |
| Knit goods | 24.3 | 34.1 | 2.0 | 46.9 | 14.9 |
| Mens' clothing | 15.7 | 6.4 | 1.7 | 41.2 | 15.4 |
| Women's clothing | 6.8 | 14.1 | 0.5 | 13.9 | 7.3 |
| Furs | 37.9 | 3.9 | 0.2 | 0.9 | 0.6 |
| Furniture | 34.9 | 11.0 | 2.3 | 49.5 | 19.2 |
| Periodicals | 14.1 | 52.4 | 22.4 | 93.0 | 33.3 |
| Drugs | 21.0 | 17.0 | 46.5 | 131.4 | 85.1 |
| Soaps | 11.2 | 58.1 | 18.7 | 323.2 | 8.0 |
| Paints | 35.5 | 23.0 | 8.7 | 235.6 | 30.7 |
| Perfumes | 52.0 | 67.0 | 10.9 | 32.6 | 14.3 |
| Footwear | 11.2 | 15.1 | 2.0 | 110.0 | 15.4 |
| Hand tools | 32.7 | 27.0 | 16.6 | 65.2 | 21.9 |
| Electrical appliances | 55.0 | 38.8 | 21.2 | 71.2 | 11.5 |
| Radio, TV, and phonograph | 43.7 | 36.2 | 20.4 | 319.4 | 111.8 |
| Motor vehicles | 60.6 | 175.5 | 375.0 | 2,482.1 | 1,545.4 |
| Instruments | 20.6 | 19.3 | 28.4 | 520.7 | 67.7 |
| Jewelry (precious metal) | 31.6 | 9.8 | 4.6 | 31.1 | 9.3 |

[a]Since the estimate of minimum efficient firm size is obtained from a nonlinear relation with the estimated regression coefficients, its standard error cannot be obtaine ddirectly. The standard errors presented in this table are derived from the first term of a Taylor expansion of the nonlinear equation around the true value and are therefore only approximate values.

standard errors of these statistics as well as the same estimates of minimum efficient plant size *MES* that were used in Chapter 6. The average sizes of the leading four and the second four firms in each industry are also presented.

Before we proceed, it is necessary to consider one factor that may distort the estimates of minimum efficient firm size. The largest asset-size class in the IRS statistics includes all firms with assets greater than $250 million. No account is taken of the possibility that larger firms within the upper size category may show higher profit rates than smaller firms within the same category. Distortions in the estimated nonlinear equation may be important where a substantial number of firms have assets exceeding $250 million and large differences in size exist among these firms. In the motor-vehicle industry, for example, much of the distribution of firm sizes is included in this single open-ended category. Although this problem is most severe in that industry, it may be significant for other industries in which the average size of the four largest firms exceeds $250 million. In these cases, some doubt must be cast on the estimates of *MEF* obtained.

As shown in Table 10.2, the standard errors of many of the estimated coefficients are relatively large. This is not surprising, since the estimates are based on a maximum of 8 degrees of freedom. At the same time, in 20 cases out of 28, the estimated coefficients do exceed their standard errors, while in 7 industries the coefficients are greater than twice their standard errors.

As expected, minimum efficient firm size generally exceeds minimum efficient plant size, although there are six instances in which the opposite relation is found. No economic significance should be attributed to the latter, since the differences are never statistically significant, and the estimates of minimum efficient scale of plant are themselves subject to error. Note also that among these six industries, four contained firms sufficiently large that the average size of the leading four firms exceeded $250 million, and therefore differences in size within the open-ended size category may have distorted the estimates.

A more interesting comparison is with the actual sizes of the 4 largest and the 4 next largest firms in the industry. In 24 cases out of 29, the average size of the 4 leading firms exceeds the size that exhausts all of the advantages of scale, and in 13 of these, the differences are statistically significant. In 4 out of the 5 industries in which the estimates of *MEF* exceed the average size of the 4 largest firms, on the other hand, the differences are not significant. In many industries, therefore, the average size of the 4 largest firms is clearly greater than that necessary to realize estimated economies of scale in both production and advertising. These statistics confirm the conclusions of earlier studies which indicate that the sizes reached by the largest firms in many industries cannot be explained on the basis of economies of scale alone.

When comparisons are drawn between the estimates of minimum efficient firm size and the average size of the second 4 largest firms in an industry, different conclusions are reached. In 26 of the 29 industries, the average size of these firms exceeds estimated minimum efficient plant scale. In 17 industries, however, the mean size of the second largest group of firms lies below *MEF*. Thus it appears that although the size of firms in the second largest group is typically sufficient to exploit all economies of scale in production, these firms, unlike their larger rivals, are frequently not large enough to have exhausted the full advantages of size. This suggests that the top 4 firms may frequently have a competitive advantage over the next largest group, an inference that is confirmed by the analysis of profit-rate differences later in this chapter.

## ADVERTISING INTENSITY AND MINIMUM EFFICIENT FIRM SIZE

In this section, we examine the influence of advertising intensity and production economies of scale on the share of the market accounted for by a firm of minimum efficient size. Various interindustry regression equations are estimated in which the dependent variables are the estimates of *MEF* expressed as a proportion of the market.[8]

A dummy variable to distinguish the three local or regional industries in the sample—soft drinks, dairy, and bakery products—is introduced into the regression equations to correct for the use of the size of the national market in the denominator of the dependent variable. Since the ratio of *MEF* to market would be substantially higher in these cases if appropriate market definitions were used, the coefficient for this variable should be negative.

In specifying the regression equations, we do not assume that the effects of advertising and production economies are necessarily additive. Where economies of scale at the plant level are quite large, the optimal firm size required to realize these economies may be sufficient to realize any economies of scale in advertising. At the same time, firms that are sufficiently large to realize in full any advertising scale economies are likely also to be sufficiently large to concentrate their production in plants of efficient scale. On these grounds, an interaction variable—the product of the advertising:sales ratio and the ratio of minimum efficient plant scale to market—was introduced. Both linear and logarithmic variants of the basic equation were estimated.

8. The estimates presented in Table 10.2 which are expressed in the volume of assets, are multiplied by the appropriate industry ratio of sales to assets and then divided by the value of average industry sales in the particular industry for the four-year time period. In order to avoid using estimates which lie beyond the range of observable sizes, the values of MEF in the regression analysis are constrained to be less than or equal to the average size of the largest four firms in the industry. For those five industries where the estimates exceeded this level, the constraining value was used to construct the dependent variable.

When all four independent variables are introduced together as explanatory variables, none of the regression coefficients (except that of the regional industry dummy variable) is statistically significant in either the linear or the logarithmic version, because of the multicollinearity among the independent variables. Hence the empirical results presented in Table 10.3 involve alternative equations with one or two of the variables omitted. In equations (1) and (2), the interaction variable is introduced alone in the linear and logarithmic versions respectively. In both cases, its coefficient is statistically significant but the coefficient of multiple determination is significant only in the logarithmic equation. In equations (3) and (4), the two component variables are introduced independently but without the interaction term. In these equations the advertising coefficients do not exceed their standard errors, although the ratio of *MES* to market is significant in one of the two equations. However, the coefficients of multiple determination are insignificant in both equations. In all four equations, the regional industry dummy variable has a significant coefficient with the expected negative sign.

The *negative* sign on the interaction variable in the logarithmic equation indicates that the partial effects of both the ratio of *MES* to market and advertising intensity are *positive*, since both variables are necessarily less than unity and therefore have negative logarithms. This negative coefficient also indicates that, as expected, the effect of advertising on the ratio of *MEF* to market diminishes as the relative importance of plant economies increases, and vice versa.[9] To examine the size of this effect and the extent to which it diminishes, we can compute the partial elasticities of *MEF/Mkt* with respect to the advertising:sales ratio at alternative levels of *MES/Mkt*[10]. Some typical values are:

| *MES/Mkt* | Elasticity of *MEF/Mkt* with respect to advertising:sales ratio |
|---|---|
| 0.01 | 0.33 |
| .03 | .25 |
| .05 | .22 |
| .10 | .17 |

9. Note that the linear equation with the interaction variable alone (equation 1 in Table 10.3) implies the opposite effect since the relevant coefficient is positive. It is, of course, impossible under this specification to have partial positive effects of advertising intensity which also diminish with the ratio of MES to market. This factor may account for the lower $R^2$ obtained with this specification.

10. These computations are readily made by noting that the relevant

$$\text{elasticity} = \frac{\partial \ln MEF/Mkt}{\partial \ln Ad/Sales} = -0.0718 \cdot \ln MES/Mkt.$$

TABLE 10.3. Multiple-regression equations explaining ratio of minimum efficient firm size to market[a]

| Equation number | Dependent variable | | Constant | Regression coefficients | $R^2$ | Corrected $R^2$ |
|---|---|---|---|---|---|---|
| (1) | $MEF/Mkt$ | = | $0.041^{c}$ (0.011) | $+\ 5.307^{b}\ (Ad/S \cdot MES/Mkt)$ (2.521) $-\ 0.048\ REG$ (0.031) | 0.19 | 0.13 |
| (2) | $\ln MEF/Mkt$ | = | $-2.530^{c}$ (0.497) | $-\ 0.0718^{b}\ (\ln Ad/S \cdot \ln MES/Mkt)$ (0.032) $-\ 1.497^{b}\ REG$ (0.655) | $.23^{b}$ | $.17^{b}$ |
| (3) | $MEF/Mkt$ | = | $0.026$ (0.016) | $+\ 0.199\ Ad/S + 0.466^{b}\ MES/Mkt$ (0.283)\ (0.263) $-\ 0.070^{b}\ REG$ (0.035) | .21 | .11 |
| (4) | $\ln MEF/Mkt$ | = | $-1.591^{b}$ (0.914) | $+\ 0.203\ \ln Ad/S + 0.323\ \ln MES/Mkt$ (0.199)\ (0.190) $-\ 1.558^{b}\ REG$ (0.682) | .24 | .15 |

*Notation*

$MEF/Mkt$ = Ratio of estimated minimum efficient firm size to market
$MES/Mkt$ = Ratio of estimated minimum efficient plant size to market
$Ad/S$ = Advertising:sales ratio
$REG$ = Local industry dummy variable; its value is 1 if the industry is local and 0 otherwise

[a]Figures in parentheses are the estimated standard errors of the coefficients.
[b]Statistically significant at the 5-percent level.
[c]Statistically significant at the 1-percent level.

These results suggest that advertising outlays interact with scale economies at the plant level to influence the minimum size of an efficient firm. Particularly where scale economies are small in relation to the market, heavy advertising outlays may increase the minimum share of the market accounted for by an efficient firm.

In this analysis, some statistical problems are encountered because the dependent variable is an estimate of the true values rather than of the value itself. These problems are discussed in the appendix to this chapter. At this point, we note only that the estimates presented above do not appear to have been influenced substantially on this account.

Before we conclude this section, it is useful to examine the 12 industries that have been excluded from the regression equations. These industries are those for which the hypothesized positive relation between profit rates and firm size did not hold. Table 10.4 presents some pertinent structural characteristics of the excluded industries. The ratio of *MES* to market is somewhat higher in these industries, although the difference is not significant. On the other hand, these industries show lower advertising:sales ratios, on the average, than those

TABLE 10.4.   Characteristics of excluded industries[a]

| Industry | Advertising:sales ratio (percent) | Plant economies of scale (percent) |
|---|---|---|
| Wines | 5.2 | 4.2 |
| Meat | 0.6 | 0.7 |
| Carpets | 2.0 | 7.7 |
| Hats | 2.2 | 10.4 |
| Millinery | 0.8 | 0.4 |
| Screens and blinds | 1.6 | 3.3 |
| Books | 2.4 | 1.8 |
| Tires and tubes | 1.4 | 5.0 |
| Household and service machinery | 1.9 | 6.4 |
| Motorcycles and bicycles | 1.1 | 12.5 |
| Clocks and watches | 5.6 | 8.3 |
| Costume jewelry | 4.0 | 0.7 |
| Average:  12 excluded industries | 2.4 | 5.1 |
| 29 included industries | 3.7 | 4.5 |

[a]These industries are those for which estimates of minimum efficient firm size could not be obtained and which are excluded from the regression equations presented in Table 10.2.

industries that were included in the regression equations.[11] This finding suggests further that where advertising is relatively low there is less likelihood that larger firms will show higher profit rates than smaller ones in the same industry than where advertising is a more important feature of industry behavior. Our failure to estimate a specific value of *MEF* for those industries may simply be indicative of a very low minimum scale of an efficient firm.

## PROFIT-RATE DIFFERENCES BETWEEN LARGE AND SMALL FIRMS

As noted above, we are concerned with the determinants not only of minimum efficient size of firm, but also of the extent of the disadvantages suffered by the firms that are smaller than this size. In this section, we deal with the latter problem by examining differences in profit rates between firms at different scales of output. This variable is used to represent the net effect of differences in both prices and costs.

Profit-rate differences are defined for each industry between various sets of "large" and "small" firms, and these differences are then related to two industry characteristics: the relative importance of economies of scale at the plant level and the relative importance of advertising.

The effect of economies of large-scale plants upon profit differences should depend on the extent to which the production of firms in both size groups is concentrated in plants of suboptimal scale, upon the average size of such suboptimal plants, and upon the shape of the production-cost curve below minimum efficient plant scale. We assume that all firms in the larger size group have fully exploited such economies, and that the disadvantages of the smaller group of firms are related to their mean size in relation to minimum efficient plant size. Note that we do not use the ratio of *MES* to market, the variable used in Chapter 6 to measure the effects of scale economies on average profit rates in an industry, because it should not be directly related to profit-rate *differences* between two groups of firms in an industry.

The effect of advertising on profit-rate differences should obviously depend not only on the average advertising intensity in the industry but also upon the relative differences in size between the two groups of firms. This effect is measured, therefore, by the product of the advertising:sales ratio and the

11. We tested whether the mean advertising:sales ratio in "excluded" industries is significantly greater than the mean ratio in the "included" industries. The *t* statistic fell slightly below the critical value at the 5 percent confidence level (1.56 as compared with a critical level of 1.68) and, therefore, we were not able to reject the null hypothesis at that confidence level. The null hypothesis could be rejected, however, at the 10 percent level.

logarithm of the ratio of the average size of the larger firms to the average size of their smaller rivals.[12]

To test these hypotheses, we estimate interindustry regression equations of the following form:

$$PD = a + b \ln(SL/MES) + c\,[(Ad/S) \cdot \ln(SH/SL)] + v, \qquad (4)$$

where $PD$ is the difference between the mean profit rate of the larger firms and the mean profit rate of the smaller firms; $SL/MES$ is the ratio of the mean size of the smaller firms to the scale of a minimum efficient plant, where both variables are measured by the volume of sales, $Ad/S$ is the advertising:sales ratio for the industry, $SH/SL$ is the ratio of mean sales of the larger firms to mean sales of the smaller firms, and $v$ is an error term. If advertising intensity and plant scale economies were the only factors affecting the profit rate advantage of the larger firms, the functional form of the equation would imply a zero intercept. The intercept is included in order to allow for the possible net effects of other factors that create advantages of size. In addition to the general equation, equations are also presented in which one of the variables, the intercept, or both are suppressed.

Profit rate differences between three alternative sets of large and small firms are examined. In the first set, we consider only firms above $MES$ and analyze the difference between the average profit rates of the top four firms and that of the remainder of the firms above minimum efficient plant scale. Although it is unlikely that profit differences between these groups are related to economies of scale at the plant level, this variable is introduced into some of the regression equations to allow for possible errors of measurement in the estimates of $MES$.

The results are presented in Tables 10.5 and 10.6. We find that, on the average, the top four firms enjoy an average profit-rate advantage over the remaining firms above $MES$ of 1.6 percentage points. This difference, which amounts to a 20-percent advantage, is statistically significant at the 5-percent level. The multiple regression equations suggest that these differences are affected by the effects of advertising adjusted for difference in average firm size between the two groups. Since the intercept is not significant in any equation, this implies that, once the effects of product differentiation via advertising are taken into account, there is no net advantage, on the average, to the largest firms. As expected, the measure of plant scale disadvantages of smaller firms

---

12. The logarithm of this ratio and the logarithm of the ratio of SL to MES are used in equation (4) because we assume that the effect upon profit rates of a given absolute increase would diminish as size increases.

TABLE 10.5.   Tests of significance of mean profit rate differences[a]

| Profit rate difference between— | Mean difference[b] | Standard deviation of difference | N | t test |
|---|---|---|---|---|
| Top 4 firms and other firms above *MES* | 0.0160 | 0.0408 | 35[c] | 2.32[e] |
| Firms above *MES* and firms below *MES* | .0248 | 0.0406 | 38[d] | 3.76[f] |
| Top 4 firms and all other firms | .0252 | .0380 | 41 | 4.24[f] |

[a]Firms with total assets below $500,000 are excluded from all calculations.
[b]All averages are weighted averages of relevant asset-size class means; the weights are proportional to total equity for the asset-size class.
[c]Six industries were deleted because there were no firms above *MES* that were not also in the top 4, so these regressions were fitted to 35 observations.
[d]Three industries were deleted because there were no firms below *MES* that were above the size cutoff of $500,000 in assets, so these regressions were fitted to 38 observations.
[e]Statistically singificant at the 5-percent level.
[f]Statistically significant at the 1-percent level.

TABLE 10.6.   Coefficients for interindustry regression equations predicting profit differences between larger and smaller firms

| Equation Number | Constant | Effects of | | $R^2$ |
|---|---|---|---|---|
| | | Plant economies | Advertising intensity | |

A. *Equations predicting the profit rate difference between the top 4 firms and all other firms above MES*[a]

| | | $\ln \dfrac{SL1}{MES}$ | $\dfrac{Ad}{S} \cdot \ln \dfrac{SH1}{SL1}$ | |
|---|---|---|---|---|
| (A.1) | −0.00130 (0.09) | 0.000475 (0.04) | 0.502[b] (2.10) | 0.12 |
| (A.2) | −0.00088 (0.09) | | 0.503[b] (2.15) | .12[b] |
| (A.3) | | −0.000244 (0.03) | 0.492[b] (2.36) | .12[b] |
| (A.4) | | | 0.488[c] (3.31) | .12[c] |

B. *Equations predicting the profit rate difference between firms above MES and firms below MES*[d]

| | | $\ln \dfrac{SL2}{MES}$ | $\dfrac{Ad}{S} \cdot \ln \dfrac{SH2}{SL2}$ | |
|---|---|---|---|---|
| (B.1) | −0.00777 (0.58) | −0.0406[c] (3.06) | −0.0233 (0.29) | .21[b] |

Table 10.6. (continued)

| Equation number | Constant | Effects of | | $R^2$ |
| --- | --- | --- | --- | --- |
| | | Plant economies | Advertising intensity | |
| (B.2) | | −0.0349[c] | −0.392 | .21[c] |
| | | (3.94) | (0.53) | |
| (B.3) | −0.00910 | −0.0398[c] | | .21[c] |
| | (0.73) | (3.10) | | |
| (B.4) | | −0.0315[c] | | .20[c] |
| | | (5.19) | | |

C. *Equations predicting the profit rate difference between the top 4 firms and all other firms*[e]

| | Constant | $\ln \dfrac{SL2}{MES}$ | $\dfrac{Ad}{S} \cdot \ln \dfrac{SH1}{SL1}$ | |
| --- | --- | --- | --- | --- |
| (C.1) | −0.0149 | −0.0208 | 0.555[b] | .18[b] |
| | (0.86) | (1.49) | (2.35) | |

*Definition of variables*

$SH1$ = Mean sales for top 4 firms
$SL1$ = Mean sales for remainder of firms above *MES*
$SH2$ = Mean sales for all firms above *MES*
$SL2$ = Mean sales for firms below *MES* (with assets above $500,000)
$SL3$ = Mean sales for all firms except the top 4
$MES$ = Estimated minimum efficient scale of plant
$Ad/S$ = Advertising sales ratio for the industry

[a]Six industries were deleted because there were no firms above *MES* that were not also in the top 4, so these regressions were fitted to 35 observations.
[b]Statistically significant at the 5-percent level.
[c]Statistically significant at the 1-percent level.
[d]Three industries were deleted because there were no firms below *MES* that were above the size cutoff of $500,000 in assets, so that these regressions were fitted to 38 observations.
[e]Both sets of industries mentioned in footnotes a and d were deleted, so that this regression was fitted to 32 observations.

is insignificant, which simply reflects the fact that all of the smaller firms included in this particular comparison lie above minimum efficient plant scale.

In the second analysis, firms in each industry were divided into those above and those below estimated minimum efficient plant scale. Here, of course, we would expect to find that the effects of economies of scale at the plant level are more important. This expectation is confirmed by the empirical results.

As shown in Table 10.5, firms above *MES* have a mean profit rate that is 2.5 percentage points higher than that of firms below *MES*, an advantage of roughly one-third. This difference is statistically significant at the 1-percent level. However, in contrast to the difference between the two groups above *MES* examined in the previous analysis, advertising plays no role in explaining this profit-rate differential. In none of the regressions is the scaled advertising: sales ratio significant, and the observed profit rate advantage of firms above *MES* is attributable largely to the extent to which the group of smaller firms lie below *MES*. The variable measuring this effect is significant at the 1-percent level in all equations. The constant term as well as the scaled advertising variable is insignificant, indicating that, once the effect of technical economies is taken into account, firms above *MES* have no net profit-rate advantage. These findings also provide additional support for the validity of our estimates of scale economies at the plant level.

Since advantages of size in relation to advertising intensity appear to be particularly important for the largest firms in an industry, an additional analysis was carried out to examine profit-rate differences between the four largest firms and all others both below and above *MES*. Because previous analysis demonstrated that the firms above estimated *MES* suffered no disadvantage in the scale of production facilities, the ratio of the mean size of firms *below MES* to *MES* was used to measure the interindustry effects of plant-scale economies upon the profit rate advantages of the top four firms. The measure of advertising intensity used in this analysis is the advertising: sales ratio scaled by the logarithm of the ratio of the mean size of the top four firms to the mean size of *all* other firms.

The estimated equation is presented in the third part of Table 10.6. The scaled advertising intensity variable is statistically significant at the 5-percent level,[13] whereas relative production-scale economies are significant only at the 10-percent level. The insignificance of the constant term suggests that the net effect on the average of other factors upon these profit-rate differences is unimportant.[14]

Taken together, these three sets of regression results indicate that product

13. In order to make sure that this interaction variable was not simply picking up the effect of size differences per se, we reestimated equation C1 of Table 10.6 with the interaction variable replaced by the logarithm of the ratio of the sizes itself, obtaining the following equation:

$$PD = \underset{(1.11)}{.0300} - \underset{(0.50)}{.0079} Ln \frac{SL_2}{MES} - \underset{(0.80)}{.0108} Ln \frac{SH_1}{SL_1}$$

$$R^2 = .046$$

As none of the coefficients is statistically significant, we conclude that the coefficient of the scaled advertising variable in the equations reported in Table 10.6 does reflect the effects of the interaction of advertising and size differences.

14. This is not to argue that the partial effects of other factors is unimportant, since the effects of separate factors may offset one another.

differentiation via advertising confers an advantage upon the very largest firms in an industry, and, as would be expected, that firms below minimum efficient plant scale suffer a disadvantage attributable to economies of scale in production.

## CONCLUSION

In this chapter we have presented the results of empirical analyses of the effects of advertising on the relative profit positions of large and small firms and on the minimum efficient scale of the firm. The findings provide empirical support for the view that there are advantages to size that are related to the level of advertising intensity in an industry. These results suggest that there are net advantages to large firms—beyond those attributable to economies of large-scale plants—in industries in which product differentiation via advertising is an important dimension of industry structure.

# APPENDIX 10-A

In the regression equations presented in the body of this chapter, the ratio of *MEF* to market is an estimate of the dependent variable rather than the variable itself. To see the importance of this factor, consider a regression model in which there is only a single independent variable:

$$Y_i = a + b X_i + u_i,$$ (1)

where $X_i$ and $Y_i$ are values for the $i$th observation and $u_i$ is the value of the random error term for the same observation. However, we cannot observe $Y_i$ but rather have estimates which are subject to error:

$$y_i = Y_i + e_i,$$ (2)

where $e_i$ is a second random error term. Therefore, the estimating equation takes the form

$$y_i = a + b X_i + v_i,$$ (3)

where $v_i$ is the sum of $e_i$ and $u_i$. Note that the error term $v$ is necessarily heteroscedastic in that it varies directly with the dependent variable. In these circumstances, as is well known, the efficiency of the regression estimates can be improved if the observations are weighted appropriately, which here would be by the reciprocal of the standard deviation of $v_i$.

Although we cannot observe the variance of $v_i$ for the equations given in Table 10.3, we do have estimates of the comparable variances of $e_i$, which are the variances of the individual values of the dependent variables in the equations. These are derived directly from the figures given in the second column of Table 10.2. Therefore, we hoped to proceed as follows: first, we would compute the variance of the estimated residuals from the unweighted equations, given in Table 10.3, from which we would obtain an estimate of the mean variance of $v_i$; next, this estimate would be used to estimate the mean value of the variance of $u_i$:

$$\text{var } (u) = \text{var } (v) - (1/N) \sum_i \text{var } (e_i) \tag{4}$$

where var $(u)$ and var $(v)$ are estimates of the mean variances of the two random variables; then each observation would be multiplied by $[\text{var } (u) + \text{var } (e_i)]^{-1/2}$.

A further difficulty involved the five industries in which the values of *MEF* were constrained not to exceed the average size of the four largest firms. When this constraint limits the values taken by *MEF*, corrections are made of the estimates of the standard errors of the coefficients. In these cases, the effective variance of the observation should be increased since the fact that the constraints are violated suggests that there may be some specification error in the function that is fitted. Hence, the estimated standard error of estimates for the constrained values is probably greater than that implied by the original estimates. The variance correction used is

$$\text{constrained var } (MEF_i) = \text{original var } (MEF_i) + (MEF_i - K)^2 , \tag{5}$$

where original var $(MEF_i)$ is the square of the values given in the second column in Table 10.2 and $K$ is the value of the constraint that is violated. Note that this formula is analogous to the formula relating mean square error to variance and bias.

When this procedure was attempted, a severe problem was encountered. Note that a crucial step is the estimate of var $(u)$, which is derived from the difference between two variance estimates, as indicated in equation (4). Both of these estimates are, of course, subject to error, and the estimates of var $(u)$ derived for each of the equations in Table 10.3 are negative, or in other words the estimated var $(v)$ is less than the mean value of the estimated var $(e_i)$.

Since this approach could not be followed, an alternative weighting scheme was used. Equation (2) in Table 10.3 was reestimated with each observation multiplied by the reciprocal of the standard deviation of the dependent variable. By comparing this weighting scheme with the appropriate one, we can see that it reduces the relative importance of observations with large variances by a greater extent than is required to correct for the presence of heteroscedasticity. But note that if observations with high variances are given too little weight in this scheme, they are clearly given too much weight where all observations are weighted equally. The estimated equation when this weighting scheme is used is

$$\ln MEF/Mkt = -1.702 - 0.112 \, (\ln Ad/S \cdot \ln MES/Mkt) \qquad (6)$$
$$\phantom{\ln MEF/Mkt = } (0.457) \quad (0.032)$$

$$\phantom{\ln MEF/Mkt = } -2.009 \, REG, \qquad\qquad R^2 = 0.78,$$
$$\phantom{\ln MEF/Mkt = } (0.744) \qquad\qquad \text{corrected } R^2 = 0.76,$$

with the same notation as in Table 10.3. Note that the coefficients remain statistically significant and that the estimates of the crucial parameter vary only from $-0.072$ in the unweighted regression to $-0.112$ in the weighted regression. Some further support is thereby provided to the results found in this chapter.

CHAPTER 11 **Conclusions**

In the preceding chapters, we have examined various aspects of the economics of advertising. It is now time to ask what conclusions can be drawn from this analysis, and to consider the general policy implications of our results.

The empirical analysis has focused on a specific class of advertising expenditures. Advertising, of course, runs the gamut from the small classified advertisements inserted by individuals in daily newspapers to the large and expensive advertising campaigns carried out by the larger manufacturers of consumer goods on network television. In this study, however, we have limited our concern to advertising by firms that manufacture consumer products. We have therefore not paid attention to classified ads, which are generally inserted by individuals and retailers, or to advertising by firms in the distribution and producer goods sectors. Although the analysis, and therefore any implications for public policy, are limited to the former class of advertising, it is also this class of advertising that has created the most controversy in recent years and has raised the most important questions for public policy.

Advertising by the manufacturers of consumer goods can be viewed as influencing various types of consumer decisions. In the first place, advertising affects the distribution of sales among the products of different sellers in the same market. In addition, it may influence the distribution of demand among different markets, thereby affecting the outputs of different industries, and perhaps also the allocation of income between spending and saving. Until recently there has been little concrete evidence on the relative strengths of these various effects, but it has become part of the economic folklore that the most significant impact of advertising lies in the distribution of sales among firms in the same market, with a decreasing impact in the further categories.[1] Although we have not attempted to determine the relative significance of advertising at various levels of consumer decision-making, we have examined its impact both upon competition within markets and upon the distribution of demand among industries.

We examined the impact of advertising on industry demand by estimating demand equations for each consumer products industry. We find that relative advertising expenditures appear to be more important than relative prices in allocating sales among industries. The evidence therefore indicates that advertising has a major impact on consumer spending decisions, and hence upon the allocation of resources.

The effects of advertising on the distribution of sales among products in the same market, and particularly on relative sales of new entrants and established firms, is perhaps even more important. It is through these effects that advertising has a major impact on market behavior and performance. Since the effect of advertising on market performance is our primary concern, several chapters have been devoted to this issue.

We have obtained empirical support for the conclusion that the heavy volume of advertising expenditures in some industries serves as an important barrier to new competition in the markets served by these industries. In the various econometric analyses reported in this study, the hypothesis that advertising has a significant effect on profit rates was subjected to a number of tests. The results show that the strong impact of advertising on profit rates is not sensitive to changes in the specification of the equation, that it prevails under estimation within the context of a simultaneous equations model, and that it stands up when rates of return are adjusted to reflect the partial capitalization of advertising outlays. The implication of these results is that heavy advertising in some industries leads directly to high price-cost margins. As a result, advertising has contributed to the development of market power in these industries. A related finding is that in a number of industries advertising appears to create major advantages for large firms relative to their smaller competitors.

---

1. In this regard, note the statement by Robert M. Solow, "I suppose ... that it must be relatively easy to affect such decisions decisions between alternative brands of the same product at given prices] by advertising . . . It must be harder to influence the consumer's choice between purchases of cigarettes and purchases of beer, and much harder still to influence his distribution of expenditures among such broad categories as food, clothing, automobiles, housing. It is open to legitimate doubt that advertising has any detectable effect at all upon the sum total of consumer spending or in other words, on the choice between spending and saving." Robert M. Solow, "The Truth Further Refined: A Comment on Marris," *The Public Interest* no. 11 (Spring 1968), p. 48.

## THE COSTS OF MARKET POWER

The conclusion that advertising has an important impact on competitive behavior within industries is supported by various analyses presented throughout this book. These analyses also permit us to measure the social costs of the market power generated by advertising and other factors. Three elements of the social costs of market power may be identified: (a) technical or "X" inefficiency resulting from actual average costs exceeding minimal average costs; (b) allocative inefficiency, the familiar dead-weight loss due to prices exceeding marginal costs; and (c) the transfer of income from consumers to the owners of firms possessing market power. The second element is the one that is emphasized in the literature on welfare economics, but it may be less important quantitatively than the technical inefficiency and income-transfer effects of market power.

Estimates of the importance of two sources of technical inefficiency are obtained: the costs of suboptimal capacity implicitly sheltered by the high price-cost margins established by larger producers, and the costs of excessive advertising outlays themselves. Estimates of the costs of suboptimal capacity are derived from the equations predicting profit rate differences between large and small firms presented in Chapter 10. The difference in profit margins attributable to firms operating below minimum efficient plant scale, together with the percentage of total sales accounted for by such firms, is used to obtain estimates of the costs of suboptimal capacity in the sector as a whole.

In Chapter 2, we examined the question of excessive advertising. Our suggested approach was to consider expenditures as excessive that exceeded those that would be made in the absence of the anticompetitive effects of advertising. Excessive advertising expenditures therefore are those made expressly to promote increased levels of market power. That advertising is excessive in some industries is suggested by two considerations: (a) the high degree of skewness of the interindustry distribution of advertising:sales ratios, and (b) the strong impact of industry advertising:sales ratios on profit rates.

Our estimates of excess advertising are therefore based entirely on the few industries in the sample with advertising:sales ratios that exceed 4 and 5 percent.[2] If we assume that nonexcessive advertising in these industries is distributed as a proportion of sales, as are advertising:sales ratios in the remaining industries, an appropriate measure is the sum of the differences in the observed ratios for industries above the critical level from the mean ratio for

2. Eight of the 41 industries in the sample had advertising:sales ratios of 5 percent or more; another three had advertising:sales ratios between 4 and 5 percent. Even by the lower criterion, only a quarter of the industries have excess advertising. Note also that the median ratio for 41 industries in the sample is only 2.2 percent.

industries below that level. That these are conservative estimates is suggested by the fact that the cigarette industry, which many would argue carried out excessive advertising,[3] has an advertising:sales ratio of 4.8 percent. Furthermore, these calculations ignore the possibility that advertising may be excessive in industries, such as motor vehicles, that have a very high absolute volume of spending on advertising.

The volume of advertising accounted for *by such differences* is an element of technical inefficiency in that it represents expenditures made and resources used to promote private objectives rather than to satisfy consumer demands. In many respects, it is analogous to outlays made to promote and defend against income transfers and is a social cost even if one takes a neutral stance with regard to the transfer itself. Thus, even if the degree of allocative inefficiency due to heavy advertising were small, there might still be substantial inefficiency in resource use associated with current levels of advertising.[4]

To some extent, excess advertising represents resources that are wasted in that there is no effective demand for the output that is produced. To some extent also, however, these outlays represent resources used to produce an output—the content of the information media—for which presumably there is an unexpressed consumer demand. In either case, however, there is likely to be a high degree of inefficiency in that resources are not allocated in accord with consumer preferences.[5]

The structural equation explaining profit rates can be used to determine the extent to which profit margins in each industry exceed competitive levels. The excess profit margin, the excess costs due to technical inefficiency, and the estimates of the price elasticity of demand obtained in Chapter 5 can together be used to calculate the deadweight loss of allocative efficiency.

Finally, the net transfer of income from consumers to the owners of the firms with market power simply involves the calculation of the total excess monopoly profit based on the measure of excess profit margin already discussed. It should be noted that this transfer is not necessarily from consumers to the current owners of the firm, since the monopoly rents have presumably

3. Nicholls concludes that "advertising is the key to the monopoly problem in the cigarette industry." William H. Nicholls, *Price Policies in the Cigarette Industry* (Nashville, Vanderbilt University Press, 1951), p. 412. See particularly pp. 187–203.

4. A related argument was made earlier by Tullock. See Gordon Tullock, "The Welfare Costs of Tariffs, Monopolies, and Theft," *Western Economics Journal*, 5 (June 1967), pp. 224–232.

5. In this study, no attempt has been made to estimate the efficiency or distributive effects of supporting the information media by advertising. Whether the level of excess advertising used for these purposes is greater or lesser than an appropriate measure of the inefficiency of current arrangements is difficult to determine.

TABLE 11.1.  The cost of market power in the consumer-goods manufacturing sector

| Loss of Technical Efficiency: | Estimates using 5% critical level of advertising | | Estimates using 4% critical level of advertising | |
|---|---|---|---|---|
| | Millions of dollars | Percent of value added | Millions of dollars | Percent of value added[1] |
| Excess advertising[2] | 656 | 1.4 | 827 | 1.7 |
| Cost of suboptimal capacity[3] | 736 | 1.6 | 736 | 1.6 |
| Loss in allocative efficiency[4] | 140 | 0.31 | 161 | 0.35 |
| Total cost to society | 1,532 | 3.2 | 1,724 | 3.7 |
| Monopoly transfer[5] | 1,070 | 2.3 | 1,100 | 2.3 |
| Total cost to consumers | 2,602 | 5.5 | 2,824 | 6.0 |

[1]Details may not add to totals because of roundings.

[2]For each industry with advertising:sales ratios above 4 or 5 percent, excess advertising as a percentage of sales is the difference between the actual ratio and the mean ratio for industries below the appropriate critical level. For industries with advertising:sales ratios at or below these critical values, excess advertising is zero.

[3]These estimates are based on equation (B.4) in Table 10.6. This equation predicts the profit-rate differential between firms above and below minimum efficient plant scale *MES*. For each industry (with the exceptions noted below) the predicted values of the profit-rate differentials for this equation are first adjusted to a before-tax basis by multiplying by 2 (since the effective average tax rate is about 50 percent) and then multiplying by the equity: sales ratio to estimate the unit-cost disadvantage as a percentage of sales of suboptimal firms. This unit-cost differential is then multiplied by the dollar value of sales by firms below *MES* (note that this includes firms below the $500,000 asset-size cutoff used in the analysis of Chapter 10) to obtain the absolute cost of suboptimal capacity.

In three industries—women's clothing, millinery, and furs—there were no firms below *MES* that were not also below the minimum size limit for the analysis persented in Table 10.6. For these three industries, the estimated profit-rate disadvantage is arbitrarily set at 2.5 percent, the average profit-rate disadvantage observed across the sample of industries (see Table 10.6). This difference is then multiplied by 2 to adjust for taxes, by the equity: sales ratio, and by the value of sales of firms below *MES* in arriving at the absolute cost of suboptimal capacity in these industries.

[4]This calculation required two measures: the estimated excess price-cost margin and the price elasticity of demand. The latter measure is the short-run price elasticity of demand from Table 5.8 constrained to be nonpositive.

The excess price-cost margin consists of the excessive costs (due to advertising and suboptimal capacity) and the excess profit margin itself. The calculation of the former is described in Notes 2 and 3 above. The excess profit margin is determined as follows. Using equation (2) from Table 7.1 we estimated a competitive rate of return in each industry on on the basis of the following assumptions: (a) the advertising:sales ratio is set at 4 or 5 percent respectively (corresponding to assumed maximum values of competitive levels of advertising); (b) absolute capital requirements are set at the median value for the sample of the industries; (c) the local market dummy variable is set at zero, since we interpret the latter variable as representing the effects of concentration and economies of scale in relation to the market; (d) the rate of growth of demand for the industry is set at its observed value, since rates of return in competitive industries may be expected to vary with rates of growth of demand.

The difference between the observed rate of return and the estimated competitive rate of return, multiplied by the equity:sales ratio, provides a measure of the excess net-profit margin due to market power. This variable, constrained to be nonnegative, is scaled by 2.083 (the reciprocal of 1 minus the marginal statutory tax rate of 52 percent in effect over the 1954–1957 period) to obtain the before-tax excess profit margin in sales.

The estimated value of the loss of allocative efficiency was measured by the familiar triangle of deadweight loss*, as follows:

$AL_{(i)} = \frac{1}{2}(M_{(i)} + CSO_{(i)} + X_{(i)})^2(-ES_{(i)})S_{(i)}$, where $AL_{(i)}$ is the absolute value of the allocative efficiency loss in industry $i$, $M_{(i)}$ is the before-tax excess profit margin on sales in industry $i$, $X_{(i)}$ is excess advertising as a ratio to sales in industry $i$, $ES_{(i)}$ is the short-run price elasticity of demand in industry $i$, and $S_{(i)}$ is total sales in industry $i$.

[5]This value is the amount of transfer of income from consumers to the firms with market power. Since the taxes paid on these monopoly rents do not represent such a transfer, we calculate the after-tax value of the excess profits drawn from consumers. For each industry this is simply the excess after-tax profit margin on sales (described in Note 4) multiplied by industry sales.

Although the value of the monopoly transfers is a cost to consumers comparable to other costs, it cannot, of course, simply be added to the previous costs to determine the net cost to society. To calculate the social cost of such transfers would warrant a separate study of its own, and for present purposes we simply ignore these costs.

---

*This sort of calculation has been called into question in a recent paper by Professor Bergson. Using a more consciously general equilibrium approach, he suggests that the familiar triangle may understate or overstate the correct magnitude. See Abram Bergson, "On Monopoly Welfare Losses," *American Economic Review*, 63 (December 1973), 853–870.

been capitalized into the value of the shares of the firms possessing market power.

Because the value of the monopoly transfer does not measure the social cost of the transfer, we have carried out two aggregate calculations, labeled respectively the "cost to consumers" (which includes the monopoly transfer) and the "cost to society" (which does not). However, since the latter measure makes no allowance for the social cost of the redistribution of income and wealth attributable to market power, it understates the true social cost of market power.[6]

Because the effects of advertising are concentrated in a small number of industries, we have carried out two sets of calculations. The first set covers the consumer goods sector as a whole, and the second covers the small groups of industries with very high advertising outlays corresponding to the alternative cut-off points. The calculations are presented in Tables 11.1 and 11.2, and

6. Ignoring the monopoly income transfer is correct only if income distribution has no weight in the social welfare function, or if there are costless means of offsetting the income distribution effects brought about by market power. Since it is obvious that neither of these conditions holds, the social cost estimates presented in the tables above understate the total costs to society of market power in these industries.

TABLE 11.2.   The cost of market power in industries with high advertising

| Loss in technical efficiency: | Industries with advertising above critical level of 5% | | Industries with advertising above critical level of 4% | |
|---|---|---|---|---|
| | Millions of dollars | Percent of value added | Millions of dollars | Percent of value added |
| Excess advertising | 656 | 11.2 | 827 | 9.8 |
| Cost of suboptimal capacity | 112 | 1.9 | 156 | 1.9 |
| Loss in allocative efficiency | 62 | 1.1 | 90 | 1.1 |
| Total cost to society | 830 | 14.2 | 1,073 | 12.8 |
| Total monopoly transfer | 148 | 2.1 | 247 | 2.5 |
| Total cost to consumers | 978 | 16.2 | 1,320 | 15.3 |

See notes to table 11.1 above.

details regarding the calculations are given in the notes to these tables. The results indicate that the costs involved constitute a nontrivial percentage of value added in the consumer goods sector as a whole, and are of substantial importance for the group of industries with high advertising outlays in relation to sales.

For the consumer goods sector as a whole, the estimated total annual cost to consumers amounted to more than $2.5 billion (at 1954–1957 price levels) and accounted for 5.5 to 6 percent of value added in the sector. If the monopoly transfers (amounting to 2.3 percent of value added) are ignored, the annual dollar cost to society is more than $1.5 billion, or from 3.2 to 3.7 percent of aggregate value added.

Of these amounts, excess advertising and the costs of suboptimal capacity each account for 1.5 percent of value added. As would be expected on the basis of previous studies, the loss in allocative efficiency is much smaller, amounting to slightly more than 0.3 percent of value added. Of these total costs, we should note that the total effect of advertising is larger than the figures shown for excess advertising itself, since advertising affects profit margins, thereby giving rise to allocative inefficiency and monopoly transfers. In addition, these higher price-cost margins contribute to technical inefficiency by permitting firms of suboptimal scale to exist.

For the two subsets of industries where advertising is above 4 and 5 percent respectively, the picture is more dramatic. The respective costs to consumers are about 15 and 16 percent of value added; and the costs to society (ignoring monopoly transfers) are, respectively, 13 and 14 percent of value added. As would be expected, the role of advertising looms large. In the first group, excessive advertising directly contributes 10 percent of value added; in the second group, it contributes about 11 percent. Because of the interaction of the high costs of excessive advertising and the high price-cost margins in these industries, the deadweight loss of allocative efficiency is slightly greater than 1 percent. The relative losses due to suboptimal capacity and the value of monopoly transfers are not very different for these subsets of industries than for the sector as a whole. This reflects the fact that other sources of market power are important among some of the remaining consumer-goods manu-facturing industries.

On the basis of these results we conclude that the costs of market power in the consumer goods industries are significant and that advertising itself directly and indirectly accounts for a substantial portion of these costs. These costs, moreover, are highly concentrated in a small number of industries.

## GENERAL POLICY IMPLICATIONS

We now turn to the policy implications of the major finding of this study: that heavy advertising creates a significant barrier to new competition in a number of important industries. Industries characterized by heavy advertising earn profit rates that are typically between 3 and 4 percentage points higher than those in other industries. This differential represents up to a 50-percent increase in rates of return. Since available evidence suggests that long-run average costs in the manufacturing sector are generally constant at output levels reached by leading firms,[7] our findings indicate that prices in manu-facturing industries characterized by heavy advertising exceed marginal costs. The costs of this performance are estimated in the previous section.

These results, however, refer only to the social costs of advertising as an entry barrier and suggest nothing regarding the social costs of promoting entry despite the presence of barriers. The policy implications of this finding depend on the social costs of pursuing various public policies as well as the social costs of permitting monopoly to remain. Indeed, if the differential costs that give rise to entry barriers represent real social costs, it may be socially preferable that entry not take place if the higher costs must be borne either by the entrant or by some supporting agency. In this case, entry restric-tions may be viewed as giving rise to a form of "natural oligopoly." To the extent, however, that policy actions can be designed that increase the likelihood of entry without entailing such costs, there is room for an increase in economic welfare.

Although a policy judgment that entry should be encouraged does not follow

7. See, for example, J. Johnston, *Statistical Cost Analysis* (New York, McGraw-Hill, 1960), pp. 44–168.

from the mere presence of barriers to entry, the social costs of restricted competition remain. Even though policies that lead to increased entry may not be desired because of the social costs incurred as a result, the policy problem of high price-cost margins persists. Although policy judgments become more difficult, these circumstances are not cause for arguing that no policy actions should be taken. For example, the setting of price ceilings in regulatory proceedings may be as appropriate in the case of a "natural oligopoly" protected by entry barriers as in the case of a "natural monopoly."

Furthermore, in these circumstances, it may be more important to emphasize policies dealing with explicit or tacit collusion. Where entry barriers are substantial, it is more important to make collusion more difficult, since the presence of entry barriers permits existing firms to achieve and maintain high price-cost margins. Where entry barriers are low, on the other hand, collusion is less likely to be effective since high profit margins would attract new firms into the market. This conclusion receives some empirical support in the analysis above, where concentration was found to have a significant impact on profits only where entry barriers are high. Thus, policy actions to promote competition among existing firms become *more* important where entry barriers are high, and greater efforts in this direction are advisable.

The prospect of designing public policies to promote competition by reducing entry barriers is greatly improved if the differential cost advantages of established firms consist entirely or largely of private rather than social savings. In this case, it may be desirable to remove entry restrictions even if the differential costs must be borne in the process. The social gains of reduced market power would in such cases exceed the social costs of the policies concerned.

Alternatively, and perhaps preferably, policies designed to eliminate or offset the effects of practices that give rise to these differential advantages could be considered. The prevention of price discrimination by the media is a difficult but not impossible task, which could be handled under existing antitrust laws. Price discrimination in the capital markets may be partly offset by appropriate tax policies designed to mitigate capital shortages faced by new firms.

Under what conditions are the entry barriers due to advertising likely to reflect differentially higher private but not social costs? Where scale economies in advertising result from the practice of price discrimination by the information media, the higher private costs of new entrants do not reflect higher social costs. Similarly, where advertising constitutes a significant addition to absolute capital requirements and where the higher interest rates charged to new entrants are due to the practice of price discrimination by the suppliers of capital, the higher private costs of new entrants again do not reflect higher social costs. In either case, entry may be promoted without fear of increased social costs.

Social and private costs may also diverge because of the peculiar nature of the demand for advertising. As indicated above, the demand for advertising messages by consumers is derived from the demand for information concerning products in the market. Because advertising by its very nature represents a biased form of information, in that it is designed especially to promote the products of particular manufacturers, the demand for advertising messages must fall below the comparable demand for messages from a more objective source of information at the same price per message and in the same style and format. However, because of the public good character of much information, underinvestment of resources in the provision of objective information may be anticipated.

The higher demand for objective information suggests that consumer welfare would be served if the same volume of resources were devoted in as effective a manner to the provision of information from sources more objective than advertising. Alternatively, consumers would be equally well off if less were spent and the lower volume of expenditures were used for more objective information than that contained in most advertising messages. Thus, the differentially higher advertising costs required of new entrants may reflect higher private than social costs.

As suggested in Chapter 2, the current volume of advertising messages is accepted by consumers largely because of the subsidized content of the information media, which is provided jointly with the advertising messages. For a large share of current messages, the relevant consumer demand price is therefore negative. The costs of providing these messages, as distinguished from the cost of subsidizing the information media, must therefore be private rather than social costs, since consumers would indeed benefit if these expenditures were not made. Although some producers would suffer, what is foregone is the monopoly profits associated with extensive advertising. It is therefore difficult to argue that the differential cost advantages of new entrants represent higher social costs where a large share of the output of these costs commands a *negative* demand price. The fact that advertising has a clear effect on consumer decisions does *not* imply that consumers require or prefer the volume of messages received; the difference between the *ex ante* demand for and the *ex post* effect of advertising explains this apparent paradox.

The prospect that a large share of the differentially higher costs of new entrants represents increased private rather than social costs suggests that it may be both possible and desirable to design public policies to counter the anticompetitive effects of intensive advertising. Policies to promote entry are desirable where the net social costs of government actions are less than the net social costs of the market power due to barriers to entry. To determine whether this is the case requires an evaluation of the set of social costs and benefits associated with advertising.

The evidence presented in this study supports the view that advertising enhances market power through its effects upon entry barriers and upon the relative positions of large and small firms in the market. As a result, there are net welfare losses associated with intensive advertising in certain industries. However, it does not follow that we would necessarily be better off with substantially less advertising but with everything else unchanged. Although advertising may create market power and may be excessive, it nevertheless provides information and helps finance the information media. Given consumer ignorance and the inadequacies of investment in the provision of public information, advertising may represent a useful solution to the twin problems of providing information to consumers and financing the provision of public entertainment and information through the media.

The effects of advertising upon consumers and upon the media have been the source of considerable controversy. To its defenders, advertising provides information to consumers on the nature and availability of products offered in the market.[8] To its critics, advertising is largely persuasive in character and has little to do with the provision of consumer information. In fact, advertising is viewed as often providing misinformation.[9] Some commentators recognize that the distinction between "informative" and "persuasive" advertising is exceedingly difficult to draw, and any given advertisement will generally possess both characteristics.[10] On this account, this distinction may provide little assistance in evaluating the social gains from advertising.[11]

An alternative approach to evaluating the social gains from advertising is to consider the distinction between the impact of advertising on the underlying

8. See, for example, George J. Stigler, "The Economics of Information," *Journal of Political Economy*, 69 (June 1961); and Lester G. Telser, "Advertising and Competition," *Journal of Political Economy*, 72 (December 1964).

9. See, for example, Nicholas Kaldor, "The Economic Aspects of Advertising," reprinted in *Essays on Value and Distribution* (Glencoe, Ill., Free Press, 1960), pp. 96–140; John K. Galbraith, *The New Industrial State* (Boston, Houghton Mifflin, 1967); and Vance Packard, *The Hidden Persuaders* (New York, D. McKay Co., 1957).

10. This position is taken in Harry G. Johnson, *The Canadian Quandary* (New York, McGraw-Hill, 1963), p. 280.

11. Note that our finding that advertising contributes to the achievement of market power in a number of industries does not rest on any assumptions regarding the "informative" or "persuasive" character of the messages provided.

structure of consumer tastes and on the extent to which consumers suc-
ceed in maximizing their satisfaction for a given structure of tastes. Note that
the second effect emphasizes the relation between advertising and consumer
ignorance, and indeed it is probably in this context that the gains from advertising are best evaluated. This distinction may also arise when tastes are
given by product attributes and specific commodities are purchased for their
attributes.[12]

That advertising has an impact on the underlying structure of tastes is
difficult to deny. What is difficult, however, is to create and defend an objective
standard by which these changes can be evaluated. To critics, advertising imposes a set of materialistic values that are undesirable in their own right.
Nonmaterialistic values are shunted aside and cultural standards left to
decline. On the other hand, it has been argued that advertising on a national
scale has an integrating effect on society and provides a more cohesive com-
munity.[13] Moreover, it has been noted that "innovations were bizarre, and
curious tastes were acquired, before advertising became a major phenomenon,"[14] so that not all complaints in this realm should be laid at the doorstep
of advertising. Whatever position one takes in this debate, it seems clear that
we have few standards by which to evaluate the opposing positions. This is
an area where personal philosophies are dominant, and accepted conclusions
sparse. If we have no way of evaluating alternative structures of tastes, we
find it difficult to determine the gains from activities that influence tastes.
Perhaps the most valid approach, therefore, is an agnostic one, and we should
aim to consider the gains and costs of advertising apart from its impact on the
structure of tastes.

When we consider the influence of advertising on consumer satisfaction for
a given structure of tastes, we are on only slightly more solid ground. If a
preference function is defined on the basis of full information on the menu of
products offered for sale and optimal choices are determined, it would seem
reasonable to posit that factors which lead actual choices away from this ideal
involve a welfare loss for the consumer. In this case, however these factors are
defined, they are necessarily associated with the provision of information or
misinformation on consumer products.

If we could be assured that advertising provides no misinformation and

12. See Kelvin J. Lancaster, "Change and Innovation in the Technology of Consumption," *American Economic Review* (May 1966), pp. 14–23; and his "A New Approach to
Consumer Theory," *Journal of Political Economy* 74 (April 1966), 132–157.
13. This argument is reported in Robin Marris, "Galbraith, Solow, and the Truth about
Corporations," *The Public Interest*, no. 11 (Spring 1968), 39.
14. Walter Taplin, *Advertising: A New Approach* (Boston, Little, Brown, 1963), p. 20.

thereby promotes consumer choices that are more in accord with those that would be made with full information, then we could argue that there is a positive gain to the consumer associated with his revised preferences.[15] Although this may be the case in many circumstances, we cannot rule out the prospect that some forms of advertising lead consumers further away from choices based on full information. Indeed, prospects for the provision of misinformation are surely increased by the manner in which advertising messages are supplied, since the dominant concern of the advertiser is to sell the product, not to provide objective information on products in the market.

Much depends, therefore, on the question of what sort of information is obtained from advertising. If the social gains from advertising are stated in terms of the consumer information that is provided, then it might be argued that only "informative" advertising provides social benefits. The content of this statement depends, of course, on what is meant by "informative" advertising. If only messages that are descriptive of the qualities and prices of products in the market are considered informative, then much advertising provides little informational value—whatever its impact on consumer decisions.[16]

To others, a broader definition of information is used, so that essentially all advertising is information. Product qualities include "all the characteristics which can be attributed to the goods and might influence a consumer, short of quickly apparent deceptions."[17] And here subjective characteristics and associations are explicitly included. The question of what should be referred to as "informative" advertising lies at the heart of many recent controversies on this subject. Its answer must affect any judgment that is made of the overall gains to society from advertising.

In this context, the information provided by advertising is valued precisely because it leads to a new set of consumer decisions. To the extent, however, that the advertising messages of competing firms are directly offsetting, there is no new pattern of consumer decisions. Since information is here defined on relative rather than on absolute terms, information would not increase in these circumstances. Thus, Marris and Solow agree that where advertising messages are directly offset by those supplied by competing firms, the eco-

15. This type of analysis is presented in Melvin W. Reder, *Studies in the Theory of Welfare Economics* (New York, Columbia University Press, 1947), pp. 68–71, where it is assumed that all advertising increases the degree of consumer information.

16. This position is taken by Boulding who believes that "informative" advertising is a small share of the total. See Kenneth E. Boulding, *Economic Analysis*, 3rd ed. (New York, Harper & Row, 1955), p. 672.

17. Taplin, *Advertising: A New Approach*, p. 47.

nomic effect of these messages is nil and there are few social gains from these efforts.[18] The information required for these market results could be provided at lower social costs and economic efficiency improved.

Whatever the merits of these competing views, the evidence presented in Chapter 5 does bear on one issue. Since advertising has an important effect on the interindustry structure of demand, we cannot assert that all advertising is wholly self-canceling. Whether the resulting interindustry distribution is in some sense better or worse than the distribution that would prevail in the absence of advertising is difficult to determine. It is noteworthy in this respect that firms in large numbers industries producing a homogeneous product or products have little incentive to advertise, so that advertising will tend over time to shift consumer demand away from such industries and products. This suggests that there may be industries in which there is relative *under*investment in advertising as well as industries in which there is overinvestment. In addition, in the absence of advertising, the rate of introduction and of acceptance of new products would be much slower, since these products depend more heavily on advertising as a source of consumer information than do established products. We are therefore unprepared, on the basis of the analysis presented above, to draw any policy implications regarding the effects of advertising on the interindustry demand for goods.

The anticompetitive effects of advertising within an industry are another matter. The evidence presented above supports the view that advertising is excessive in a limited number of industries within the consumer goods manufacturing sector. This excessive advertising is provided to consumers at an effective negative price, and serves to establish or augment the market power of the larger firms in these industries.

A final possible source of the gains from advertising results from the "payments" to consumers who receive these messages. In effect, advertising is used to subsidize the remaining content of various media, and these subsidies must be included in the gains from advertising. For the broadcast media in the United States, advertising revenues represent the entrie source of funds, whereas in the case of newspapers and magazines the advertising subsidies are only partial.[19] Although these subsidies are important and cannot be ignored, this source of revenue has important implications for the performance of various media that are not always desirable. In this case, the costs from these

18. Marris, "Galbraith, Solow, and the Truth About Corporations," p. 39; and Solow, "The Truth Further Refined," pp. 48–49.

19. See Nicholas Kaldor and Rodney Silverman, *A Statistical Analysis of Advertising Expenditures and of the Revenue of the Press* (Cambridge, Cambridge University Press, 1948), pp. 38–52.

subsidies must be subtracted from the full value of the subsidies to determine the net value that is added to the gains from advertising.[20]

Although it is difficult to add up all the costs and benefits from advertising, it is appropriate to ask whether the benefits might not also be obtained even if some of the costs were lower. The issue here is not whether all advertising should be supported or attacked, but whether some changes might be made that would limit the social costs without subtracting from the potential gains from advertising.

All sources of consumer information must necessarily use the resources required to supply messages to consumers, but all information sources need not serve to restrict the degree of competition. Indeed, as we have seen, this latter phenomenon is concentrated in a small set of industries within the manufacturing sector. In this case, the major policy question is whether certain areas of advertising might be limited in order to reduce the social costs of increased market power without restricting the potential gains from improved information and from media subsidies. In our view, this question has an affirmative answer.

## TOWARD A COHERENT SOCIAL POLICY

To the present time, public policy toward advertising has been made with little reference to the possible anticompetitive effects of high levels of advertising expenditures. The major policy actions in this area have focused on the content of advertising messages and the issue of "truth in advertising." Little attention has been paid to the implication of the volume of advertising for the degree of market power exercised in the American economy. The recognition of these effects represents a new set of considerations in the determination of social policy, and one that is long overdue.

It is, of course, easier to suggest that the anticompetitive effects of heavy advertising must be considered in the formation of effective public policy than it is to indicate which specific measures should be taken. It does not appear, moreover, that a solution to this problem is easily approached within the conventional framework of antitrust policy.

To the extent that policy actions in the past have influenced the volume of advertising, they have had a stimulative effect. The subsidy present in low

20. One such cost in the case of television is that the value attributed to a specific television program reflects primarily the gains from advertising rather than the utility provided to the ultimate viewers. This is particularly important since the support of television by advertising has effectively eliminated the prospect for the sale of television programming to individual consumers. For further discussion of the economic questions raised by the use of advertising to support the information media, see Johnson, *The Canadian Quandary*, pp. 273–275.

postal rates for second- and third-class mail, and the current income-tax provisions that permit advertising expenditures to be expensed rather than depreciated, are two elements of this subsidy. In both cases, public actions have served to augment the heavy volume of advertising that we observe. These measures need to be reconsidered in the light of the major findings of this study. Furthermore, public actions may be needed that move in the opposite direction.

Specific policy studies are required to determine which actions should be taken in this sphere and how the current and past effects of heavy advertising can be reduced. The provision of impartial information would tend to reduce the impact of advertising on consumer decisions and thereby the entry barriers created by heavy advertising. Information that correctly reported that competing products are equally good or equally useful would make an important contribution, for this is a type of information that is rarely provided by advertising. Government regulations that require product standardization may be possible and beneficial in a limited number of product areas. These and other actions should be designed specifically to increase the ability of consumers to evaluate competing products and thereby reduce their reliance on advertising.

In addition, it may be necessary in some circumstances to adopt policies that limit the volume of advertising expenditures. Whether through new tax policies toward advertising or through expanded enforcement of the antitrust laws, actions of this type may be necessary. In this connection, Turner suggested "that it would be quite appropriate to impose, for a period of time, an absolute or percentage limitation on promotional expenditures by a firm or firms that have obtained undue market power through violations of the Sherman Act. A classic purpose of a remedial decree in such cases is to dissipate the consequences of unlawful acts, and if limitations on promotional expenditures would help, they are appropriate even though the promotional expenditures as such were and are lawful."[21]

Whatever is decided regarding specific policy measures, it is evident from our findings that factors which promote product differentiation may be as important as those which influence the size distribution of firms in their effect on the achievement of market power. Current policies that emphasize the role played by market concentration need to be supplemented by those concerned directly with the nature and extent of product differentiation. Policies dealing with these matters would be an important component of a general policy designed to promote competition.

21. Donald F. Turner, "Advertising and Competition", *Federal Bar Journal*, XXVI, no. 2 (Spring 1966), 96.

# Index

Aaker, David A., 2n
Advertising messages, 8–9; consumer demand for, 10–14; price of, 14–16; market for, 16–19; and controversy over excessiveness of advertising, 19–21
Alexander, Sydney S., 127n, 221n
Almon, Shirley, 174n
American Motors, 52–53
Autocorrelation, problem of, 78–79
Automobile industry, advertising expenditures of, 52–53

Bain, Joe S., 41 and n, 43n, 44 and n, 45n, 50n, 61n, 110n, 112 and n–113, 121n, 122n
Barriers to entry, 21, 41–43; advertising and product differentiation, 43–45; advertising and absolute cost advertising, 45–49; advertising and economies of scale, 49–53; advertising price structure and economies of scale, 53–61; overall impact of advertising on, 61–63
Bauer, Raymond A., 24n
Baumol, William J., 13n
Benjamin, B., 51n
Bergson, Abram, 243
Blake, Harlan M., 54n
Blank, David M., 54n, 55n
Bliss, Perry, 24n
Blum, Jack A., 54n
Bogart, Leo, 61n

Borden, Neil H., 50n, 141 and n
Boulding, Kenneth E., 250n
Brand loyalty, 13–14, 23–24, 46
Brozen, Yale, 41n, 47–48 and n
Buchanan, James M., 14n

Capital investment, advertising as, 169–174. *See also* Goodwill stocks; Rates of return
CBS, 55
Chamberlain, Edward H., 50n
Christ, Carl F., 10n, 158n
Chrysler, 53
Consumer choice, 22–23, 39–40; advertising and consumer ignorance, 23–25; a model of, 25–31; and price discount, 31–32; sources of information in, 32–35; and required advertising investment, 35–39
*Consumer Reports*, 12, 33
Cost advantages, absolute, advertising and, 45–49

Day, George S., 2n
Dean, Joel, 49–50 and n
Demand equations, overview and summary of, 88–92
Dorfman, Robert, 44 and n, 79n, 142 and n, 143 and n, 147
Douglas, Susan P., 14n
Doyle, Peter, 13n, 141n
Durbin-Watson coefficients, 69, 77, 78–79

255

Reder, Melvin W., 250n
Robertson, Thomas S., 23n
Rothschild, K. W., 142n

Scherer, F. M., 43n, 52n
Sherman, H. J., 127n, 219n
Silverman, Rodney, 251n
Simon, Julian L., 50n
Simultaneous-equation models, specification and estimation of, 79–85
Single-equation estimates, specification and presentation of, 68–70
Solomon, E., 175n
Solow, Robert M., 239n, 250–251n
Somers, Anne R., 11n
Somers, Herman M., 11n
Stauffer, Thomas R., 175 and n, 181n
Steiner, Peter O., 16n, 44 and n, 79n, 142 and n, 143 and n, 147
Stekler, H. O., 221n
Stewart, John B., 50n
Stigler, George J., 10 and n, 41n, 61n, 110 and n, 111 and n, 222n, 248n

Studebaker, 52–53
Survival Technique, 112–113

Taplin, Walter, 154n, 249n, 250n
Taylor, Lester D., 2n, 65 and n, 66 and n–68, 71n, 77n, 92n
Television, network, extent of quantity discounts in advertising messages on, 54–61
Telser, Lester G., 8n, 18n, 19 and n–20, 46n, 169n, 248n
Theil, H., 70n
Tullock, Gordon, 241n
Turner, Donald F., 253n
Tyler, William D., 2n

Urban, Glen L., 54n

Weiserbs, Daniel, 2n, 71n
Weiss, Leonard W., 6n, 53n, 112 and n, 113n, 170 and n, 171n, 219n, 221n
Whiteside, Thomas, 3n
Williamson, Oliver E., 146n